WOMEN OF T

Women of the Land

*Stories of Australia's rural women
as told to*

ROS BOWDEN

an
ABC
BOOK

Published by ABC Books for the
AUSTRALIAN BROADCASTING CORPORATION
GPO Box 9994 Sydney NSW 2001

Copyright © Ros Bowden 1995

First published 1995

National Library of Australia
Cataloguing-in-Publication entry
Bowden, Ros.
    Women of the land: stories of Australia's rural women.
    ISBN 0 7333 0446 X.

    1. Rural women—Australia—Social conditions. 2. Rural
    women—Australia—Interviews. 3. Women in agriculture—
    Australia. I. Australian Broadcasting Corporation. II. Title.
305.40994

Designed by Helen Semmler
Photography by Ros Bowden
Edited by Nina Riemer
Set in Schneidler 10/13pt by
Midland Typesetters, Maryborough, Victoria
Printed and bound in Australia by
Australian Print Group, Maryborough, Victoria

1695-7

5   4   3   2   1

CONTENTS

PREFACE

The idea for this book came from ABC Radio's Rural Department, which in 1994 launched the ABC Rural Woman of the Year Award, and I was delighted when Nina Riemer of ABC Books approached me to interview a number of farming women who had participated in the inaugural award. For many years I had been involved with oral history for broadcast—both for ABC Radio National's Social History Unit and, before that, the Coming Out Show—and Nina's idea was for me to interview a number of the women whose remarkable stories of courage and achievement had been uncovered by the Award.

I travelled all over Australia to interview the women on tape and Nina edited the transcribed tapes in such a way as to retain the character and the 'voice' of the speakers—a technique she has used successfully in other ABC books based on Social History programs.

By happy coincidence, Mark Cranfield, head of the Oral History Section at the National Library of Australia, had indicated to me his interest in non-metropolitan subjects, so the master tapes and transcripts of interviews will be added to the Library's collection. Their generous support contributed significantly to the project's success.

Some of the women I interviewed were already leaders in their rural communities and active in farmers' organisations, others were battlers on small subsistence farms, but they all had stories to tell. I hope this book can bring more of their experiences to the attention of the general public and perhaps help bridge the gap of understanding between city and country. I hope it will also give recognition to the essential role played by women in Australia's rural industries.

Thanks are due to the staff of the ABC's Rural Department for their advice and for making telephone and other facilities available to me, to Dawn Webb, Isabelle Fogarty and Rose Eagleton who transcribed the tapes so speedily, to the people of the ABC Ultimo switchboard who cheerfully connected me to a string of country numbers often early in the morning or at night.

But, most of all, I thank the rural women for their patience as my microphone intruded into their busy days and for making me welcome. And also for the many images of rural life which I could not record but which will stay in my memory.

Ros Bowden
Sydney, June 1995

RURAL WOMEN

I *heard for years the stories of my Italian grandmother having*
to cook three hot meals a day for gangs of cane cutters—maybe
twenty men working on our farm at the one time. Yet she never
appeared on the legal paperwork, her name wasn't on the title
and her contribution was never recognised. I hope that doesn't
happen to my generation of females.

Lisa Palu

In cities the battle for recognition and reward for women's
work has been going on all this century and for some time
before that. In rural areas, however, with their strong
emphasis on family and traditional values and the passing
of land from one generation to the next, women's work
often continues to go unrewarded and their stake in family
farming enterprises frequently is not legally enforceable.

To raise awareness of the contribution women have always made in Australia's primary industries, the ABC in 1994 introduced a National Rural Woman of the Year Award, but the idea for some sort of recognition and encouragement for rural women came a year earlier from a young agriculturist and ABC Rural Reporter, Lisa Palu, whose description of her grandmother's situation headed this chapter.

In my early days as a Rural reporter for the ABC when I travelled around the regions and went to an awful lot of farmers meetings— cattle producers, grain farmers or fruit and vegetable growers—I saw the same pattern at every rural industry sector. There would be a hard-working woman as the secretary of the organisation. She would take all the meeting minutes, do the agendas, write all the letters, but would never stand up at the meeting and say anything.

When I spoke to these women after the meeting I realised they had a lot to say and a lot to contribute. They really took a lot of information in because they were reading all the material that was sent to their local branch and were writing letters. They were a tremendous resource but were never being used.

Generally most of the women who attended the grower meetings were down the back making the cups of tea and scones and I asked them why they didn't join the meeting and why they didn't get up and have their say. There were a range of answers and basically it all came back to self esteem. They felt that they weren't valued and their opinions weren't worthwhile, that the men would ridicule them if they stood up and gave their point of view. Yet as far as I could see, their opinions were even more valid than those of the men who were standing up hogging the floor.

The idea of an award just came into my head one day. I thought about it for a couple of years and approached various people for

2

sponsorship, my idea being to run it at a local level. I approached the local bank, the Qld Industry Development Corporation and the local agricultural show and got a mixed response. Some people told me I was mad; others that it was a great idea and they would love to help. This was in 1993, when a new organisation of rural women was forming called the Queensland Rural Women's Network.

I worked closely with Jan Darlington, the lady who really got that off the ground, and at her property one day when I was doing some Landcare stories I mentioned that women's contribution wasn't being recognised and that women were a wasted resource to agriculture because they didn't have a voice. We had similar concerns and beliefs and I said we needed an award. She thought that was a tremendous idea, and I guess she pushed me to push people above me to get it going.

I was doing a stint on the Country Hour in Brisbane when I formally approached my supervisor, Edwina Clowes. It was really her motivation, her enthusiasm, her ability to move mountains that got it going. Otherwise good ideas can be just that: they can remain on paper unless there is someone with the drive and motivation to make things happen. It was a good idea at the right time with the right people behind it.

Edwina Clowes is Executive Producer of ABC Radio's Country Hour in Queensland.

The idea was in keeping with a recent review of Rural Department's output where one of the main recommendations was to have more rural women on the programs and more coverage of the issues that affect women.

It was all pretty new as far as the Rural Department was concerned. We were basically playing it by ear and developing it as it went along. We had a great marketing team (Kay Nicol and Anita Warren and Robyn Gifford) who put a lot of work into it. We had some strong support from the Queensland Women's

Network and Jan Darlington who were instrumental in getting right behind it.

The ABC's national editor (Rural) Lucy Broad took it on and was strongly supportive. So the next cab off the rank was New South Wales followed by Western Australia, Tasmania and Victoria in some sort of order, then South Australia and Northern Territory. So it went national state by state, culminating in the National Award.

By the end of the day Queensland had 100 nominations with 500 nationally. We thought that was a pretty good effort. I think that all of us in the Rural Department were terribly gratified to meet and get to know women of such achievement who yet were so humble and so incredulous at receiving what was really such a small amount of recognition.

I think probably one of the big achievements of the inaugural award was the network of support that has now been established. All the regional winners in Queensland, and there are nine of them, keep in touch on a regular basis. A lot of them are involved in other networks like the Rural Women's Network and all of them have said that the award has given them recognition and encouragement to continue their pursuits. Some of the State and National winners say it has opened doors that wouldn't have been opened before and has made them set their sights higher for the benefit of rural women in their industry.

It's really hard to quantify but that slow build up in confidence, recognition and support, that network that is now forming, is fantastic. Men have been doing that for years.

Lynne Johnston is a farmer/grazier in partnership with her husband David. She has a background in teaching and in 1994 she was the Western Australia State winner of the inaugural Rural Woman of the Year Award. She took up full-time farming when the existing family partnership was dissolved in 1977. Lynne is on the executive of a number of rural committees and is a campaigner for a better deal for women in the rural sector. Her speech launching the 1995 ABC Award outlined some interesting perspectives on the status of women in rural areas.

It is often difficult for professional people outside agriculture to fully understand the peculiar circumstances of women in agriculture. In your professional world, I acknowledge that there remain hurdles and glass walls and ceilings, but the disadvantage of women in agriculture is their lack of access to the fundamental resources of their industry—the land and the knowledge.

In agriculture, despite the fact that women make up thirty per cent of the nation's farmers, they own a mere three per cent of the resource, the land. Our access to knowledge is curtailed from birth, and despite the increase in young women attending agriculture colleges and schools, the number is still infinitesimal. Potential women students are quickly made aware of the limited career path available to them following graduation.

When you marry a farmer you rarely become a landowner. The land is sacred and stays in the family of which you are not really a part.

The law conspires to make it difficult for women to access this power of ownership of the resource. Until recently the State Stamp Duty legislation made the cost prohibitive for a wife to be included on the land titles. That problem has been overcome but there remains the Federal capital gains legislation that prevents many of us from receiving the due reward for our input into the property. If a property is owned pre 1985 then it is free of capital gains. Should a farmer seek to include his partner's name on the title, a transaction will be deemed to have taken place and half of that title will then be subject to capital gains in the future. Should the land have been acquired post 1995, then capital gains would have to be paid even though no capital gain would have been received.

The corollary to this absence of public acknowledgment is an absence of financial acknowledgment and on this farm, this woman who is so essential to the viability of the business does not appear in the farm books as a labour cost against the business. This maintains the power to distribute largesse in the hands of the man. When a woman pushes up for crutching, her replacement from the paid labour force would cost at least $110 a day. A shift on the tractor $120 a day.

If a part breaks in a machine in a factory in Perth, an employee is sent to get it—time and travel costs are real. On a farm it's, 'I need a part urgently for the tractor, just hop into town and get it for me while I strip the machine down'. Hopping into town means twenty, forty, sixty, eighty kilometres and back—half a day, $60, plus travelling.

The ABC has taken the first step in highlighting the role of women in agriculture—the next is up to us. Nothing will change unless we make it change and women will no longer accept that change will happen of its own accord. We need the three Rs of agriculture: Recognition, Representation and Resources.

There is another side to the problems women can experience down on the farm. Lyn Sykes has been looking at social changes in rural areas. She is a Relationship Counsellor with the Family Life Movement in the western New South Wales country town of Dubbo. She has a personal connection with the country having grown up in a small country town and eventually trained as a nurse in Wagga Wagga. A large proportion of her clients are farming families trying to accommodate the very different expectations of three generations in a cooperative enterprise—the family farm.

When I looked at my statistics for 1992, a third of my clients were second generation farming women, where the first generation was still on the farm. Many of these young women were often not from a farming or country background. They came to us when they decided that they needed to meet as a family and needed a facilitator to chair those family meetings.

Out of that need to have some professional help has grown an awareness that help is available and that it is not too socially unacceptable. The other thing that has prompted people's action is that in the rural community, like any other, a third of long term relationships come to an end.

As farms become more vulnerable they are actually less financially able to cope with marriage breakdowns and so the whole issue of the daughter-in-law has become very significant. Many farms see the daughter-in-law as a real threat to farm viability. Of all the things that threaten farms, a relationship breakdown, particularly if there are a few kids and the departing partner takes the children and a large swag of the assets with her, can mean the demise of a farm. But unfortunately, when farming families treat these women like outsiders, that's how they behave and so then they are not reluctant to remove assets from the farm family.

I've seen farm families taking what I consider to be extreme precautions to protect their assets from the daughter-in-law. Probably in time it will be the son-in-law. The unfortunate part is that, frequently, these people can be an enormous asset to the enterprise. They have very substantial talents to bring to the enterprise and if they are not encouraged to do that there is a real frustration for them in being able to see something that could be done more effectively and more efficiently and never having the opportunity to have any input.

A whole lot of my clients were second generation farming women—mostly young women but some women in their fifties— where the first generation were still living on the farm. Parents may have been in their seventies or eighties and this middle generation in their fifties were waiting to get the farm.

In one of the families I know, the ownership of the farm missed that generation completely and went from the grandparents to the grandchildren—not without some hostile feelings, of course, from people in the middle.

Certainly, being caught in triangles—the persecutor, victim and rescuer—is a very common pattern that I see: daughters-in-law presenting as the victims, with husband or partner the rescuer and the in-laws the persecutor.

I asked Lyn Sykes whether she finds that parents are beginning to accept their daughters-in-law. I had heard some extraordinary stories about patriarchs who seemed to think they could control their daughter-in-law's movements.

Often they measure distances on the car's meter and watch how often their daughters-in-law go past the farmhouse! I've had women tell me they find alternative tracks out of the farms so they don't have to go past the farmhouse.

I'd like to be able to say it's changing as a general rule, but I couldn't honestly say that. I had a phone call only last week from a very educated young woman who's thinking of moving into a farm family and, in fact, is engaged to the son. When she had dinner with the family she asked them what they expected of her when she came into the family. Her interpretation of what they said was something like, 'Well, you have to keep our son fed and amused, and basically that's your role'.

This is a woman highly qualified in a rural field. That was last week, so it doesn't encourage me to think that attitudes are changing too quickly.

I have the opportunity to speak at seminars about this sort of thing and I am suggesting that families look at these women more, look at what they can offer the enterprise. Rural communities once used to look purely at the financial viability of any management decision. In the last twenty or thirty years perhaps, people have been encouraged and are happy to look at the environmental issues related to their management decisions, so they are not only looking at financial sustainability but environmental sustainability. I think the third of those management prongs—the management of their human resources—has been slow to move into farming. When management decisions are made, frequently extensive research is done on the implications on the financial sustainability, and frequently on the environmental sustainability. But rarely do they look at the impact on human resources of the operation.

These rural women, Lisa Palu, Lynne Johnston and Lyn Sykes, certainly gave me something to ponder. I am essentially a city person, although like many people of my generation I knew people on the land and spent holidays on farms from time to time. I will always remember the joy of drought-breaking rain when once I was working in Wagga Wagga. It resulted in floods, of course, but the spirit in the town was quadruple the spirit at Christmas.

Nowadays it is no longer common for city people to have friends or relatives in the country. The huge drop in farm income has meant decline in the rural workforce and a big drain of country people into the cities in search of work. I no longer have longstanding friendships in country areas, my children have never been on a farm holiday.

Travelling around the rural areas of this country, often driving hundreds of kilometres between interviews, I had time to reflect on the disintegration of the city-country link. Drought relief appeals have certainly brought an understanding of the difficulties of country life but what is missing is personal contact. Country people are beginning to be regarded as almost another culture, a different kind of Australian, stuck in Akubra hats and the ways of the 'sixties.

Such people may well exist but I only met cheerful and

strong women and their families, very aware of contemporary issues, especially as they affected their industry. Modern communications technology means that information comes to them just as quickly as it does to Sydney and Melbourne. They use computers and reproductive technology to design cattle to consumer demands. They follow trends in the colour and flavour of fruit and plan their orchards accordingly, and they visit their counterparts in other countries and other states so they do not lag behind. The number of field days, conferences and information meetings that farmers attend, often after an exhausting day on the farm, is mind boggling. The financial margin on farms is so small they cannot afford to leave anything to chance, and all members of the family work with a frenetic commitment to the land that seems to hold their life force.

Meeting these rural women and collecting their stories was a most rewarding assignment. Not all the women were award winners. But all are big contributors to their country and to the new image of the farmer. And Lynne Johnston is speaking for all of them when she says, 'I am the farmer, not the farmer's wife'.

PATRICIA LEIGHTON

*Patricia Leighton was brought up in the city as was her engi-
neer husband, Russell. I asked her if she was brave or just
foolish to take on undeveloped land in the Cape Rich area of south
Western Australia in 1966. Their story is one of hard work and
courage as they gradually cleared the land and introduced crops
and stock. Their first home was a shed built for shearing. It
remained their home for twenty years until Patricia, with help from
their now grown children, dug and poured the foundations and
built a number of freestanding structures out of a local white
spongelite rock. Currently they are replanting some of the trees
they cut down in ignorance all those years ago.*

There wasn't much time or money for going out and doing
things when I was a child in suburban Sydney in the
postwar years. We had a wonderful bush paddock down

11

behind us, and I think that's where I grew up. My grand-father had a couple of blocks at the back of Wahroonga, down towards Kuringai Chase I suppose, and he used to grow vegetables down there as well, so we used to go and help him on our bikes and come trundling home with, say, an enormous watermelon on the back of the bike. My brother became a jackeroo with AML&F Company way back in those early days and worked his way through to have his own property, so although I was always connected with him, I was very much a suburban dweller, and my work in Sydney when I was teaching was right in the inner city area in Redfern.

Tell me about your first taste of being a farmer.

After I'd taught in Sydney for twelve months I really wanted to get out into the backblocks. I wanted to go some-where like the Northern Territory but in fact a job turned up in Tasmania so I went to Tasmania in 1958 and started teaching near Hobart. During that time I met my husband. He was an engineer from England who had come out on a working job with the Hydro-Electric Commission in Tas-mania, and I was very keen on getting out in the bush and took up bushwalking, and that was really how I met him. We used to do a lot of bushwalking and skiing in those early months when we knew each other, and we were married at the end of 1958 back in Sydney. We then went back to Hobart.

I continued teaching and he was still working, but after renting a flat in Hobart for some months we decided to buy a farmlet at a little place called Snug, in those days about twenty-five miles out of Hobart down the channel. We had about thirty-six acres of a mixture of pasture and bush and a little old ramshackle cottage, and it was there that we stayed for the next seven years. He continued to work with the Hydro and I gave up work when my first baby arrived. I sometimes milked four cows in the morning, we had 250 hens and thirty sheep, and we had Herefords, ducks and geese. It was really a storybook farm, and I had four of my children in Snug.

We gave up all our bushwalking and our skiing; all our spare time was spent fencing and rushing off down the highway to bring in our straying sheep and our cattle and so on. And then one day on 'The Country Hour' I heard that they were opening up land in the Kimberleys on the Ord River, and I thought, ooh, this sounds exciting, so I wrote off for information and along with that information came information about the south coast.

When it all came back my husband said he thought he would prefer the cooler southern part of Western Australia and we made further enquiries about what was then known as the Cape Rich area, which is about 100 kilometres north-east of Albany.

We had no savings; we really had nothing behind us except one little farm that we still owed money on. These blocks in this district are what's called Conditional Purchase Blocks, so they were put up for application, and I think there were about ninety-six applicants for the thirty-six blocks that came up. We decided after much discussion that we'd give it a go, it would be our next adventure, perhaps. Russell travelled across on the train and attended a Land Board sitting on a property not far from here. My eldest daughter has now married the son of the original owner of that property, so it's gone around in a circle.

They all slept in the shearing shed there and they were all interviewed, and when Russell came back after this great adventure right across Australia he just said, 'Look, we haven't got a hope; they're all from big farming backgrounds and they obviously have a lot of money behind them', and we just sort of put it in a back box and forgot about it. Then I was listening to 'The Country Hour' another day and the announcement came that we had got a block in Western Australia, and it was just the most startling surprise. I can remember ringing him and we were stunned, but also very, very excited. It was very thrilling.

Was it a fairly daring or a foolhardy thing to do? You didn't have a great deal of background as a farmer and your husband is English and I guess had no experience of the sort of businesses and country that you find around here.

We'd always worked very closely with the Agricultural Department on our little thirty-six acre farm in a very small way. We had a lot of backing from them in those days and I can remember one of our referees was one of the Ag. Department people from Hobart.

We had very little experience. Russell was a mechanical engineer so he had a great deal of experience in machinery and that was our big trump card, I feel. That was 1962 and in the next three years he managed to get an old Caterpillar tractor from one of the Hydro towns way out in the bush somewhere and an old Albion truck, and I think it would have been in 1963 he loaded the old Caterpillar tractor on to the back of the Albion truck—I can distinctly remember it trundling up onto the truck (laughs) on the steep slope of the driveway at Snug—and off he went, heading for Western Australia.

In those days, of course, the highway across the Nullarbor was just a dirt track and it was a real adventure for him. There wasn't a main road, either; there were only diversions where people had gone round bogs, and I really didn't think he was going to get to the other end, but in fact he didn't have any problems and finished up towing some other fellow a vast distance across to Norseman.

That was the first tractor, and he purchased a plough in the West at the same time. One of the sons of another local who had moved into one of the nearby districts did the first plough for us and before the first plough happened all the bush was knocked down with chains or logs.

But it wasn't until 1965 that we felt that the time had come to start looking westwards and Russell resigned from his job at the Hydro-Electricity Commission and took up a job with Goldsworthy Mining, who were just starting off their development in the Pilbara.

I stayed behind and we put the little farm on the market. Also, I'd just had a fourth baby so we felt that she had to be at least three months old before I travelled with her. We eventually sold the little farm—'Noonameena' it was called and there are many stories related to leaving it. I had the old Ford ute and on the final day my mother was so worried about me travelling across on my own with the children that she actually came down to join us, but we still had to get there (laughs) in the ute. So we had my brave mother with one of the children on her knee, two children sitting on the seat between us—I'd made home-made seat belts; there were no seat belts in those days—and, horror of horrors, the baby was in a little tiny bassinette thing on the back shelf.

We set off and caught the ferry across to Melbourne. My father had come down from Sydney to make sure we got to Melbourne all right and waved us on the next stage. We stayed in on-site vans in caravan parks and had one night in a motel—that was our one luxury night. We travelled very slowly: I think we were doing about 100 miles a day with many stops for feeding babies and children, but it was a lovely way to come across, slowly but surely feeling our way westwards.

We stayed with a friend in Adelaide and my mother flew back home at that point, and we put the ute on the train at Port Augusta. Russ was waiting for us in Kalgoorlie with an old truck he'd bought, so we thinned out the load in the ute a bit and had one more camp on the side—in a gravel pit, I remember, on the side of the road on the way to Perth. He had rented a unit in a fairly new suburb north of Perth and so we moved into this little half-house. He was still working with Goldsworthy and was away a lot, but I sat in this little half-house from, I suppose, August through to January. Penny went to the local kindergarten and the children had a wonderful time at the beach, and we had odd trips down to 'the block' as we called it.

I can remember the first trip down. We were all piled in the truck and the bassinette this time was on the floor under all our feet. We had the old army disposal tent as well and down we came. I can remember driving along this dirt road for miles and miles and miles and suddenly swinging into the bush, trundling, bumping and thumping along, and then Russell said, 'We're here'. It was late at night so we piled out and pitched the tent, and I can remember the calls of the birds from the bush first thing in the morning at the first light and thinking, wow, my God, what have we come to? There just didn't seem to be any trees. It was, of course, mallee country and it was just so different to anything I'd experienced; it was just like sand or gravel to me and I didn't think that anything could possibly grow.

The actual Cape Rich area was pioneered in the 1840s, way back in the early days, and the descendants of that original family are still in the district. So there were people in the area, but the country that we had taken up had not been developed at all; it was just virgin mallee country.

We had a little campfire and still, whenever the odd bit of blackboy goes on the fire or the stove these days, it brings back vivid memories of that first trip down and sitting there in the middle of this bush that to me seemed so drab and so poor after the lovely chocolate soil in Tasmania. I must admit at that stage I wondered whatever had we done.

Penny was due to start school in the February of 1966 so I said to Russell, 'That's when I want to move down'. He was still working and away up in the north a lot of the time, but he had organised that a shed be erected to be ready for me to move in in time for Penny to start school. So at the end of January a neighbour helped me to load things on the truck and I came down with the family and rolled up to what was to be this lovely new shed which we were going to have as accommodation, to find it was only half-finished (laughs) and the workmen were still there with wet concrete everywhere. I can remember it was late in the afternoon and we ended up in a sort of lean-to in what is now the work-shop, and I had children being ill, I suppose from the long trip down, and there really was no water. Again I thought, what have I done?

Penny would have been turning six that year to start school and Sam would have been five, Jim three, and Sylvia at that stage was nine months. So there we were in this half-finished corrugated iron shed. They had cleared and ploughed all the area around it so it was sitting in the middle of this bare ground surrounded by mallee trees in the distance. The workmen were wonderful; they did as much as they could to help, but they were still laying concrete. They had a water tank full of water which they were using for making the concrete so we were able to boil some of that and use it.

Russell arrived a couple of days later and everything was speeded up. The roof was on and we were able to move into the large end of the shed—it was built very high because it was to be the future shearing shed. We put little double bunks all along one end and we had some old second-hand wardrobes which we put down the middle. We just used kerosene primuses and basins and so on until we'd been in to Albany and collected some more second-hand stuff, but at that stage we were really just camping on the concrete floor in this end of the shed.

That was fine, and then the time came for Penny to go to school some few weeks later so I piled them all in the car and headed off in the direction Russell thought it was— up and down the highway and that main highway was just a rutted track. So up and down I drove and we were late, and a car appeared in the distance and this welcoming face rolled up and said, 'Are you looking for the school?' We were shown this little track in through the bush and a tiny box sitting in a little cleared area, a one-roomed school with two tiny boxes out the back where the pan toilets were housed. So that was Penny's first day at school. In fact there was a school bus that bumped and jostled along the tracks and came to our front gate which was very convenient.

Russell had then left his work up north and we got on with generally settling in. He assured me that the time in the end of the shed was to be short-lived because it would be the shearing shed, but I must say that twenty years later we were still in that end of the shed. The priority was outside and we continued very slowly.

Going back to the shed, what were the changes and improvements that you'd made to your home in those twenty years while you were in the shed?

Well, to start with, let's just look at the ablutions. At first it was two buckets, one to wash with and one to throw over to rinse with, and then we moved on to an old two-handled tub which the ducks now use, which meant you could at least sit half of yourself in, even if the other half was out. We'd move the tub around to the down-wind side of the shed, which was quite convenient—it was amazing the number of satellites we used to see in the sky then, too. We had an old fuel copper for hot water and a couple of tanks up on tank stands. We'd put down a mill and we had bore water but it was very alkaline, so we were also able to use that, which meant that there were no soap suds, and when it was boiled up in the copper it all came out rather rusty (laughs).

We then moved on to a wonderful old bathrub which sat between the tank stands—we still have that, too—and I can distinctly remember the queueing up for a turn in the bath. The one that got in first, of course, got the fresh water and the one at the end got the very revolting water. There was also the possibility of being caught out there when somebody rolled up—I think it was the aim of some of the people in the district to catch us out in the bath (laughs)—or being caught in a thunderstorm. Being in the bathtub was quite an adventure, as was the little toilet house which was just a wired-down tin box with a hole in the ground and a little seat that wobbled back and forth. You can imagine trying to toilet-train children in a wobbly hole-in-the-ground toilet which was about eighty metres from the shed.

And inside—did you try to line it or do anything glamorous like that?

It was always going to be a shearing shed—well, that was initially, I suppose. We put in some old carpets and built in an old fireplace at one end, which invariably smoked so the whole shed was filled with smoke and we got a Metters No. 1 stove up the other end and an old sink. We then moved up to Tilley lanterns, which were the hissing, very bright ones, and that was quite a move up. Some time after that we got a low-voltage generator which was just outside in another part of the shed, and when it was on there was a thumping noise which reverberated right throughout the shed, and eventually we got a bigger lighting plant which was situated further out and that was a great improvement.

There were, of course, no telephones in those first days. There was a little old telephone line that connected up the original farm, but it was really a private line and when the telephones actually came in that was one of the biggest breakthroughs for the district: it was just wonderful to be able to contact your neighbours just by dialling a number.

Eventually the power came in and that was just miraculous! We originally had the kerosene fridges but they also smoke, and they either freeze everything or defrost everything; there never seemed to be a happy medium and they were a real problem. So to have the electricity for the fridge and then the freezer was just miraculous.

In those days the mail was dropped in once a week and now it's three days a week, which is quite amazing. We had a wonderful old mailman; he used to pop the odd jelly bean in the mailbox for the children, and we'd get bread delivered out once a week from Albany.

Eventually Sam started school, and the school by that stage had a little verandah on it, and then Jim started. But before that we began a little kindergarten. At that stage the school had moved up more into the actual town site and had become a two-teacher school and the little old original school was empty so we established a kindergarten there on

20

one day a week. A neighbour and myself started it up voluntarily and we had children from far and wide, and their mothers. The mothers would park around in the bush somewhere and have their own little session, and I think it was as important for the mothers all to get together as the children, and the children would gather as well. We had a little library exchange and it was the greatest fun. Jim was one of the foundation members of that, and Sylvia, the number four baby, joined in as well.

But, just looking at the whole district, I was only one of many women all doing the same thing. Some of them were just in little lean-to shanties, they were in caravans, some were in Nissan huts, some of them went straight into houses and we thought they were very spoiled and in great luxury—they were only simple houses but we thought they were very luxurious. But everybody supported everybody else. It had to be that way, because you were all so dependent on each other for your development and for your family security, so it was a great big family. That was something that I treasured very much in those days. It was like a great big extended family, and that included the men and the women, and it was something quite special.

The nearest doctor was in Albany. I had a wonderful doctor and when we got the phone I could ring and give him the symptoms and he'd say, 'What have you got in your medical cupboard?' and I'd say, 'This, this, and this', and he'd say either to give them that or put them to bed and let them get over it, or come straight in, and it was very comforting to have that back-up. A child health nurse used to come out in those early days fairly irregularly, but it was certainly a great back-up.

At this point, I suppose quite unexpectedly, baby number five was on the way and I couldn't think where we were going to put a baby because we were still in this undivided, unlined shed. But it all worked out so easily, somehow. At that point Russell had gone back to working with the Main Roads Department in Albany and we'd set up a little old caravan at Emu Point in Albany where he would stay during the week—he'd come home twice a week—and it was during this time that Kylie was expected. I must admit that I did spend many phone calls saying, 'Help, I'm sure it's about to happen, you must come out!' But, of course, this eased off and she eventually arrived in a very easy way when we were in the caravan in Albany taking the children to swimming lessons, so that was fine.

When I brought her home, again it seemed quite natural to have a baby in a shed. She lived in this wonderful, two-handed basket, and there were so many other children to give her plenty of stimulation and help with her. At that point every day we were out working on fence lines or whatever, and she just came with us in the little basket and was just always part of the work scene. She fortunately was a very placid baby, so we wouldn't have missed her for anything! (laughs)

Tell me about the sort of development on the farm. What were you doing in these first few years?

We originally had to chain or log the bush down, leave it for a time to dry out, put a burn through and then a first plough would go in. Of course, it would be very spiky and that's where our Caterpillar tractor was great because you didn't have your rubber tyres puncturing all the time. Then we'd always do a second plough and all the debris would be raked up and burnt and then it would be ready for seeding. At that stage we'd bought another old second-hand tractor: in fact, Russell drove it from Perth to the farm one

Christmas, I can distinctly remember. He didn't quite make it and we had to go and collect him from somewhere up above Mount Barker and we spent Christmas Day going back to retrieve this tractor that hadn't quite made it the night before (laughs).

We bought an old second-hand seeder and Russell would seed it down and add fertiliser and all the trace elements that were missing. That's what really opened up this country, when they found out which trace elements were missing. There was such a demand for sheep in Western Australia—with all this new land being opened up sheep were very short—we got our first sheep from South Australia. I can well remember that first truckload coming up the driveway to go in onto the first area of ground that we'd developed.

You were seeding for pasture, then.

Yes, for pasture; for clover, perennial rye grass and annual rye grass. I must say that when the Agricultural Department people came out in those very first days I'd say, 'What have you done? This is just terrible, nothing will grow here', and they would assure me that I would have clover up around my knees by the spring and I'd just look at them disbelievingly. But in those early years it was so: it just came away and we rolled in this wonderful pasture. Mind you, it's not quite the same these days with all the pests that have moved in, but in those early days when the pests were not into the pasture it was just a most amazing growth.

You were still pretty well rookies with farming, weren't you? How did you learn what to do? Did you get a handbook from the Ag. Department and follow it?

This was new country for everybody; nobody really

23

knew, it was all fairly experimental. The Agricultural Department were very helpful. We had very good back-up from them and they were giving advice all the way, but it was trial and experiment. You just looked at what your neighbours were doing; they had field days; you saw what was working for somebody and not working for somebody else; you worked that into your budget—and we were always obviously on a very tight budget—and it was just learning as you go. A lot of it involved machinery, of course, and that's where Russell had the advantage.

A lot of it must also have been fairly hard physical work in places where machines can't always operate.

Yes. Nowadays we have a front-end loader to do a lot of the lifting but in those early days we didn't have one and we did a lot of very hard work. The children were all expected to work and holiday time was work time; there weren't many holidays or much time off.

What was your bank managers' attitude to all this. Were they supportive?

They were very concerned about the whole area, because a lot of us were really battling. If Russell hadn't had the opportunity to get off-the-farm work and another income we wouldn't have had a chance, so the fact that he was able to go back to his engineering was essential.

Coming up towards 1970 the crunch really did come for us. We had a very dry year, we were losing a lot of sheep and wool prices had dropped. People all around were having to just get up and leave their properties. We asked two neighbours to keep an eye on our place and we loaded, very sadly, all our second-hand goods and chattels onto the back of the old original Ford Ute and the old Bedford truck and

24

wended our way to Perth. It poured with rain all the way. I'd enquired about accommodation in Perth—we'd decided that we wanted Penny to go to a particular school—and we ended up renting a lovely little house in a very pleasant suburb of Perth. We were completely ignored by all the well-to-do neighbours for many, many months: they just didn't know what to make of this family with the two barking dogs and the masses of children and the truck and the ute (laughs). It was just a bit much, but eventually we got to know them and it was fine.

This would have been the first time you'd lived in a house for some time.

That's right, it was quite luxurious for me. Russell went back to his engineering work with another company that was up in the north-west, and after some months—at that stage Kylie was a toddler of two—I got a job as a teacher with a kindergarten that they were setting up in the Crippled Children's Hospital for spinabifida and muscular atrophy and various other crippled children. They were called crippled children in those days and we should now say disabled children, which is a better word.

So we were in this little cottage, the river was just down the road, and I used to deliver Sylvia to kindergarten in the old truck with the dogs barking on the back and head off over to the hospital, which was nearby in Cottesloe. It was really fascinating, working with these children in the ward. But the fact was that I was able to go back to work and make an income, as was Russell, and we used to travel down to the farm most weekends. We'd load up on the Friday night, work all weekend and drive back on Sunday night and back to work on Monday morning, and it was tough, really hard.

The trip would be a good five hours plus, in the vehicles we were using in those days—we'd drive pretty slowly. Shearing and crutching had to be fitted into holiday times, so the children's holiday times were fun work times, as always, and I think it was for about seven years that we went on like this. We'd be back, of course, over the long summer holidays, and mine being a teaching job I always had those long school holidays down here as well.

I eventually became a pre-school board adviser and then an early childhood education adviser and my work took me all over Western Australia developing a program for families with pre-school children, which was a great experience. I went out across the Nullarbor in a different way this time, on the tea and sugar train, and connected up with families up there, up through the Kimberleys and the Pilbara and the mining towns, places like Wittenoom and so on, so it was a tremendous experience for me, just widening my knowledge of families in all corners of Western Australia.

Russell came back in 1978 and my big decision, my conflict, then was, do I go back to the farm with my husband—I had five children and at that stage Kylie was Year 7—or do I stay with the children? That was a hard one. We didn't want them to go to boarding school; we wanted them to stay together as a family, and after much travelling back and forth I decided that the farm and husband was the way to go. At that stage we had bought a house in Cottesloe, Penny was at University, and we left the children to ... well, fend for themselves. I really shudder when I think back to it. I feel somewhere deeply troubled that I left Kylie at such a young age, but they'd always been very independent children and they'd always been resourceful, and it worked. We had problems and the phone ran hot many a time, and we had interviews with headmasters over odds and ends, but the schools knew what was happening, they knew the background, and we had made it quite clear that if there was a major problem we would be on the spot in a very quick time.

What ages were the kids? The eldest was at University and would have been nineteen or something?

I'd have to look up the dates, but Penny went on to do Agriculture at the University and she'd have been about in her third year, so she'd have been nineteen, twentyish, and Sam was just about to leave school and Jim two years behind Sam. Sylvia would have been Year 9 or 10, so they were very crucial ages and stages for the family, and I admire them for the way they handled it, even though we had some traumas which were obviously inevitable.

What was the right decision? I don't know, but it was a hard one, that one.

In those early days when we were still in the shed, we used to have to shear the sheep on the next-door neighbour's property. So at shearing time we would trundle the sheep through bush tracks and round obstacles and over to the neighbour's property. There was no telephone and the shearers would have said they would be there at that time, but you'd get the sheep there, all set to go, and no shearers would turn up. Because it was on a neighbour's place you'd have to bring all the sheep home. Or you'd set off, and half-way across the rain would come and you'd have wet sheep. The shearers would be there but they wouldn't be able to shear them because they were wet. So shearing on a neighbour's property was another major trauma time.

When the children left school they all had a year off and returned to help us on the farm, and it was during Sam's year off that the shearing shed was built and the final paddock developed. In Jim's year off another big storage shed was built. They all travelled and had working jobs as well, because we wanted them to know what it was like being out there and earning their own living on a working job. But back here we first of all built a little bathroom up the other end with Barker stone which is spongelite; it was formed under the shallow sea that used to be in this area. Then, as they all got to that late teenage stage, they all built themselves a little sleeping hut. So even though we were still converging in the shed for eating, everybody was gradually getting a little cabin that they slept in. It was their spot; when they had friends it was somewhere to withdraw to.

We had six little sleeping cabins scattered around, and because Russell and I eventually felt we were being left out, sitting up there in the shed (laughs), we built one ourselves as well and, finally, when I came back to the farm, I decided that we would have a community centre, and that's what this building is—a lounge-dining-kitchen combined. If you'd visited in those days you would have been given some mortar and a trowel. People come down and say, 'Oh, there's my stone!'. It's a bit higgledy-piggledy but everybody lent a hand. Russell thought it was just a huge joke and my little game and he pretty well ignored it until it got to the roof stage and I said, 'Right, now it needs a roof', and he had this skew-whiff sort of building to put a roof on. He'd bought all this old timber from structures that they'd knocked down in Albany, so none of the timber he was working with was straight—a lot of old kauri and jarrah full of old notches and things—so he not only had to fit it onto my crooked structure, he also had to fit in this crooked timber. But it sits there and it's proved to be a great venue.

It's certainly a lovely room to be in. You didn't hew the stone as well?

No, it comes from a quarry. In the old days the first ones were 18 inches x 6 inches x 9 inches so we had that basic size, and then if we wanted to fit in a little bit or an angled bit you could saw it with a bushman's saw. It's quite light to handle, so it was possible for us all to lift it. Kylie helped me to put all the windows in and, a of course, nothing quite fitted; we still had to fill in little gaps and so on because none of the stones were quite perfect. I wanted to feel as if I was outside when I was inside and we'd got accustomed to the open feeling in the shed where even if you were cooking you were still part of all the action. That's why it's this open style with windows all round.

Going back to the kids, I'd like to talk a little bit about the involvement of children on farms and their being part of the labour force. At what age did you decide they could be useful?

I suppose the first major job that I could do with the children was fencing and putting droppers on fences, so they all got their little dropper tie as soon as they could handle a bit of wire and a little implement and they'd lift a dropper up onto the fence line. The minute they could follow what everybody else was doing they were there. I suppose they were five years old when they'd be doing the odd little jobs. There were always jobs to be done—wood to be picked up, root picking.

Root picking was a constant occupation in the paddocks because even though it was raked up there were still mallee roots, which had come up when you ploughed the soil, scattered all over every paddock. Even little three-year-olds and two-year-olds could get quite adept at throwing mallee roots on the back of a truck. There were always fires to be lit and constant sheep rounding up and sheep work to be done. In the early days we'd do all our sheep work on a tractor with children running hard on foot, but eventually they all got their little bikes and they were able to be quite useful in the mustering operation as well.

Safety is a very big factor on farms in these days and certainly children are much more restricted in what they can do with machinery, but in those early days if you felt your child was able to handle something, they were there, and I must admit that our young children were very good at driving vehicles, motor bikes and tractors at a very early age. As a grandmother now I'd be horrified if my grandchildren were doing the same thing, but in those days, without the seat belts, they'd learned to be very self-preservative and we never had any sort of a broken limb or a major accident. They've always been very careful but very able to handle any sort of machinery or vehicle. In fact, we couldn't have done without them. They were the unpaid work force. We used to say 'This is building up your future; this is going to pay for your education' to the poor things—a sort of bribery, I suppose.

Then, of course, when it came to leaving school they were all quite happy to be farmers, but we said, 'No, you must go away and study and get yourself some sort of a qualification and then you can certainly come back', and of course that's just what they did. So here we are, on our own with all the children out happily in their own professions and occupations. I still think that they have a great interest in the farm, and I'm sure that one or some of them will always be involved, but at this stage they've got their own little families growing and they're doctors and engineers and what-have-you scattered over Western Australia.

That kind of upbringing was quite an advantage. A lot of people complain now that they can't get their kids to do anything, not even the washing up.

I think it made them very resourceful and very independent, and possibly that was why I was able to leave them in Perth, because I think we were pretty tough. In those early days if you said, 'No, because it's dangerous, you don't do it', then it wasn't done. I think we were pretty bossy probably, and it made the children resourceful. I regret that there wasn't more time for sharing stories together, for those sitting on knees and cuddling times and chatting times. It was survival and it was adventure in those early years, but there wasn't much time for soft gentleness and just sharing emotions, if I can put it that way, and I regret that. But I find that it's lovely to watch them now developing that with their own children. But for a lot of us in those days you were on that survival line. As I keep saying, it was a tremendous adventure but it was very tough, too. Many times, I must admit, I would just get in the car and drive, just leaving; but I never quite got through the front gate (laughs).

There were wonderful up times, each stage of development was a wonderful up time, and there were certainly very down times. It's amazing how you forget them but when we sometimes reminisce something will bring back a memory and you realise that there were some really tough times. But I think it was all worth it.

I found a great love of the bush here. I'm sure it goes right back to my childhood when I grew up in that bush block at the back of the house in Wahroonga. When you get into the mallee bush here and the understorey and you start recognising plants, you realise what a tremendous variety there is, and I developed a great love for the bush and for the coastline. My time off was exploring the bush and exploring the coast and the children and I would pop on our backpacks and do trips along the coastline with our little tent. I suppose that was the beginning of doing my studies with my local Historical and Heritage Committee on the local flora and fauna.

The time in Perth had taught me a lot and it made me appreciate very much more what we had done here. I think that was quite an important stage in my life. Also, Russell was always optimistic and could look to the future; when I was feeling down he would always be right there saying, 'Onwards, onwards!' I was also drawn to the district, not only its environment but also the people here who were very special to me, we'd all grown together. It was wonderful to get back and it was also wonderful to eventually have the house to live in, which provided a haven. Looking back, the shed really wasn't ever a haven in the bad weather, and it was great to have a fire that didn't smoke. A haven, that's the only word I can think of for it.

I suppose it was at that point I became more involved in the community. Once we'd put up the dwelling I had more time in between all the sheep work and farm work and I was involved in the establishment of a local Historical and Heritage Committee. We looked at all the families in the district and after much trying and failure and trying again we got a story from every family in the district, whether they had been the first schoolteacher or the bulldozer driver who put in the first dams on the farms, and we published a book. That was the beginning. We also had many historical events; we were involved in the re-enactment of the bringing of the wool down to the coast and the loading on the sailing ship. The sailing ship *Leeuwin* came in, and the horse and dray took the wool down to the beach and we trundled it down and it was quite an occasion. There's a very colourful history of the 1840s onwards of the district here and it's been wonderful to discover all that.

Then we looked towards the heritage side of the area and

first of all we did a survey of the birds and produced a little book on the birds of the district, then we went on to the eucalypts of the district. This straggly old mallee country produced a vast number of eucalypt species which, again, was a fascinating study involving everybody in the district who was prepared to go out there and peer at gumnuts and buds and so on. Then we looked at the banksias of the district and produced another little book on that, and right now we're involved in a mammal survey. We have a federal grant and we have families all throughout the community finding out what mammals we have left. I'm very involved in that. I seem to spend a lot of my time on hands and knees digging pit traps in and involving children, which is the exciting part of it. The interest of the children has been just wonderful, so has getting them sorted out with their reference books and their little check-off sheets and so on. That's been a really exciting part of the involvement in the district as well.

I noticed on the way in here that you've got strips of young trees growing up. Is that part of the development of the place?

Ever since the early days it was all clear, clear, clear, and of course it's in recent times that farmers are realising that it shouldn't have been clear, clear, clear, it should have been clear and leave, clear and leave. We always left some patches of remnant vegetation but we didn't have the money to fence it off in the early days so a lot of it was ravaged by grazing, but towards the end of our development we were able to fence off some quite worthwhile remnant vegetation.

We have quite a wide road reserve out the front of the farm and that planting up the driveway is actually a corridor linking it with other corridors around other paddocks, with a large strip of vegetation we've left alongside a creek, which was a wonderful surprise we found in the early days. We had a creek with all these permanent pools strung along it which we just stumbled on in the bush quite out of the blue one Christmas. In fact, Russell took me in there and showed them to me as a Christmas present. It was the most wonderful Christmas present. We left the children down on the back fenceline in a sort of sandy patch and said, 'Don't move!' and he took me in to these wonderful pools.

So that is part of linking up bits of remnant vegetation and making corridors for the wildlife. But I suppose as a result of all this interest in the bush and being a battling farmer—we've always been battling farmers, I think—and having such a love of the natural vegetation, I was just automatically drawn towards the Land Conservation District Committee in our region and I've been fairly closely involved with that since it was formed. There are many projects going on but I think my contribution to that has been the balance between farm production and the preservation of what we have left in the environment. And there are the people: they always come number one, as I've learned very thoroughly. If you're trying to achieve anything in the district it must come from the people themselves; you can't impose anything on them, certainly not in a community like ours, where everybody including us—my husband in particular—is their own boss and makes their own decisions. Nobody can impose anything on you.

In the early days the shed was just in the middle of this vast cleared land and I would pick up little bits and pieces I found in the bush and transplant them. I've grown my own seedlings from seed every year, and after many failures from sheep eating them and grasshoppers ravaging the whole thing year after year, we've eventually achieved a fairly haphazard garden around our dwellings. I didn't even know what a lot of it was going to grow into. Quite crazily, there are great big trees sitting behind little huts because I didn't realise they would be tall, but we've never been quite able to cut them down so we spend our time trimming back these enormous trees that are hanging over little tiny stone huts. So growing the local natives has been a big part of my interest as well.

Thirty years is a long time to have worked and worried and agonised about a bit of land. What does it mean to you?

It's just been my life, I suppose. The end is obviously in sight. I find that very difficult to contemplate. At this stage we have gone into the growing of bluegums, which is a bit of an experiment for this far east of Albany, but a Tasmanian bluegum which they've developed is proving to be very good for the woodchip industry and at this stage we're finding we can hang on here and cope with the physical work by balancing it out with growing trees. It's providing a great balance for the land as well in many ways—after all the things we created by clearing the land, putting trees back on is quite an exciting concept.

I'd also like to look towards, perhaps, oil mallee production. Some mallees produce a eucalypt oil and, ridiculously, Australia is importing a lot of its eucalyptus oils, so I can see a great future, perhaps, for this area in growing mallees for oil production.

Tell me how that Rural Woman of the Year Award affected you.

I was only runner-up. The girl that was selected was a very wonderful person. She has worked very hard for the wool industry and she's at quite the other end of the scale to me. I regard myself as a grassroots person in my own community.

I was a reluctant participant but the backing of some very strong friends and my wonderful old mother in Sydney finally urged me to take the plunge. I felt when I did it that I was representing all these women along the South Coast who have probably done much more than I have.

And when I came back here the joy of many of the women in the district—it was *their* achievement just as much as mine—was a tremendous joy to me.

ANNE GILFILLAN

*A*nne Gilfillan, like many women who were left with a farm
to manage when their husbands died, had to fight negative
predictions from bank managers and friends. But Anne is a stal-
wart. She educated her five children, four of whom were at school
at the time, and with skills gained at TAFE and farm field days,
increased her own knowledge of farming and farm management.
Now in her late sixties, she is always up early, active on the farm
at Tarlee in South Australia. Recently she introduced Murray
Greys to the cattle herd. 'You can't stand still', she said.

My family have owned this property since 1866 and the
house was actually built in 1872 so it goes back a long way.
I married the man next door and, in 1961 when my father
died, my husband bought back again the property that
belonged to my people.

As a child growing up on the farm, at what sort of age did you start helping with farm work?

Very, very young, because there is a photo of my brother and I holding lambs for the tailing and we wouldn't have been any more than three or four. The little school was just down the road and we walked or we rode our horse—three of us on the horse—to the school. When I was four I used to ride down with them and bring the horse home again and then she wouldn't ever go back at night to get them (laughs), so I used to have to kick and kick to get her to go down there. It's only three-quarters of a mile away but it's closed now. I went to school when I was very little because the others went to school. I used to have a sleep in front of the fireplace because I was only about four-and-a-half, I used to get tired and in front of the fireplace was the coolest place. When I began it had about twenty-five children and it eventually ended up with eight. It used to be fifty-odd but most of them only came when it wasn't harvest from round about, but there were a lot more houses and a lot more people about then.

It was only a one-teacher school. I went through the whole seven grades on my own in the class, so I had knowledge of the higher classes. I think for three months I had some company in that class out of the seven years. Then I went off to boarding school with thirty-two in my class and I wondered what had hit me. Apart from being sent away from home, to go to boarding school with a class like that was such a change.

When you were at primary school and you came home from school and on weekends did you have people around you could play with?

No. There was no transport very much. We had church and Sunday school, that was our outing. We went to Sunday school on Sunday afternoon and to church in the morning at eleven o'clock and that was about all we did. Then in the wartime there was no petrol and my sister and I ran the Sunday school and used to drive in a horse and sulky down to Giles Corner where the church was. But Giles Corner was quite a living little entity in those days. There's nothing there now, but it had a tennis club and a croquet club and a church and a hall and a youth club and a Fellowship. During the war there was a Comforts Fund and Red Cross and competitions and grandmothers competitions and lots of things going on. But I don't even know my neighbours now; it's very sad. I made a New Year resolution to go and visit them but I still haven't done it.

Going back to when you were at primary school, after school and on weekends did you help on the farm?

Yes, there was always something going on, there were lots of people about, and we helped drafting sheep and we grew up doing those chores and liking them.

Was there any difference, do you think, between you, as girls, doing those chores and the sorts of chores you did?

Not a lot. My elder sister was not very keen on the outside work but my brother and I were into everything and there was not a lot of difference made between us in those days; it wasn't until later that there was. I went away to school when I was twelve and it was never the same afterwards. When I came home at fifteen I was expected to work as hard as any man.

We had cows and we got up at six o'clock, we started milking at seven o'clock, we had to clean all the milking machines and we started milking again at four o'clock in the afternoon. It was long hours and hard work and we were

expected to do it. Then when the war ended I was supposed
to be a girl again with all the graces, and there weren't any
(laughs) except that the corners got knocked off. I think
perhaps my father thought that violin lessons would keep
me being a lady!

I was a pretty poor violinist. I had started at the boarding
school—my father wanted a violinist and I did it to please
him. I didn't really want to do it, but the violin lessons
were ... well, it was a chance to get away. I used to catch
the train at Tarlee, which is six miles away—about eight
kilometres—and I had to drive the horse and sulky to catch
the train at eight o'clock in the morning, so I had to leave
home at six-thirty at least and it was often wet and cold
and miserable. Sometimes in the wintertime it was almost
dark when I left. We also had a list a mile long of all the
farm things, all the business, all the repairs, the parts and
everything that we had to do, but the train journeys were
nice; I used to talk to people and meet people, which I didn't
ever get here on the farm very much, so it was an outing. I
went once a fortnight, which was not enough, and I was
always very excited before I went and absolutely dog-tired
afterwards; it took me days to get over it. I had one of the
very best teachers in Adelaide who taught me at the boarding school and he went on with me. Poor soul, he must have
been very disillusioned, but we had a good friendship and
away I went and had a good old chat and a bit of a lesson
and came home again (laughs).

*Do you remember much about the house that you lived in as a
child and the sort of services and things that were available in it?*

It was this house but it's been very much altered. There
was a big, big kitchen with one table to work on, and the
family ate at the other table. It had a slate floor and a bread

oven and a great big wood stove. That was the only stove, and when I was a child there were no lights. They'd had a big gaslight thing but it had long since gone and there were only Aladdin lamps.

There were great dust storms when I was a child, something like we had in January here, but they seemed to happen and we'd come home from school at four o'clock and the Aladdin lamp would be lit because it was so dark with the dust because there was fallow everywhere and the ground was worked up, and that was a big contrast. We went to bed with candles and I used to put a pillow against the door so nobody could see the light under the door when I was reading late at night. Later on we had a thirty-two volt electric plant but there was limited electricity and you had to put the lights off, and when the engine stopped there was nothing very much to keep the power going. It wasn't until the late 1950s that we got the power into this area, so it was a long, long time without it.

We didn't realise how deprived we were. We had the cellar—that's where you went up and down with the butter, and up and down with the jelly to try to set it—and then we had a cool safe and that was a great innovation, because that was in the kitchen and you didn't have to take the butter down the cellar.

In those days the family ate separately from the workers and there were always lots of people about. Before my mother died we always had somebody living in the house, and there were men who worked on the farm. There were so many people about it's unbelievable to look at it now. We can't afford to even get casual labour because the cost is so high, and the risks are high. But there are four houses on the 2000 acres that my father owned and they had families in them with three or four children and those children went to the school.

When you were growing up did it ever occur to you that you might do something other than farming, that you might have another choice of career?

I think my father wanted me to do teaching but I was most unhappy at boarding school though I did very well at the primary school—because I had specialist attention, I suppose. There weren't very many of us and I was in my own grade on my own for the whole seven years. But I fretted away at the boarding school. I went into the second year and instead of starting off and taking three years to do the Intermediate I tried to do it in two years and got overwhelmed with the work. I got sick and I carried on a treat: I was a real disaster!

I loved the farm and I loved the farm work even as a child and I didn't want to do anything else. When I eventually got a job I got a job at the Botanic Gardens and enjoyed that very much, but I didn't stay there very long. The work outside and the work with plants and animals was what I wanted to do.

At one stage my father wanted me to go off and do nursing, but I didn't want to do that. Sadly, my elder sister begged and begged to go and be a nurse and he wouldn't let her go. It was a bit peculiar. He thought that I could have done teaching but I begged to come home and since he was very short of labour that's what I did.

This was in 1942. I was at boarding school from '39 to '41 and came home in the holidays when Darwin was bombed. One of my fellow boarding house friends—her people had the post office at Darwin—went home for the holidays and was killed, and that was the closest we had come at that time to the war. It was a terrible blow that someone we knew was killed in the Darwin bombing.

My father was a Gallipoli veteran and very patriotic. He encouraged my brother to go off to the war at eighteen when there really wasn't any need; he could have got out of it and there really wasn't any necessity, but my brother was keen and my father was keen for him to go, and so my sister Helen and I had to stay home and do the work that my brother would have done.

They still tried to make us ladies because we did a week outside and a week inside. My stepmother was a wonderful housekeeper: we washed on Mondays, swept on Tuesdays and ironed, I suppose, cleaned on Wednesdays, but there was a wonderful routine. She was a great housekeeper and she ended up with a whole houseful of people that we had to keep house for—later in the war there were six prisoners of war—and not much help. They would kill a beast, or cow, and they would bring it in and dump it on this great big kitchen table in front of her and she had to sort out which was which and what was what and we girls had to help her. My father built an extra room on the house for the six Italian prisoners of war. They didn't use the house amenities but they ate in the kitchen.

The men would come in with the carcass chopped into quarters, and she would have to oversee the preparation. There was an Italian cook in amongst all of it. Sometimes there was a Southern Italian cook that didn't get on with the Northern Italians, and then there was a fellow who had come from Addis Ababa in Abyssinia and he was a pastry-cook. My stepmother had to oversee what he cooked and how he cooked and it was all done with this blazing big Simpson wood stove; it wasn't an Aga or anything comfortable. And there was no washing machine; the washing had to be scrubbed on a board and the clothes were pretty dirty. This is just for the family, but washing was a major operation. Everything was boiled and the copper sticks had to be picked up and the copper had to be boiled because there was no power. There was a big underground tank so there was a reasonable amount of water, but washing was a major operation.

Every alternate week we used to have to come inside and do the household chores, and I'd have a book in every room and would get into trouble all the time. Saturday morning was a major cooking day and we had roast leg of mutton—not ever lamb, it was always mutton—and some old ewe because you didn't kill a young one, that was money. She was a wonderful cook and we always had roast leg on Saturday and on Sunday, of course, we had the cold meat. It was a real ritual, and she brought us up and taught us the housekeeping routines and things that she had been taught and she taught us very well, because she was wonderful at it. But on the week that I did my 'cow' week, well, I seemed to lose all the incentive for the housework and that was the way it was. They seemed to think that by doing the week about we didn't get terribly involved in anything, but it was up and down. It was a funny old business.

Did you have any social life at that time?

Quite a lot of social life in that we had to go off and do this playing at all the local functions. We were brought up to be Methodists and, of course, nobody taught us to dance, but we'd have to go and play at a concert somewhere and then they'd have a dance afterwards and we were out of it, but some of the dear old chaps would teach us to dance at these dances. It was quite often; it depended on how much petrol we had whether we could or couldn't go. My father used to get petrol for the milking machine engine and I think we got some of our outings on the milking machine engine petrol, but it was always touch and go how much fuel you had, and if you didn't have any fuel, well, you went by horse and sulky.

When the war finished what happened to the work you did?

Well, the 1945 drought came. 1943 was a poor year, 1944 was a little bit worse, and in 1945 the season didn't open until July. My father had bought another property and had let the big tractor go: he had a Caterpillar tractor and it was part of the sale of the property, so he went back to horses. That's what he was used to and he went back to a horse team. My sister and I had to drive the horse teams, and we had some bolts. I was scared of the horses; they were so big and they were so heavy and they were always fairly fiery because he bought brumbies and broke them in and if they got a spook, well, they went, and we did have some notable bolts with the team. I was dead scared of them. He went back to that, but when the '45 drought came he'd also sold all the hay, which is a very sad reflection now because we do manage our droughts better, and the horses died. Some of them were shot and some of them died and he agisted all the sheep away. They were down the bottom end of York Peninsular and they came back, and then we got big rains and they died by the hundred because they were in poor condition. It's a whole sad story, that '45 drought, and I've been scared of drought ever since.

Anyway, my father bought wheat for the sheep and he didn't have so many sheep left because a lot of them died, so he planted everything and when it all came up and was seeding he had a good finish in '45: it was a bad start but it had a good finish and we had all these crops of proper wheat. It was all different colours, and I said to him, 'What sort of wheat is that?', and he said, 'Hope! Hope it grows and hope it yields' (laughs). We got out of it with all this planting, but by that time he had bought for a song a very old crawler tractor and he worked night and day himself. He worked most of the day and most of the night but by that time we had to sell the cattle because we had no feed for them. We fed them on potatoes to start with and kept them alive and then we sold them for a song, for £5 a head, and they followed me all the way to the railhead. I had one sheaf of hay in the back of the sulky and the whole mob followed me all the way, they were so hungry. We put them on the train and they went to the abattoirs and that was the end of the dairy.

You got married soon after the war?

I got married in 1951. I got the job in the Botanic Gardens but I was again very homesick and I used to come home at the weekends. I had a lovely job but I didn't like living in the city; it was not my scene at all and I was engaged to the man next door so I came home. We were engaged in 1949 and married in 1951.

In those days, when you started off life as a young married couple on a farm, did you have separate roles? People seem much more now to have a team management where they're both doing things. What was your role when you started off as a bride?

I was still very much the wife of the man, but because of my background I had a lot of interest in things. He was a great talker, he was a wonderful conversationalist, and he would share with me, and I think that was a very great asset because when I was left on my own I did know what was going on, partly because of my interest but more, again, because of his conversation. And I think that I was not even then a very normal, a usual sort of wife, but I had a baby boy in the first twelve months and then a couple of years afterwards a baby girl, and I was pretty well tied up with the children. But while they were little we often did things together. My husband's farm was not very big; he did have a married man but he lived at the other end of the property and I was often called on to help with drafting and sheep work and things. And the children ... the little boy had an absolute fixation for doing what Dad did and so we were often outside with the farm work even in those years. But by the time I had three children I did usually have somebody come to help me and then I got outside even more. We moved one property to the other property and I had two more little girls, and I tell you, with five children that was about enough.

But at the same time I was expected to do sheep work and to keep an eye on things, and often I would be involved in the decision making then because he always liked a sounding board. I remember one very dry year he hadn't put in a paddock, he was going to leave it out as fallow, and I said to him, 'Well, you won't get anything out of that if you leave it out for the whole season. Even if you plant it with oats it'll be feed.' It was just an observation because I knew enough, and he went ahead and did it. I don't think I actually got the credit for it afterwards, because it was very successful, but I did hear him telling somebody else that Mother had suggested that, so I suppose that was about as much credit as I'd ever get!

You have worked hard most of your life on the farm, and I guess you're not alone in that; a lot of women have done a lot of hard work beside their husbands or fathers or whatever. What sort of credit do you think people get for that?

Well, now, far more than I ever did think was possible, really. I remember when I first started off and I had maintained the farm for a number of years, one of my contemporaries said to me, 'Oh, if you can do it anybody can do it', and that really flattened me. Debbie Thiele [winner of the inaugural ABC Rural Woman of the Year award] said, 'You have to have the will, the opportunity and the encouragement', and a good many of us have the will and the opportunity but very few of us get the encouragement. I think that's the thing that's been sadly lacking, the encouragement, and I hope it's not going to be lacking in the future.

What about the Rural Woman's Award itself. Have you noticed any effect in the community or around the women since the inaugural award?

The Rural Woman's Award has received a good bit of publicity and a lot in the farming magazines, which is good because there was nothing in my early days, nothing. I was expected to do the education and my husband would do the agricultural politics. At one stage I had children in four different schools and by the time I chased around the education that was as much as I could manage. But since he's been gone I've done the politics and I belong to the Farmers' Federation and go to the meetings when they have them and take an interest in my grandchildren's education. I don't know what else I can do.

It was a surprise to me that my brother, who lived on this property and who comes and tells me what I should and shouldn't do, much to my annoyance, though he's a good friend of mine, applied for my Rural Award thing and I was very, very touched by that. He knew things that I had done that I didn't even know he knew. I did a management course after my husband died; I went to Gawler every week at night and, I tell you, after seven o'clock at night to go off to Gawler to a course once a week was hard.

In the wintertime it was always foggy coming back. I did that for two years and it gave me the jargon. I found that the bank managers were some of the worst people that I had to put up with. I went in to see the local bank manager and he sat back in his chair and he said, 'You don't think you're going to run that place and leave it to four daughters? You must be mad!' I was so angry I burst into tears, which is a woman's failing, and walked out, but I did have the guts to go back the next week and tell him to mind his own business and that's what I was going to do. And that's what I have done.

I was angry because he was not a local man; he had come from some other place to relieve at the bank, and we had good credit; my husband had no debts when he died. We had lost between $55 000 and $60 000 in death duties and we had no assets on the farm left except a very small share portfolio which I've added to. But we had no free assets left. They valued the place and then they came in from the Commonwealth and then re-valued it on a hobby farming basis, and twenty years afterwards it's nowhere near a hobby farm situation in this area. I should have fought it—they wouldn't allow me then; I would have fought it now. It was a very, very difficult time. It took them three or four years to clear up the estate and we'd lost pretty well everything, plus which I had lost my breadwinner and I had to give away one-third to a sharefarmer. I had to organise the work and the sharefarmer that came in has been a very loyal supporter.

So, over all, how well equipped do you think you were, having lived on a farm all your life, for managing a farm when your husband died?

I was probably a lot better equipped than a lot of my contemporaries because I always did the banking. I went into the local town; he didn't go out a great deal and I always did the banking. He was very frugal and I always knew that if it rained I could spend the money and get the children clothes and I could do what I wanted to do if it rained. So I learnt, and I also learnt how much money there was in the bank so that I could do the shopping that I needed. I learnt to manage that way as well as having a working knowledge of the farm, but I was very out of touch when he died with the whole set-up; I had to learn just like anybody else had to learn.

What did you do so that you could retain the farm and bring up your daughters here?

I learnt that you couldn't do it from the kitchen; I learnt that you had to be out there and because it was my nature and my background that was no hardship to me. I had two daughters going to high school at that time and they were both very good and very helpful. I remember when the cattle got out one night at 7.30 in the dark my youngest daughter helping me to put them back into the paddock. They had worked with their father as well, and they were very good, they were very helpful. My sharefarmer lives in the local town, at Tarlee, so he was here during the day and he proved to be very capable and we also learnt to talk, he and I.

When he first started off he was doing the cropping and doing the sheep work by the hour and he was not used to sheep. He didn't like sheep. When I decided after my brush with the banker two years after my husband died that I had to go and learn the words, learn how to talk to the people that held the finances, that was a good decision. I was able to go off and do that management course, and I realised when I was doing it how much I had in my head. You don't when you first start; you think that there's nothing there and I was very woolly; I was woolly with grief and over-whelmed with problems and it was hard to think. But doing the course I said to the lecturer, 'How could we sharefarm the stock?' and we worked out from the figures I had that my sharefarmer could make a go of his side of it by the net return from the stock, and that was a great success because it gave him an incentive and the more he put into the stock work, which he was better at, the more he got out of it.

Communication is most important, as well.

I guess for a time you were just holding even, then there must have been a time when you decided that you wanted to make some alterations, to move ahead to do other things.

Because of my sharefarmer's position we took on five years instead of the usual three years because the five years got me to the end of my daughters' matric. and I didn't want to move them out of the home that they were used to because of the mental difficulties of that. So we made it five years and he was agreeable for five years, and by that time I expected that perhaps my son would come back on the farm from his station, but by that time he was killed in an accident on the road along the Darling. We decided to do another five years and I decided to do that for myself, and having got into that sort of situation where he was making a living and I was making a living we decided to do another five years and we've just finished another five years.

That's how many?

It'll be twenty since he's been doing the sharefarming. He took over in August/September of '75 when my husband died.

51

You must look back on those twenty years with some sort of satisfaction.

Yes, I do. There were some ups and downs and there were some really difficult times, and there were times when we had to borrow the money to pay the shearers on the wool, times when it was *that* close. But I have always put the money away and we have learnt to get through the year with the money allocated without, I'm afraid, doing the budget that the banks want. But I have learnt to do all the costs as you go along, to know when the costs are going to come in and to know when to have the money ready and to have the projects that will bring that money in, to have it ready when the costs are high. That's worked out well.

DOROTHY BRENTON

*D*orothy Brenton arrived in Australia from the UK at the tender age of two-and-a-half. Her parents had come to a Group Settlement scheme in West Australia. She married George during World War II and when he came home the couple were able to buy twenty-five acres of land just out of Denmark in Western Australia. They added to this later with a Conditional Purchase grant. Although the Brentons are theoretically retired, when I arrived they had just finished delivering several large rolls of hay to the cattle and Dorothy was about to begin preparations for Bed and Breakfast guests later in the week.

My husband and I both came to group settlement with our parents. I was only two-and-a-half so I don't really remember much. I think the first thing I remember really clearly was being in the Peel Estate which is south of Perth. We were there for about four years, before we came to Denmark. That was a disaster; it was just sand and absolutely hopeless for dairying in those days without any irrigation or anything like that.

We arrived at Fremantle in April 1924 and after the Peel Estate we relocated to a farm three miles out of Denmark. The only school I ever went to was the Scotsdale School which is on the Scotsdale Road near Denmark. And George went to the Parryville School which is just down the road here, and that is the only school he ever went to. We both left when we were fourteen because in those days it was impossible to go on. If I had gone on to high school I would have had to have gone to Perth and stayed with an aunt, which terrified the life out of me, and there was just no question of continuing all those years ago.

My father was a dairy farmer and in the early days he milked by hand, of course. I remember we got our first milking machine in 1937. And we had pigs and just a very small area. It was a continual battle I suppose, everbody was in the same boat in those days, really.

In his earlier years my father had worked with horses. He worked for a transport company so he was used to the countryside, he was used to animals, and latterly he drove the first steam wagon in Glasgow. That's where I was born, in Glasgow.

But my mother hated it for the first seven years in Australia because she was from Manchester, she was used to the city and she had no contact at all with country life. I think it was much easier for the ones who had been rural in England and had some background of farming. But my mother adapted and afterwards she said she would never have wanted to go back. She got used to the countryside and she loved it really, and she lived to a good age and they both retired off their farm in Denmark.

Both George's parents and my parents retired and handed their farms in Denmark on to their children which is something that not too many group settlements people achieved.

Do you remember when they first moved onto that land. Was there a house there?

No. When they came it was all the same. There were small shacks—I believe they had earth floors—and there were only the two little rooms. They cooked outside, they washed outside and there were really no facilities at all. It was just like a camp until the houses were built, I think eighteen months or two years perhaps after they arrived.

The house on this farm here—where my daughter lives now—was built in 1926 and so was the holiday cottage ... the one we use for a holiday cottage today was built in 1926, two years after they arrived in Denmark.

People from England obviously thought it was grim, but it wasn't considered to be by the locals who had been here some time. Everybody was in the same boat. You think now, how did they get by? And how did they manage without shopping? Perhaps once a month they got an order.

But when we were in Peel Estate we did go into Perth, into Fremantle once a month on 'the Charabang' or whatever you call it. It was the bus. And because my father had a brother who lived in North Perth, when we did our shopping once a month we visited them. I've got photos of myself taken at their place when I was two-and-a-half.

You must have led a fairly happy life.

We did. We were carefree. Ours was a big school, a two-teacher school. I think sixty-four was the most children we had, but it was all in one.

When I left school I went home on the farm and helped with the milking and worked in Denmark. I relieved at a shop while a girl went on holidays and I also worked for some people I knew pretty well. One lady had had an operation and she was ill and her husband wanted someone to come and give her a hand. I went and looked after her, helped her for about three months and then another friend had a second young baby and I went there.

From that I saved up and went to Perth for a holiday, to stay with my aunt. I'd met George by this time and then, of course, he went into the Air Force. I worked in Perth for a few months and then it got really nasty and looked like the Japs were coming down the coast. He was away by this time in the Air Force—over East finishing his training as an airframe fitter. I came home on the farm and I helped Dad. There were a couple of fellows who grew vegetables for Kalgoorlie and for the Army and I helped them with tomato growing and all that sort of stuff.

George went into the Air Force in 1941 and we were engaged. He didn't want to get married until after the war but I said, 'We get married now or you'll have your ring back', because I had a feeling we should get married then. So we did. Then he went off, over east, and that was when I came home, so we were married actually five years before we came and lived together on the farm. We'd been very briefly together in that intervening time.

When he came back did you have a farm of your own?

By that time we had acquired this one, accidentally you might say, because a lot of these group settlement farms were abandoned. Unbeknownst to us they were reserved for war service land settlement. George's father—who lived down the road in those days, where his brother is now—

he wanted to lease this particular property to run his cattle in the winter. And he asked George to sign this form so that he could lease it.

We were up in Kalgoorlie just before the end of the War. George was stationed there for a while and we signed the form, he went back to the Air Force and next thing we got a letter from the Agricultural Bank—as it then was—to say that our tender had been accepted. 'Please forward eighty-five pounds and it will be at ten percent deposit ... ', and it would be ours.

We were absolutely flabbergasted, we didn't even know we'd tendered, and that was really how we came to get the home farm here. We've added a lot to it since. So when he was discharged we went and looked after Mum and Dad's farm for two weeks while they had a holiday in Perth, and then we came out here with our Dodge utility. Everything we possessed was on the back of it including, I remember quite well, a green enamel wood stove that my parents had bought for us for a wedding present five years before, and just the basics of what you could buy with coupons—the linen and all that sort of thing. That was how we started off.

The old cottage was there. It was structurally sound except that the verandah boards, the windows, the doors were all gone, they'd all been taken—or people had helped themselves to them—the tanks were rusted away, you couldn't use the stove to cook. We had to start off from scratch and build it all up from that. And it was all bush except twenty-five acres which had been partially cleared. All the big dead kauris were still standing and all the ferns had grown up. We started from then and today it's about five hundred hectares of mostly totally cleared land.

The mills came in and cut all the timber, there was a lot of kauri, a lot of timber on this property, and they used to come in the winter time because it was high and dry and they could work right through the winter. They had access to the timber, the government got the royalty. We didn't have the timber rights—nobody did, except the ones who were before 1900 or something like that, they had timber rights. So the timber was all taken and we were left to clean up the mess. You could stop the government from using your drive, they had to make alternative arrangements to get in if you wouldn't give them access through your main driveway, but we did, of course.

The 1950 fire—which was devastating—cleaned out all the timber that was left. It hadn't all been taken then but it really did make a big mess of the timber that was here. Now all the regrowth is beautiful, it's fifty years old and we have locked away perhaps fifty acres (in the old terms) under the Remnant Vegetation Scheme for thirty years. No one can touch it. It's growing up to be beautiful forest . . . the understorey is all coming back and it's really delightful. We're very pleased about that.

When you came here in your Dodge ute, where did you start?

The first thing my husband and his brother did was put a rainwater tank together. We bought the tank in sections, if I remember rightly, because I've got a photo of them doing it, to catch some water because we had no drinking water. There was plenty of creek water but no drinking water. On the 6th of December we came and put the tank together, but it didn't rain until the 6th of May that year so we were carting water for drinking and for washing for six months.

And then we put the stove in so we could cook and we made two rooms liveable, and we spent all our time burning up logs. There was so much work to do, you didn't really know where to start. We made a mistake really; I wanted to buy some cows immediately—my father had Guernseys—and we bought some Guernseys off him. I had the choice of the ones in the herd because he didn't agree with me which were the best cows. We bought eight, I think. But we really didn't have enough feed for them and we had to put them down on the coast hills the first winter, but we managed, we got by. I've still got all the records of our first milk cheque.

We built on those original cows and bought pedigree Guernsey heifers from the Rutherford girls at Torbay, and we started a Guernsey stud which we had for probably twenty years, I suppose. We went into Friesians and had all Friesians for the latter time of the dairying period.

And we had a lot of pigs—you had to have a lot of pigs to drink all the skim milk—and before we went onto butterfat we had anything up to 140 pigs. We really started the first intensive piggery—the remains of it is still there—where you had them under cover, on slats, and we used to have sows and reared our own pigs. My husband would take the truck to Katanning in the autumn, or when we needed, and bring a truckload of weaners home and we would fatten them. There's always been good demand for pork. We'd sell them at the sales in Denmark and I never ever remember getting a poor price for pigs.

What was your job in this?

I always helped with the milking, right up till we stopped five years ago. Sometimes we employed people in latter years, but one of us was always in the dairy. We didn't leave the dairy to employees. When we were potato-growing I worked on the harvester; I cut the seed.

I was lucky in as much as I had four daughters, five years apart, and they were all good cooks. As they grew up I'd go in from milking in the evening, I'd have my shower and dinner would be on the table. So, I had a bit of an advantage in that way, having girls in the house who were—although I say it myself—very good housekeepers. They're also very good gardeners—there's nothing they can't do, the four of them—but it was a case of necessity, I think, in their childhood.

Had the house been fixed up when you had your first child?

Not really. She was born after we'd been here about a year. We did the house bit by bit, you know, and I think after about the first five years it was reasonably comfortable. It was probably the same as all the other farm houses around here at the time.

You're obviously well-known for your gardening and you've got splendid gardens out here, when did you feel you could take that up?

I've always loved gardening. When I was home up in Mount Shadforth in my teenage years I always had a garden up there. It's something I've always had an interest in. If I'd been a man I think I would've liked to have been a land-scape gardener, if not an architect or something like that. I think it's very challenging to create a beautiful garden, a beautiful situation. It's very important to me.

What sort of person makes a good farmer?

You have to love the land. You have to love the life, the outdoor life. You have to love the challenge. Farmers are born, they can't be made, I don't think. I really do believe that. I think we're very *lucky* that we had the opportunity when we were young to have grown up with it. I think there are so many people in the cities who would've made wonderful farmers if they'd had the opportunity.

People come and stay with us here from all over the

60

world. We have a lot of English people—I do Bed and Breakfast—and they always say, 'It must be such a wonderful life.
So free'. Well, it's very demanding but you can't have it both
ways, can you?

We've also been very fortunate in as much as we've always
had good health. If you didn't have good health and good
stamina and the desire to work, you wouldn't succeed. If you
weren't physically capable of it, you just couldn't do it.

*You left school at fourteen and I guess you didn't have the advan-
tage of going to an agricultural high school or any of that sort of
thing. How did you learn it all?*

I think I was lucky perhaps in that my parents were very
well read and we read a lot as children. I think that helped
a lot. And it's ongoing experience over a lifetime. You pick
it all up. You get a vast knowledge which only time and the
interest in it give you.

There are negatives, of course. There's all sorts of negatives. First of all you've got the seasons. We are very fortunate here, we live in a very favoured rainfall area. I'd hate
to farm in a marginal area where you were watching the
clouds for months at a time. It must be heartbreaking to see
your animals suffering and see no end to the financial strain.
I don't think I could stand that.

So, we're very lucky. We farm in a very beautiful, very
rewarding part of Australia—the best part of Australia, I
think myself, having seen nearly all of it. Then, of course,
things go wrong, you get major machinery breakdowns and
it costs you a lot of money you haven't probably budgeted
for. All sorts of things come into it. A few years ago the
cattle price was bedrock, there was no demand. I remember
I came home one afternoon—it was when we were still
dairying—and George had sold one hundred and ten

animals I think it was, which I had reared on the bucket, for less than $700. It was just a pittance, you might say. I was absolutely furious, but he had to do it because there was no point in keeping our dairy cows hungry to feed all these young animals which were twelve months old or so. He had to get rid of them. So things like that go wrong.

When they do go wrong, do you have a view that it'll get better?

It can only get better, can't it? I remember when we had our first big dam made on the creek for irrigating potatoes. We had a flash flood one night and the next morning I looked down the valley and I saw all this brown, and I thought, whatever is going on? The dam had gone. George had put a big diesel motor down there on a concrete slab— we didn't have power in those days—and the heavy rain had started washing around the slab and it cut the middle right out of the dam. We were depending on this dam to irrigate the crop and I remember running up the hill bawling my eyes out, and George said, Whatever is the matter? I was devastated because we were so dependent on water that year to irrigate the potato crop which was on the hill here. We had to get the dam replaced and replace the motor. That's the sort of thing that at times crops up. It does in anything, doesn't it?

What else has gone wrong? Well, we lost our only son when he was three. That was a big blow, but you come to terms with it. I never ever thought I would but I remember at the time the Church of England minister here—who was a very nice fellow—said to me, 'In time you'll remember him with joy', and you do. It happens eventually.

What about the community life around here?

We would like to have taken a much closer interest in the

community life but we're a fair way out of Denmark and as far as going to CWA or that sort of thing, I was always too busy. I mean, my husband was very much involved in the Farmers' Union in the earlier days. I used to do the milking while he went to Bunbury and he was also a director of Sunny West Co-Operative Dairies for quite a few years. I've always been too much involved on the farm here with the work that had to be done and bringing up a family to be greatly involved with community work. My husband did three years with the Denmark Shire in the 1950s and he was very active in the Farmers' Union for many years. He was also a Director of Denmark Co-Op. for many years. But we were involved with sport. I played hockey for thirty-odd years until I was in my thirties and I couldn't catch the seventeen-year-olds. I had to stop playing hockey. We played tennis, we went to all the dances and had a lot of fun. We went to picnics on the beach—we always went to the beach on Sundays in the summer, either Peaceful Bay or Boat Harbour or William Bay or wherever.

When a decision has to be made, how is that arrived at?

Well, fortunately, we always seem to agree on what decision has to be made. The only time we ever disagree is when we're handling cattle and we never ever agree on that. We do it completely differently, and that's the only time we ever have an argument. We've never had an argument about finance or the children or anything else but working with animals can be very frustrating at times. You think the other person isn't doing it the way you would do it. But it was only superficial, really, nothing of any consequence.

And you now live in a house that was made from your dairy.

Yes. It was only eight years old and it was double brick.

When we decided that we would go out of dairying—we'd been in it for forty-five years—we thought it was time to take life a bit easier.

I always work outside, there's always something to do outside. At the moment, Pat and Dawn—our son-in-law and daughter—are away at Rottnest for a holiday for ten days and we're just feeding the cattle. We feed out the big round bales to four different mobs every morning, we've got about one hundred and fifty calves now, and we feed the mob of springers and also all the young stock. We're very lucky, I think, that in our seventies we can both do that. George is seventy-seven and there's not many men of his age who are able to do what he can do still.

Did you ever have holidays like your daughter has?

No. In the first thirty years we were here a weekend in Perth would have been all we'd ever had. But when George got to about sixty, he said, 'Well, now is the time'. We've had some beautiful holidays—we've been overseas three times, to England, Europe and Scandinavia, and spent a lot of time in Scotland where I was born. We went first in 1980 and then in 1985 and then in 1989 for three months but we've also been to New Zealand, Tasmania and all around Australia twice so we've done pretty well for holidays.

Was that after George was sixty?

Yes, and by this time we had family at home. We had our son-in-law home—first of all Gay and Stan for a few years and now Pat and Dawn, so we've got family at home to carry on while we go for a holiday.

You're coming on to your fifty-year anniversary of moving onto this land. What does it mean to you?

It's hard to put into words, really. I get a bit emotional when I think about it. It means an awful lot, because when you've made it yourself from bush it does mean a lot and it'll always be in the family, I hope.

Dorothy, you've got a bed and breakfast business—it seems to me you're always into something new.

After going overseas and seeing Bed and Breakfasts—not that we stayed in many since we had relations and friends to stay with in England and Scotland, but we did stay in a few—I thought that would be a good thing to do, it would be interesting and you'd meet a lot of people.

I wanted to do it when we were still dairying back in the late 1980s but George said, No, there's no way. You haven't got time. You can't do it properly. Eventually he relented— in about 1989 or something—and the first year I had it the Tourist Commission came out and inspected the house and everything first, and in that year I had three couples. I remember them all quite distinctly. I started from that, and then it grew.

I probably spend more on the house, getting everything going, than I actually make out of it as far as finance goes, but I love it. Read the Guest Book and you'll see that we get invitations all over the world, and people do appreciate coming onto a farm in this part of the world. And we always take them on a farm tour. We just take a drive around and show them a bit of the district because some places they wouldn't know or where to go to see a lot of things that are worth seeing. And it's great fun.

I've got three guest rooms and they have their breakfast here and I'll do them dinner in the evening if they wish to have it—I have to cook for George and me. He complains because he gets three courses when we've got guests—he says he's getting too fat—but that's up to him, he doesn't have to eat the soup if he doesn't want it.

I enjoy cooking and it's another challenge, I suppose. It's good fun and I like things done nicely. The cottage is self-contained and they do their own food down there. And Dawn, my daughter, looks after that. She cleans and looks after it, so we share that between us. That's very popular too, it's been very very busy this last twelve months. We've got ponies and people love to come and see the calves and when there are kiddies they have a ball because they can run all over the place and go mad if they want to. And it's secluded.

And this is what you call slowing down a bit is it?

I don't consider I'm slowing down; the last thing I want to do is slow down a bit. Why should we if we're able to do things? I realise I can't do what I used to. I'm running the house, chasing cows and the next thing I know I'm sitting down puffed-out. But you've got to expect that haven't you?

ROSALIE BENNETTS

*R osalie Bennetts, a farmer most of her life, was over forty
when she nervously faced the prospect of off-farm work in
an office. Her husband had developed a serious illness and they
had three children to support. But her move was successful and
she is now General Manager of Farm Shed, an exhibition of Australian rural life, designed for international visitors, at Toner in
Victoria. Skills learned during her childhood on a dairy farm have
been invaluable.*

I grew up virtually in East-Gippsland. I was born in the Traralgon Hospital—not the Traralgon Hospital as it is now, but
the original Traralgon Hospital which was a lovely, big old
rambling house, still there today.

My parents were dairy farmers. My father was always
very partial to Jerseys.

At about age five we started helping to rear the calves and to work in the shed. My father was a very kind person to animals and to the children, but we all had our work to do, and some of the jobs were getting up early of a morning and getting all the cows in ready for milking.

I was reading something—a tribute to my father—recently, and one of his brothers was talking about when he went for the cows at 4.30 in the morning. I'm happy to say I never went at 4.30 but usually around about 6.00—between 5.00 am and 6.00 am—and that's when I still wake up. I like to start the day between 5.00 am and 6.00 am.

Was it hard having to go to school after that?

No, you didn't think of it, and we really did love it. We learnt to play tricks on Dad: we'd say we had to be excused to go over to the toilet, and we'd stay home and have toast and everything, and then we'd think, Perhaps we've been a little bit long, so I'd make Dad a nice hot drink and some toast and take it back to pacify him.

But I don't ever remember it being hard. The only negative thing—and I notice even now with my little nieces because they're dairy farming—was that if you went somewhere at the end of the day you had to go home and miss out on the rest of the fun. That's the only thing that was probably a bit of a negative as you got older.

If you wanted to go somewhere—or Mum and Dad went too—at 2.40 everybody would be just getting into the swing of the picnic or the fete or whatever, and Dad would say, 'Okay, cow time', so you knew you just had to go.

We'd go to Port Albert fishing of a Sunday. Mum would get up—it would still be dark—and because we were a large family, at that stage probably seven children, she would cut a little case full of sandwiches. I remember how horrible it used to be because the smell of petrol from the little vehicle that we had would get into the sandwiches and then they would sit them on the sand and one of the babies would throw sand in them. I used to think that the worst part of the day was having your lunch because it was smelly and all gritty. But we'd have a wonderful time—picnics and fishing and boat rides, because Dad loved fishing.

Of an evening we had the pianola. We were all taught to play if we wanted to at age ten. I was the first one to master that and I really loved learning to play the piano. Dad played the violin by ear, and Mum used to sing so we always had music at home. They were both very avid readers so that books and music were how we relaxed of an evening.

We had a wireless and I grew up on 'Blue Hills' and probably 'Pick-a-Box' with Bob and Dolly Dyer. They were fun things that we were all allowed, but you weren't just allowed to listen to it when you wanted to, it was something that Mum and Dad had control over. We just had to learn to enjoy what they enjoyed.

I guess the radio must've been one of the few outside influences to come into your lives, was it?

Yes it would have been, because my parents got papers but not every day. They came on the cream truck. My parents were always very politically in tune and conscious of world events. My mother was English and very loyal to the Monarchy and they were interested in everything that was going on around them.

Were you able to live at home and go to high school as well?

Yes, we lived at home. I remember walking in the dark to catch the high school bus to go to Traralgon. I don't know what time it would be but I used to have a torch, and I think I probably had to walk two or three miles to the bus.

Did you ever think that you might, when you grew up, not want to be a dairy farmer?

I always loved farming. I was my dad's little shadow and little helper. His first love was horses and cows and I shared that with him. I knew that I didn't want to milk forever, but I never ever saw a time when I wouldn't have animals in my life, because I really do love the animals—especially horses and cows and the odd pet lamb.

My father moved many times with share-farming. When he worked on the land at Madalya there was a man from Western Australia who was all the time talking about the Golden West, and my father had this dream of seeing it. He waited until he had seven children and then, before there was any bitumen road, we drove across the Nullarbor. He pulled a little trailer with a tent on it and we pitched it every night. We stayed in the West for well over three years but our grandmother got very ill and, in fact, died before we came back. Mum was so distressed that we moved back to Victoria, closer to her family. I did not like changing schools . . . I found it so hard. You would just make friends and you'd be torn away from them.

When I left school I first went up to Mildura to work on the grapes for an uncle for twelve months. He had a vineyard, 'a block' is what you called it, so I worked up there helping them. They had had a tragedy—their first little child, a little girl, drowned in the irrigation channel. I went up to help my aunty because she was having another baby, and I stayed there for twelve months and saved up money to go to college. Then I went to college and graduated from Business, and my only regret was that I did so well I did it in twelve months: I would've loved to have been there for two years; it would've cost more money but it was a lot of fun. I enjoyed that.

I always wanted to be a teacher, but in later years my father said that he had never had the money to be able to send me to Teacher's College. I couldn't understand that because in those days you could be a student teacher. I think you could alternate your teaching and your training, but because we lived so far out, Dad just knew that he didn't have the money, so it stopped there. I often used to wonder what would've happened had he looked into it, but that was where my heart lay—in teaching children.

What about the Business course? Has that been of use to you?

It was a Secretarial course plus Business and yes, I loved it, absolutely loved it. I worked for youth leaders as well as an export manager of a company and I enjoyed that. I have no regrets—in fact, I seem to enjoy everything that I do.

And marriage brought you back to farming, did it?

When we married, Lyle had an interstate truck and then he wanted to do logging. When he decided to go into farming, because we had moved so many times, I couldn't imagine making my children shift from school to school. We had to find something where we would stop. But Lyle wasn't really a farmer, so he kept drifting back to the trucks and we were between farming and trucks and trucks and farming.

Who took care of the farm while he was driving the trucks?

I did the farming and some of the milking and I think some of the times he tried to do both. I think the last time I was milking we went up to seventy cows. At that stage Lyle had an uncle and his uncle's brother was still alive and they had properties, so we had access to agistment land. I'm not sure what we would've been caring for, but possibly two or three hundred acres with cattle on them. Then, as the uncles got very elderly, the properties had to be sold up and we got back to our own acreage which was a hundred and something. At the moment we're just under a hundred acres and since my husband has been sick we've gone over into beef instead of dairy, which has been much easier.

In those days when you were dairying did you have to do every-thing for the cattle?

I can remember the first time I delivered a calf with a pair of panty hose and forgot how much stretch there would be. We had this cow calving and I had to go down and check again and I could see that she was down on the ground and that distressed me. All the cows were milling around—as cows always do—and I had been to church, I think, so I took off my pantyhose. I noticed that the head was just through but she was getting so weak that she just didn't have enough strength.

I tied my pantyhose around [the head] and I started to pull. Now I had tied them safely and well, but I kept backing back and back and back—it seemed to be hundreds of metres—and the pantyhose were coming with me. But eventually I got the pantyhose taut enough and I was so proud when I delivered that calf and it came out. It took a lot of oomph. The cows were milling around and so that I wouldn't distress her and get her up, I got down on all fours on the ground so that I wasn't obvious to the cows. They were more intent on her moaning and the blood that was around than they were on me. So I got away with it.

Probably the hardest thing to take is in the cold weather when the sun comes up. Isn't it strange? Before the sun comes up you can jump out of bed in the dark and do everything, but when the sun comes up, you nearly freeze. I don't know why it is.

Did you have to do fencing and things like that?

I never ever did fencing, I just looked after the milking, and the cows, and the calves, and the children. And when the children were little I would have the carry basket in the car and the car would be parked right beside the yard where the cows were so that I could run up and down, wash my hands and pop the dummy in and come back down again if they were getting distressed. The two bigger ones were inside and because the house wasn't that far away, you could run over and tap on the window if they were fighting or whatever, then whiz back before the machines were finished each time.

They didn't come out with you at dawn to milk the cows when they were tiny?

No, never. And they still don't. And putting hay out and things like that, I don't think I ever took them then, either, because I was always very safety conscious and liked to know where they were and what they were doing. Little bit of an overprotective mother.

I guess the business experience that you had would have stood you in good stead with the farm books and things?

Yes it did, although my husband says that I was never much good on the books because, if you wanted a balance, we used to be better off than I used to tell him we were.

Did you breed cattle as well?

Yes, we had our own calves. We would rear a certain

number of replacements every year, and as the children got older, that's one thing that they used to help with a little bit. The eldest son would come over and milk but he would invariably leave the gate open where the cows get milked on the herringbone, so while he was doing one side, the others were quietly going past him. And then he'd say, 'Boy! I can milk much faster than you, Mum'. And I'd say, 'Yes, just look around and see what you've done'. Once you let cows out of a milking shed you can never get them back. They think, 'Right, we're home free!' So you have to make sure that you milk a bit earlier the next morning or they are absolutely bursting.

Are any of your children interested in farming?

Yes, the youngest one. The two eldest weren't at all interested in it. They love the land, and Dean loved his motorbike and loved all the area for riding and playing and doing things. And Kim-Marie loves coming home on the farm. But Jarred's been interested ever since he was tiny—perhaps because he spent a lot of time with me. He never went to kindergarten; he stood on the railing and counted how many cows I had left and how many I would have in each time. He set his little toy animals up in little paddocks, and to this day he's our little farmer. Now, at seventeen, he's left school and he's doing a farming apprentice course. He's also working on our property two days a week and working on a commercial Angus property for two days a week.

So you have someone to hand over to when you get sick of it?

He doesn't see it as handing over. He sees it as what he's going to be doing.

Tell me how you came back into the normal work-force.

That was a result of sickness. My husband has an insidious disease which attacked both of his kidneys. When he was in his forties, the doctor thought that perhaps because of his age, because he was helping with the farm and driving trucks, it was blood pressure. But no one looked further. So for twelve months he battled on until one day they did a test and found that he vitually had two weeks and five days to live, because of the amount of toxins in his blood.

He had to go in to Fairfield Hospital and then Prince Henry's to have his kidneys and everything checked out. To this day we don't know how he got this disease. He panicked and thought he was going to die and he sold all of our milking cows to pay off the farm. He said, I would just have to go back to work, that there was nothing for it. That was quite terrifying to me at my age—I was into my forties then. A friend of mind told me about a position up here—not the position I'm in now, but in the souvenir shop. So I started back in the work-force. And for someone who loved the land, loved working with the animals, with the children, loved being at home, and was very much a home person, it was a very traumatic experience.

What frightened you most about coming back to work with other people?

The unknown, just the unknown. I was very proficient as a typist but we were talking about computers. You might as well talk about spaceships to me as about computers— that was probably the most terrifying thing.

How long did it take you to get used to it?

Eight weeks. I went to school two nights a week for eight weeks. And while I didn't feel extremely intelligent at the end of that, I'd completely lost my fear.

You've now taken over as General Manager of the Farm Shed.
Tell me what the Farm Shed does.

My most fascinating role, besides General Manager, is
that I am the personnel person. I care for all of the staff. I
care for the day-to-day running and I support the Managing
Director. He is a very astute business and financial and
mathematical person. I'm a very practical person, very
methodical and very practical. So we seem to have a good
working relationship.

Three years ago our marketing manager left so now I'm
the international marketing person and probably going to
Korea. I've been to Japan twice, I've been to Thailand, Indonesia and Singapore with marketing. That's probably where
I've had the most pressure because, this being private business and being on a farm myself, I am very much aware of
how much money is involved. You want it to be viable and
you want to do your best.

The marketing manager I took over from was younger
than me by ten years, and I thought for me to step into his
shoes, a senior lady with grey hair, trotting around doing
what he used to do, was such a contrast. I just felt fearful
for the Farm Shed. But as it's turned out I have been thrilled
with the reception I've had and the results that we've had
back.

So you go and see tour operators and tourist people bringing
people ...

Yes, travel agents and tour operators and wholesalers. We
work in with the Australian Tourist Commission and also
Tourism Victoria—they're very supportive and arrange trade
seminars. When you go to South-East Asia there could be

350 Australians all there at that one time and you set up your booth like a world trade show.

So, when they come here from South-East Asian countries, what do they like to see? What are they most interested in?

They're probably most interested in being in the country and seeing the animals.

Are there farmers amongst them?

Sometimes they might be meat buyers, but not always. A couple of years ago we had a major chain of reception houses. Instead of getting bonuses all of their staff in their reception rooms in major cities will all be sent through Australia on this tour.

It's a sort of a 'get to know Australia' kind of.

Yes, it's a reward for them: a beautiful tour to see Australia. And the Farm Shed has been happy that we've had such a large number of people coming.

First of all they see the one-hour show which we have twice a day. We have eleven breeds of sheep and we start off with those that are the best for the wool and then have the meat breeds. They are all interested in that and we have translated sheets for them so that they can follow.

They have an introduction at the beginning of the show but after that they virtually have to listen to their guide and every group has an Australian, English-speaking guide with them, but the guide will talk in Japanese or the language of whichever country they're from.

Then they see a sheep shearing, then we have hand-milking and machine-milking, and then we go outside and there's a sheep-dog working. We have the lambs fed and a whip-cracking demonstration and that's all part of the one-hour show.

We have a paddock of kangaroos and the gardens which are always very neat and tidy and picturesque. We also have displays inside and then we're very proud of our little shop that we have here because it is pure Australian Made. We don't have anything in there that's not made in Australia—it has taken a long time to get it to that stage.

We have a magnificent barbecue restaurant which can seat two hundred and ten. When the Japanese students come they like to sit them in their grades and we're very popular for the student market because we're so spacious and roomy.

Do you ever use the skills you learnt when you were farming, here as general manager?

Yes, I do. The stock staff we have out the back need guidance, and it's my position to hold everybody together so they come in and report to me. I can relate very well to the needs of the cattle, to the needs of the dog, to the care of the dog, to the care of the cattle.

One day they came and said, 'We have a problem, we have nobody to crack the whip', so I said to them, 'Well, that's fine, bring it in and I'll crack it for you', and they said 'You?' and I said, 'Yes, that's fine'. And they said, 'How would you know how to do that?' and I said, 'Well, I guess I've been doing it since I was five and I wouldn't think I'd forgotten, because it's like riding a bicycle, you never forget'. I have one rule, though: I will only do it inside under that great big tin roof where the noise is tremendous; it sounds really great. I explain how a whip is made, I explain what it is used for, that it is not something ever to be used cruelly, it's only a measure of discipline and safety for the animals.

When the animals hear the crack from that one flick and feel the sting, their minds get it together immediately: they know when they hear that they'd better do what they were supposed to be doing. I explain all of that—especially to the children—and then I crack it and, believe-you-me, under the tin roof in there it sounds great.

You're in your mid-fifties now, but you seem to be enjoying your new working life.

I do enjoy it but sometimes I think it'd be beautiful to stop. I'm hoping by the time I'm sixty I can stop and do something that I would really like to do, but in the meantime I never ever get up and feel as if I'm going to work.

I have a couple of little secrets and one of them is that every morning and every evening I walk for thirty-five minutes, usually at 6 o'clock. It's dark now, I have to take the torch, but I walk on our little country road and I talk to the cows and the sheep and whatever is around and look at the trees and enjoy everything that I love outside before I have to go and be shut inside for most of the day.

Then at the end of the day, especially if it's very stressful, it's terrific to have another little walk. I'm back in the dark this time of the year and that's why I like the summer, but I find that walking keeps your mind bright and makes you feel better as well. I think I'd be full of aches and pains sitting in a chair watching TV if I didn't do my walking.

GAIL GUTHRIE

Gail Guthrie was attending to customers in her wool and craft shop when I called in to see her. She and husband David decided to develop wool that did not itch from their own soft Merino fleeces. It was a way of adding to the value of their own produce when the wool prices collapsed. The couple and their children live at Kent River in the lush south west of Western Australia but travel frequently to promote their unique knitting yarn at shows and field days.

I grew up at Kojonup in the central south-west of Western Australia on a wool growing property, so I've always been in wool, which is our main thing now. And from there I went to boarding school and the usual things for a country girl, then to Ag. College at Muresk. I had two years there. Came home, still undecided what to do, but wanted to continue in agriculture. I had six months of carting water for the middle of the drought, which was rather interesting.

Was this for your family?

On the family farm, yes. And from there we changed direction a little and bought a holiday resort at Walpole which was caravan park, holiday cottages and that sort of thing and it was very very interesting. I was there for fourteen years so I must've liked it a fair bit.

What's interesting about running a caravan park?

Meeting people and it's a bit like farming in that you're farming people not sheep. But it was meeting the people from all over Australia, all over the world. We were getting people in from everywhere and that was what I really missed when I left the caravan park.

When you say they're the same as animals, is that your observation of behaviour?

Yes, there's a real distinction between caravaners, between people that stay in cottages and people that camp. Some are very demanding, others are very interesting, and those from overseas were very keen to learn about what was going on. The caravaners seemed to be wanting to get up and go the whole time and they missed so much that you really wondered if they saw the countryside at all.

And so they came here because it's a very rural kind of area.

Yes. Walpole and right through Denmark is very scenic. You've got the Valley of the Giants, the huge timber—the kauris and the jarrah—and that's probably the main attraction of the south-coast. It's the land of a lot of variety and I think that attracts a lot of people.

But you decided to swap the people for animals in the end.

Yes. You can only deal with people on a continual basis seven days a week—which it was—for a certain length of time. And my husband had been farming the whole time anyway, so we decided to sell out of the caravan park and move back and concentrate on the farm. And in the meantime we'd already built this home. We'd started off living at the caravan park and he was travelling all the time, then we changed direction, lived on the farm and I'd do the travelling. Then it was time to move on and concentrate on the farm.

We also took over the family farm at Kojonup. My parents had retired down here to Nornalup, and so we had a bigger enterprise to run. We're still running that.

Why do all the places end in 'up'?

'Up' is an Aboriginal term meaning 'place of', usually in association with water because that obviously drew the Aboriginals, but in the case of Nornalup it's the 'place of black snake', Kojonup—'the place of blue rock'. The blue rock at Kojonup was a major meeting and corroboree place.

So you came back to the farm ... this farm. What did you do? What was your 'place'?

By then we had four kids, three when we moved back here. I was still running the park but I had four by the time I finished. But I very much had a place in that I've always done all the books for both properties from before I left school, as I was a partner with my parents on the home farm, and then with my husband when we took over that place again. I've done the books right through but also kept in touch with what's happening in agriculture.

My husband reads what magazines he can, but I also have to do a lot of the reading, otherwise we wouldn't keep in touch and often if he couldn't go to meetings I'd go. I became involved in the local land conservation group and then, of course, as we became more and more involved in the wool, I was going off attending meetings for that as well. We became involved in the Wool Foundation, and we started researching for this business that we're doing now of evaluating our own wool right through.

Just going back to the meetings for a minute. I've always heard that it's really quite difficult for women to be heard in some of those farmer meetings.

I haven't had much difficulty, but then, perhaps I'm a bit more outspoken. They're obviously very male-dominated a lot of the time, but that just didn't stop me. I speak up when I've got something to say and it's usually heard. I can't always say that I agree with the final results but then you can't have it all your own way.

We've got eight hundred acres here at this farm. When we came back there were beef and cattle but as time has gone on we've gone more and more to wool production. I wanted to specialise in that.

Of the eight hundred acres about six hundred are pasture, quite a viable little unit for here. Smaller than that it's very hard to make ends meet in this area. Kojonup is a different place; it's only about eighteen hundred acres of which about seventeen hundred is pastured—that's probably small for that area up there. But again, it's fully-developed and it's a good operating unit. So, between the two it works very well. What we've been doing up until now is lambing here and then shifting our lambs up to grow out at Kojonup, combining the two units. Where a wet year here is usually too wet, so the farm is not as good and production is down, at Kojonup it's an ideal year. A dry year up there when we usually end up with a drought, is a good year here. So, the two work well together.

Tell me why and when you decided to do something with the wool and add value to it.

Well, we had seen evidence of people starting to value-add their wool and that was the coming thing. We'd sold one line of wool to a chap at Boyup Brook who was making jumpers, that was only our combing line, which is the second line, but we realised that we weren't going to get any more for doing that than if we'd put it through the market.

Plus, we'd heard so much over the air about people complaining that they used to be able to buy good wool and couldn't do so now that we thought, This is silly. Our wool coming off our sheep is just so beautiful and soft, it doesn't itch, it's beautiful stuff, yet it's not getting through to the customer. So I thought, well, we'll research it.

We did trips to the East looking over all the mills, and there was a big seminar in Albany called 'Beyond the Bale' which was probably a catalyst. We saw other people doing things, it gave us a lot of ideas and it was probably a jumping stone for us in working out what we were going to do.

I came home and decided that we would go into knitting yarn, that there was obviously a demand there from people wanting a good quality knitting yarn that was nice to feel, nice to work with. We carried on contacting mills but it took us a long time to persuade them that our 21 micron wool could be made into knitting yarn. They all threw their hands up in horror to start with and said: 'You can't do that!

You put 26-28-30 micron stuff into knitting yarn'.

But we were lucky in that one of the mill managers we met on our trip over East retired shortly after we met him and agreed to do some consultancy work for us to help us design the yarn. That got us through a lot of hurdles that we would've probably otherwise floundered at.

Some textile mills are very closed. We'd go and see them, we'd get to see their display but we couldn't even get through to see the mill. It was a very closed shop and there just aren't many people doing what we're doing. There's one in Sydney now, Australian Fine Wool, who started after we did, and there's the people at Mudgee doing what they call 'woollen system'. So, really, no, there was nobody doing what we're doing we could talk to; they've either come since or they've taken off in different tacks. Ours is a completely 'worsted system'. They actually card and comb the wool so they're taking out all the short fibres and you end up with a longer set of fibres, very even, and a much smoother, polished sort of yarn.

When did you think you had researched enough?

I don't think you ever do. We're still doing it ... continually following up leads. We visited the mills last year, we'll do so again this year. We're going over to Melbourne in April to do a Trade Fair and we're still learning about processing and about the marketing because, of course, that side of things is completely different too. We'd always grown our product, sent it off and it had been marketed. *We* hadn't marketed it.

Did you have to make changes in the genetics of the sheep?

No, because we were already going for a soft white wool. What we've found is that what we were doing by feel and look is now being reinforced by what the CSIRO have learnt, especially in regard to their prickle factor, but actually we were on the right line; we just know more now about what we were doing.

The prickle factor has probably been the major break-through from the CSIRO. They found that when fibres over 30 micron hit the skin they don't bend, whereas, under 30 micron they do, and therefore that can have very much of an effect. They found that if you've got less than five per cent of those broad fibres then you'll have a prickle-free wool. So, that's something that we've built our line on.

So, part of it is in the manufacturing. You were already growing the right sort of wool . . .

We were growing the right sort of wool, but when it leaves us normally it gets batched with a lot of other wool and most of that wool would not have that low prickle factor. So you'd end up with our wool being lost in the system and therefore not finishing with a product that's got that feel. When we follow our own wool right through the system we're able to control that quality and we don't batch it with other people's, and when we get to the stage that we can, then we'll bring in people with similar wool so that we still don't upset that lack of prickle.

You're a reasonably small operation so that must be quite difficult and expensive to organise.

It is and it's taken four or five years to get to the stage that we're now doing commercial sized runs through the mills. They're still small by their standards but they are com-mercial runs. It needs four tonne of yarn for the spinning mill to do a run of any particular line, and we just get into that now. We've done one four-tonne run, we'll do another one next year. So, it's about an annual run at this stage but it will depend on how good our marketing is as to how quickly it then expands from there.

It comes out of the mills as dyed yarn?

Dyed yarn, in balls ready to sell through the shops. We then sell it retail through our own little outlet here, by mail order—we've been building up a mail order system through shows and all that sort of thing—and wholesale, direct to the retailers. Of course, we're putting a certain proportion into craft kits. We've found that the 8-ply splits down beautifully like an embroidery yarn and so we're making up wool embroidery cross-stitch and tapestry kits and getting another market there for it as well.

I guess that's something that people who class themselves as farmers don't really expect to do, that sort of intensive marketing.

No, and this was completely and utterly new to us. As I've said, we've learnt a heck of a lot since we started. We thought we knew wool and yes, we knew wool, but we didn't know anything beyond the farm gate.

How do you run a business which needs to be nation-wide, I guess, to do any good at all, when you're stuck down in the south-west corner of the country?

I suppose we've got the best of both worlds. Now, with modern communication, the Fax machine, the computer, the telephone, we can be in touch whenever we want. We've got a time advantage, actually, with the Eastern States: we can get up early and do all our phone calls before our peak rates come into operation, plus we live in a beautiful spot, so, I suppose we've got the best of both worlds.

Technology has made the difference. I don't think we

could've done it without that. We may have done, but it would've taken a lot longer, a lot more trips to Perth and a lot more cost would've been involved. At least you can hop on a plane to go to Sydney and hire cars, whereas once we would've had to have driven the Nullarbor. It's relatively simple these days.

Most of your product then is for people who want to knit themselves. Is that a craft that there's a lot of interest in?

It's a little bit in the doldrums at the moment, it's very seasonal. We found with the last two very dry winters that people haven't been inside doing craft and it's not just knitting, it's all craft. But, there's a group of younger ones out there starting to take an interest again and I think it's going to be like a wave action, it'll come back, especially as it gets the concept of being a craft—not just something that the grannies do.

And that means more decorative and more imaginative design?

Yes, I think so, things that appeal to the younger ones, plus the natural fibres. They can go into shops and they can buy their acrylics and synthetic fibres but in six months it looks terrible, and they think, 'Well, we've spent this money ... ', and they've spent so much time knitting but they find they haven't got a product that they're proud of.

So I think it's something that will come back. I've noticed some of the schools are now bringing back knitting into their curriculum. The CWA have been good in doing that. The little local school my daughter goes to is a Steiner school and part of their curriculum is knitting and crochet. So, there are groups that are starting to bring it back in, and I think, as it gets more accepted as a craft and not something that's old-fashioned, it'll have a resurgence.

What about colour? Colour is so fickle, in one year and out the next year. It must be very difficult to judge ...

It is. We've been lucky. It was rather funny when we decided to choose our colours. I went and got all the paint charts and for about a month, if anybody had touched my dining room table I'd have killed them. I had all the colours cut out and laid out in their colour runs, selected from about fifteen colour runs. And we chose a couple of colours, sometimes three, from each of those, then we've brought in extra colours as they've been asked for. And it looks like we have the right selection. People are happy with our colours.

We drop out some of the more fashion colours that come and go and we bring new ones in as the demand exists, but I think the main thing is to have a range that will suit a lot of people. You've always got your classics and then you have a few of the fashion yarns that come and go.

You're the sort of person who seems to be changing careers a number of times during her life. Have you got anything else on the horizon?

No, I'll concentrate on this at the moment. I think probably something that I really want to see is the awareness of agriculture being taken up in the schools, that feeling of being proud to be Australian and being able to identify with the products Australia produces. Wool obviously is a major one of them but there's others as well.

That's something our education system is lacking. I'm on a committee with the office of the Minister for Agriculture for Western Australia and we've all got the same aim, I suppose 'rural awareness' is probably the phrase for it, but it's still all agriculture and wool.

There is a huge gap of sympathy and understanding between people who live in big cities and country people.

Yes. Something I learnt is that Canada and America have their products as part of their curriculum. They know what their products are for the country, they're very proud of these products and they support them. That doesn't happen here, and I think it's something that we've got to get going.

I've started collecting up all the information I can for Grade 5 in Western Australia, I don't know about the other states but that's the level they study their local district and their local area and products. They've got a wide variety—they study the Local Government and that—but not things that are going to make them proud to be Australian. I'm looking at pulling together a type of curriculum that they could then pick up on using wool. I think that would work.

If you take a city like Sydney with a big immigrant population, a lot of people don't know anybody in the country, they've never been outside and it's a very difficult gap to bridge, isn't it?

Yes, that's something we discovered when we had these meetings in Perth: twenty years ago everybody had relations in the country or new friends in the country or people who had moved from the city to the country, so there was a connection. That doesn't happen now, and this is where I think it's so important to get that knowledge into the schools and make them aware of what Australia has got; build that national pride. By the time they leave school it's too hard to reach them.

KAYE EBSARY

K aye Ebsary and her husband had been in Adelaide to the theatre and were staying with friends just outside Gawler, so instead of going to her home near Snowtown we agreed to meet at the Gawler Post Office. It was a very hot day and we sat in the shade on the roots of a giant fig tree. She proudly showed me a photo of her eldest son, Shannon, who had just turned eighteen. He is autistic and the eldest of four children.

I was brought up on a farm at Clement's Gap, which is near Port Broughton, mid-north of South Australia. Before I was married I spent twenty years on the family farm there. I was brought up with six children, including myself and an older brother who was crippled. I dearly wanted to be a school-teacher. Not doing all that well at Port Broughton in the last year, I went to Port Pirie High School to have a go at an alternative leaving certificate. Halfway through the year the headmaster said, 'We're not going to accept alternative leaving students for Teachers College', so that teaching dream of mine went out the window. Then air hostessing sort of flashed in my mind, but once I met my husband that was it. I was married at twenty-one and began a family at twenty-three, then by the time I was thirty I had four children. The oldest one is autistic.

Our own farm is a mixed farm. We're nestled in the foothills near Barunga Gap. We have 1200 acres and it's mainly wheat, barley, lupins, peas, and we have merino sheep for wool, of course. We have a few cattle at the moment, not a lot, we're not cattle kings but we're dabbling in that, and we also have pigs and I, with the children, rear our own meatline or buy day-old meatline chickens and raise them as meat birds and sell them around a little bit, too. But basically it's just the usual farm, I suppose. We're not big farmers, but enough to keep us busy.

All these other things that you're doing, like the chickens, is that to try and keep afloat in these times?

I guess, in a way, it can help. It's not a big, big concern; we only have 200 chickens roughly every four months, and as well as just being extra meat for ourselves we do sell a few to different people and I guess it's handy, the little bit of money that does come in. We're also involved a little bit with yabbies as an aquaculture. We have a big farm dam that just relies on run-off water form the hills—it's a deep dam and we put a few yabbies in there twelve months ago. I'm currently secretary-treasurer of the Mid-North Yabby Association up in the Clare Valley, so we're dabbling in that, too, and maybe looking at yabbies and marron in a tank culture situation. But I think you have to have your finger on the pulse of everything these days, as far as farming goes. Not just women, the fellers too—they're always looking at different options.

What's your position on the farm? What sort of work do you do?

I'm the slave, Ros (laughs). No, just the usual home duties. Shannon, our autistic son, needs a lot of attention and care. Even though he's physically able, mentally he's not, and he needs help dressing, feeding, toileting—he's not toilet-trained. But I do help out farming with Peter, not a real lot now because of our other children growing up—they take over from me now.

I help with the sheep, I've loaded pigs up and taken them to market before when Peter hasn't been around, I clean the pigsties out, and, in fact, I've taken the tractor for Peter in the dinner hour so he can come in and do other important things if something crops up; not always, but to give him a spell for a little while. I do the books on the farm and we've recently acquired a computer. Peter is dabbling in that so it would be a big load off my shoulders if he can have a go as he has done now.

So I guess generally I do what most farm wives do and most people that know us, and particularly me, know I never stand still, I'm always on the go. I do propagate our own trees, I forgot about that. I collect seeds, because our farm had very few trees on it at all, and I joined Trees for Life, became a member and found it interesting—time consuming, but in a way time-out for me to get out and relax, not that I get a lot of it. So propagating trees and plants is another avenue I try to fit in but, as I said, there's not always the time. I plant the trees round the farm for windbreaks and erosion control—that's another sideline I forgot!

So the tree planting is successful—they're growing up?

Yes. In fact, that really wet, horrible year we had when the crops were all ruined three or four years ago was the year Peter had built the big, big dam. We thought we'd never ever fill that, and, of course, that real wet year it got filled and we also planted roughly 1000 trees. So, if nothing else, with all of the crops failing and it being almost a complete disaster, it was a wonderful year for all the trees that we planted, so it was good.

Have you done any formal training? How do you learn all this?

I read a lot. We get the *Farm Journal* and, of course, the farm bible, the *Stock Journal*. Any farm books at all I always try to read. As far as trees go, I was just keen to join Trees for Life because trees don't grow overnight, as we all know, and I think if we get to the stage where we can hand the farm down to our son Jarrod, and if we can set it up nicely with trees here and there for him, eventually, hopefully, in his generation it will be a big benefit. But really I just taught myself. I did go to a Trees for Life day that came to Snowtown, and I went to a computing course at TAFE to learn how to use the computer three years ago and, of course, forgot it all (laughs). But any little avenues that I'm interested in, if I can find out more and if it's in our area, yes, I will try to chase it up.

Tell me about your son, Shannon. Were you aware he was autistic right from the start?

No. Shannon was born normally and, as with all autistic kids, they all look normal-looking kids. Autism usually presents itself in the first three to four years in life. It can even be from eighteen months to, say, three years of life. We weren't aware Shannon was autistic—well, he wasn't actu-ally labelled autistic—until he was nearly four. He was a real handful, constantly on the go, never sat still, as though he was a super, super hyperactive child. Another thing was there's no eye contact; he won't look at you when you're talking, he never had any speech, just constantly naughty, pulling clothes out of drawers, getting things out of the fridge. And toileting ... looking back now I've got no idea how the hell I managed. And generally they appear as though they're deaf—they're not—and they appear as though they're blind, they can't see, but they're not. They can be very clumsy, but of course if diagnosed young and with a lot of constant one-to-one help and understanding about the disability and special ed. they can learn. But it's a long road.

Twenty years ago what sort of help was available where you live?

Not a lot. In fact, at the local kindergarten in Snowtown Shannon was a special enrolment when he was three-and-a-half, and all we knew of was the Autistic Children's Asso-ciation and that we had no idea what this autism word meant. All we knew was that we had this lovely blond-haired, blue-eyed bombshell of a son (laughs) and he needed help. He did finish up with a special teacher one-to-one at the kindergarten at Snowtown for, I think, two years. We fund-raised to get money for that with the Autistic Chil-dren's Association help in Adelaide, and then following that he spent five years in Adelaide, three at the Autistic Asso-ciation, which meant, of course, Shannon leaving home. Of course we had Jarrod before we realised that Shannon was actually autistic, and he'd wander off and get lost. He loved the sheep and he's taken off numerous times. He's one of those Houdinis who could escape anywhere, anytime. One day home on the farm he had gone and we couldn't find him. It was a hot day and I guess I was the usual panicking mother who couldn't find him. Because they can't speak they don't respond to you and I thought he'd perhaps fallen into the pigs' tank or dam, or that a snake had bitten him.

It took us over three-quarters of an hour to find him and he was down a back road of ours, no shoes on. They can't sense pain, autistic kids, so there were many trials and tribulations about being lost. There are days when you cry your eyes out.

I remember one day Shannon had been at the fridge and pulled out eggs—he loved to smash the eggs—and tipped the milk out, just being completely naughty. Of course, with proper education and behaviour management training in the program you can fix all these things, or try to fix them, but there were days I could have just bashed the door in (laughs), but I'd end up laughing, because if you did let it get to you you wouldn't be here.

It must be extraordinarily frustrating, that sort of thing.

Well, Shannon just took up so much of my time. He was an early riser—I must say he was a good sleeper—but if he didn't sleep and I didn't, well, if the mum or the wife doesn't get her rest I think the wheels can fall off.

Did the wheels nearly fall off a couple of times?

I got pretty tired but not too much hassles me. I don't really get cross. In fact, when I have got cross once or twice I think Peter and the kids wonder what on earth is going on—you know, Mum's getting mad. But, as I said, I'm human; we all are and we're allowed to get cross.

Nearly twenty years down the track Shannon's made a big improvement. A slow improvement, but he's certainly more manageable. He's still only toilet-timed, not toilet-trained, which means he relies on us. There's some speech—he's certainly more aware—but I guess through having Shannon and growing up with my older brother, Ian, who has cerebral palsy, accepting the handicap was perhaps easier for me.

Like I say to other parents that I've come across in the disability field, it's just those first few steps at the start that are the hardest to accept—that you've got this problem, or this handicap, that it's not their fault, it's not our fault. This autism or whatever it is just happens in some families so just go about it by helping them all you can.

What's the situation now with him?

Shannon always will need one-to-one care. Unfortunately, I guess he could be one that's in the 'too hard' basket as far as funding goes. You have to have carers or someone with Shannon all the time and, naturally, it costs time but, more importantly, if Shannon was to leave the farm and do something, where's he going to go? Who's going to look after him? When it is one-to-one care you're talking dollars. We would dearly love to have Shannon home on the farm, even in something like a training centre or log cabin set-up. He's an outdoor person, he knows the home and our environment, he's happy there and, to me, if you're happy, no matter what you're doing that's the biggest plus in life. I guess we're lucky that there are lots of people still happy to follow Shannon's progress, people who come out and help, so maybe we can tap into some volunteer networking there with Shannon with the tree propagation, a few pigs and meatline chooks ...

He can do some of those sorts of things?

He can with you prompting and guiding, but slowly.

When you've got a child that requires pretty well full-time care, plus others that need some care as well, how do you manage to fit in all those activities and interests that you obviously have?

Well, I guess I do fit them in, but I don't know how. Like with the trees ... I should be there transplanting trees now and putting more seeds in, which I don't have time for. I'm very thankful that I have a husband in Peter to go to the other children's netball, basketball, tennis practice, and, at times, music. We do talk about things a lot with the kids and I think that's important, too.

When the kids are doing something and I find I can't go if Shannon's crook, or if he's got some behaviour problem and is just a bit hard to take out, I will opt to stop home. It's easier to stop home with Shannon than go to football and run around the countryside chasing him: I come back exhausted. I guess the children understand if I say, 'Do you mind if I don't go today, kids?' They say, 'Mum, it doesn't matter; don't worry'. You've got to be very careful there, too: it can be quite touchy, but half of me wants to go with the other kids and the other half knows I can't because I've got to be there for Shannon, too. Some families find it very hard and I guess eighty-five per cent of the time where you have a disabled child in the family the mum is the carer. Some siblings of handicapped children can be very bitter towards the mum, because obviously that child needs you one-to-one and you have to be careful. You've got to spread yourself around and make time to talk to the other family members, your kids or whatever.

You don't feel resentful that you're missing out on things?

Not really, because in a way I still can divert myself into

meatline chickens or the trees. I get out in the garden a little bit, not a lot, because gardening is my biggest relaxation. I think, in a way, deep down somewhere or other I found that my niche is maybe helping other disabled children or, if not children, parents. I get phone calls and even go to see other parents just as a mum, not professionally.

Is there a network of people like yourself who have children with difficulties?

Yes, there's a new group at Clare which I'm involved with now. I spent many years just myself and Annette Davidson, Shannon's one-to-one teacher in the Snowtown early days, because nobody had heard of autism. It was a new word. We spent three years going around our area talking. I spoke on just being a mum with a handicapped child, what it was all about, and just making other people feel that they can do it. I'm involved on committees, but also I guess I'm just a shoulder, a mum who's been there, for other mums now coming on with little tackers that do have problems, and mums that are just finding it so hard to cope. So I guess I'm a gopher if they want a hand or just a cup of coffee or they want to talk—no professionals or anything, no bigwigs. Parents aren't scared to talk to another mum.

There are some who can be very down, there's no two ways about that—I've been there myself at times—but it's a bit like the power of the mind I guess. 'Certainly', I said to this mum, 'You're allowed to cry, you're allowed to get mad. If you don't want to get up this morning and do the program for your son or daughter, don't do it—you don't have to. We're not robots. And don't feel bad if you don't want to do it—forget it and go and do something for you, within reason; get out in the garden or do something different.'

Yes, there are lots of sad stories out there. They just want encouraging.

What difference do you think there is between living in a rural area and the sort of situation you'd have in the city?

A plus in the country is that country people know everybody. They generally know all about you and they're happy to help out most times, even though the resources aren't always there and there's maybe more help in the city.

But I wouldn't swap the country for the world. It's peace and quiet. Resource-wise, though, and being involved just recently with a Carers' Association, we're looking at networking other carers that want help—us carers sticking up for ourselves and saying, 'These kids want help in the country. Why should us country bumpkins or our children have to shift and go to the city? They're country born and bred, they love it, give them the chance to stop up here and you guys come and help us.' But you get the same story: because of the isolation, with not a whole heap of handicapped kids in one central place, you can't have a support worker or a resource centre in one place, it has to spread all around the place in the country. People don't understand the isolation in the country, it's so different to the city, but we're looking at it, and, I think, getting there slowly.

You'd have to lobby the politicians and that sort of thing.

Yes, certainly, but if a whole mob of parents lobby, I'm not going to say we're going to get anywhere, but we're going to try.

Did you ever consider moving your whole family to the city, or closer to the resources that might have made your life a bit easier?

Not really. I think we did wonder in the early days. I must

admit both Peter and I went to lots of training programs in the city to try and help with Shannon. I might have vaguely thought about it but we thought if Shannon could get help there it might mean him going down, and, as I said, he was in Adelaide for five or seven years and then we thought we'd try him home on the farm with us in the country providing we could all cope, providing I could manage with Shannon and Peter and the other three kids and it all could work in. Yes, deep down we felt we'd give Shannon the chance because, even though he can't speak, I think that's what he'd like to do. So for the past seven or eight years he has been home and we're managing but (laughs) wearing out, too.

Do you dare look very far into the future?

I guess I've been a mum that's always looked into the future even when Shannon was first home, realising that especially for disabled kids you don't get help overnight. And sadly, in a way—I'll be honest to you—when Shannon was first at the special school, it was brought up that, as parents, let's make a push for when these little kids leave school, thinking five, six, seven years down the track, but I was just one voice. Nothing against other parents because you can't tell other parents what to do, but that vision I was thinking of was well down the track—if you plan now, in five, six, seven years' time we'd have something set up. But I guess it's just me climbing brick walls looking for something.

Now, though, we do have our twenty-year-olds leaving school and where is there for them? And now the parents want to do something. I feel if we'd had that push a few years ago, if they could have foreseen that in the early days, I think it would be better now, maybe.

It would have been a bit scary, though. Do you think that's why they don't look ahead?

Yes, certainly, and I can understand that. You've got to want to look ahead, but I guess, in a way, you've still got to look ahead without getting too far ahead. Just take each day as it comes and see what works out.

But, I'll tell you what, through Shannon and being involved with different circles you learn a lot of things in life are certainly taken for granted. Take sport. You might go to sport sometimes and hear some parents on the side-lines revving these kids up and getting into them: they've got to win, which is fine and they say, 'Why didn't you do this', and 'Why didn't you do that?', and I think, Look, darling, I'd love to give you Shannon for a week. I guess they have this sort of vision and I see things a little differently.

What about your own future? Have you got anything that you'd really like to do?

I'd like to still get out on the farm and still have a farm to be there. As I said, we're not big farmers, we're only little farmers, and we just sort of quietly, steadily go along. Money certainly helps but it's not always the be-all and end-all. Yes, I know we've got to have it, for sure, but happiness is the most important thing: being happy in what you're doing, having peace of mind so things don't get on top of you, having that all in perspective.

What about the kids? Are they going on the farm?

I think Jarrod's keen to be a farmer. He's a mad motorbike fanatic but he wants to be a farmer. In fact, Karlie, the eldest girl, is a bit keen to be a stock agent and is going to have a go at doing work experience at the local stock agent at Snowtown. I'm not sure what Lauren will want to do, but Karlie would be a good farmer, she's quite handy—a bit like me. She's out with Peter all the time, which is good.

Do you see the Rural Woman of the Year award as a useful thing to get recognition for women's work on farms?

Yes, I think I do. I think women are underestimated on the farm. We're more than dishwashers, we're more than cooks, we're more than carers. Most of us can have a useful role and some valuable input. I'm not saying all of us, but I think generally we're very underestimated.

I don't think any farmer would have made much of a go of things if their home life hadn't been ticking over all right.

That's right, but I know when farming first went bad, back quite a while ago, when money was tight, interest rates went up, and it wasn't easy for the fellers, I'd just say to Pete, 'Look, there's two of us, not just one, we're all in it. You don't have to do it by yourself.' I know you can always say these things but I believe you've got to think positive. It could be heaps worse. There's always someone worse off than we are, and that's what I say to other parents of disabled kids. And likewise with the farm, I guess. It will be a long, hard road, but we'll get there; we can see the light at the end of the tunnel.

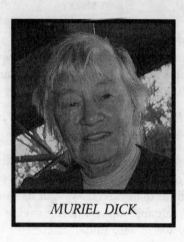

MURIEL DICK

*M*uriel Dick says she's greedy for living, and that old age is a myth! At seventy-three she runs the farm in southern Victoria by herself and takes an energetic interest in everything that comes her way from new farming techniques to politics and world news. Her cattle are very fortunate, she respects their natural instincts and allows them to roam between paddocks leading a sort of 'alternative' life style.

My mother came from Omeo; they were farmers, but she married a man of the city. He was a carpenter in the Railways actually and when he retired he went up to Warburton and bought twenty acres, split them up into little housing blocks, built houses on them and sold them off. I was his labourer, which I didn't mind at all because it gave me a terrific lot of freedom and he was very proud of me, which gave me a sort of self-assurance: he gave me strengths that usually are given in a male world. I had two dancing classes—skipping around and riding racehorses. It was a wonderful teenage life.

So you had no gender stereotype; you weren't forced to conform to one thing or another as a child.

Not really, and I think that's where I get my strengths from now. Back in my day women suffered a bit from being pinpointed but it didn't seem to worry me: I just sailed through life.

Did you learn carpentry from him, too?

No, I don't think so. I could drive a nail and I could saw but outside of that I don't think so. I think I was just filling in time and doing what he wanted to do, because he adored me. He had lost his older son when he was eleven in an accidental drowning and, of course, the focus came on me then. There were others behind but they were quite a bit younger so I had a few privileges.

Was it marriage that brought you to the country?

Yes, although when I first got married we lived in East Melbourne. My husband had come from farming stock and he really wanted to get back into the country. We didn't have any money, so we had to start from scratch, but when he sold his slow racehorses he had a little bit of capital and he leased a property. Then one day we were talking and he said, 'I'd like a property'. All the farmers owned their farms or were on the way to owning them and we had a certain pride and I said, 'Yes, okay, that's what I want, too', so we went for it. We just channelled everything into moving into properties. Yesterday I was on a forty-acre property that we owned once and I didn't know, because a new house has been built on it. The Women on Farms had a gathering there yesterday and it was a nice feeling, stamping around that ground.

When did you own this first property of yours?

About thirty years ago, perhaps more. We bought two little properties, one twenty acres and one thirty, sold those and bought here, which is eighty. My husband's brother lived on 100 acres down the road and he died but because it had to go through bloodlines and his wife couldn't inherit my husband got half and his sister got half. Then he bought her half but there was a debt on the property and he paid that debt to the widow, and that was like buying his share.

Was your husband a veteran of World War II?

No, he didn't go to the war. He lost two brothers in the First World War and I think there was that bit of heartache in the family and they were against war then. I don't know how he managed to get out of all these things but he thought he was too old in the Second World War, because he's quite a bit older than me: he's about nineteen-and-a-half years older than me. Everybody was so surprised when they found out how old he was because they thought he was only a few years older—but he joined me, I didn't join him. It was a good marriage to this extent: that we both were able to grow in our own way without being intruded upon.

So when you moved to a farm, you'd had no real experience of farming?

Not really. It was just as well we didn't go dairying when

I had those two young children. They were twenty months apart. My son was born about eleven-and-a-half months after we were married and then twenty months after that a daughter—I was overwhelmed. I can remember wanting to get home from hospital so much ... so quickly, to share this little boy baby with my husband, though when I did and I said, 'Pick him up', he said, 'Oh, no, that's your responsibility'. I cried with disappointment. He walked around, looking me over, and said, 'Look, even a heifer can look after its calf!' I was devastated (laughs). I had the weight of responsibility on my shoulders, but then I gave over to the children so that's what I did for those years.

When we bought this twenty acres and the forty acres, my father, the carpenter, came over and put up a funny little shed to milk cows in, and that's when we started dairying. We got a little herd together and I helped then, and that's when it all started. I got quite fond of the cows. I could pat them and talk to them, and I found I had an affinity with them, and I was glad. It filled in some part of my life, actually. My children were off to school, that was the parting.

So you took charge of the dairy. Were there any other crops or other cattle on the property?

My husband used to get jobs here and there but no, not really. I think we must have looked pretty poor but I used to knit, sew, cook, garden; I was very energetic, so I didn't even notice that because my life was so full. I've been like that all my life. I seem to be sort of able to make the best of what is and I pour all my energies into making it better.

Did you take charge while he was at work?

No, I wouldn't say that. He was the dominant factor; he was the one who knew it all. I was always two paces

behind, giving all the support. He used me like a cattle dog—
'Go way back, stop that bull, stand your ground, woman'—
oh, my God, with this great thing thundering at you!
(laughs) But I soon learnt to cope with all that. I just picked
it up myself. I was quite ignorant after he died. I used to
stand around while he was up the windmill doing things; I
wasn't very interested in that because being the kept
woman I was out playing golf and just helped. My place
was in the house, really, and the garden, and with the children, but if he needed help, you know, you worked like a
dog (laughs).

My life really centred around my children, my house, my
garden, out there in the community, following the children
through school. They went to Scouts, Guides, pony clubs,
cricket, football, all that sort of thing, and I used to run them
about. I was very keen, very ambitious, for my children to
move on and I gave them all the support. So it was up to
me; he was quite happy about that situation but when he
needed help I had to be out there.

I played golf for about twenty-five years, I suppose, and
I was captain, president, handicap manager, running the
show. It was great. And I used to be the one that put on
the school concerts and things like that. I trained quite a lot
of debutante sets and that took me right into the young
world, which was good, because I loved dancing. Of course,
it was country dancing back in those days.

What happened to the farm when your husband died?

Well, it was left to me eventually, after a bit of contro-
versy about 'You don't leave farms to women; they'll lose
it, they'll get married again and the guy will take off with
it'—all this sort of talk. This was his attitude, and I said,
'Okay, what about if I should die before you? You'd have

somebody in to do the housework because you know what you're like with housework, and before you'd know where you were you'd have her into bed, and where's my half then?' I think he had to think about that one, and then he said, 'Oh, yes, I think you're right'. I don't think he was very sure of how I could manage, but I did—I'm still here!

I remember the day of his funeral—he died fourteen years ago—I went to the back door and stood in the sun for a minute and I felt bereft; I felt as if I was in the world on my own. I thought, I don't know how I'm going to keep going, how I can walk. The little back gate was open and I thought, I'd better shut that, so I walked down towards it. Then the thought floated through, well, at least I'm standing up and I'm walking. I determined then that I would create a pathway for myself and walk along that alone, and I did.

You were a helper on the farm but did you know anything about running it? How did you begin to run it?

One thing that stood in my favour was that he was rotten with figures and books so I had the books to do, although I could never ever write a cheque for myself without standing on the mat and demeaning myself by asking for money—I think all women were in that situation in my day, and still are—so I had a good, functional idea of how things ran. I was pretty shrewd in a lot of ways, too, because I was aware of what we were trying to do with paying off the properties and getting there. I knew how to channel money and move in that direction so I had a lot of years of experience in my favour.

A friend of my husband from the Department of Ag. came and said, 'We'll go through your herd and we'll put eartags in their ears for identification'. He showed me how to keep information on them all in a folder, and from then on I could identify the cows and when they calved I could write down the calving date and whether the calf was male and female. I had a comments column for anything they were treated for or anything that went wrong.

That wasn't without a lot of pain and a lot of thinking and a lot of growth. I grew very rapidly through these years. I wouldn't like to go back there again, but no way in the world would I have missed this journey. It's been wonderful, because what I've really done is walk into myself; I've found myself as a person. It was a very painful journey but it can be done. You don't die; you suffer a lot of pain, but you get there if you want to.

Did you find people were encouraging you to keep the farm, or did they say you should sell it and go into the town?

I remember playing golf with a woman who was into Yoga, and she said with a smile in her eyes and her voice, 'Muriel, you know 99.6% of women in your position would sell and go to live in the town'. She was quite amused about the fact that I was the sole operator on a farm out there. I said, 'No, I'd shoot myself within a week' (laughs).

I like the challenges, so that's how it was. But if it hits your pocket you learn very quickly. I don't know that I had too many disasters—I was too careful for that with my background of years of getting it together. I just thought about it and when I made my moves I seemed to be doing the right thing all the time, and I did it my way, too. I think a lot of farmers are quite brutal with cattle. I'm not judging them; it's just a way of doing things from way back. But I'm tuned into nature and I'm very aware that we are only another species on this planet and you must have respect for everything on this planet, so I'm very caring with my animals.

What sort of practical things did you have to learn in relation to the cows?

Well, my job is sort of checking out. I have pulled calves, although I'm not really mad about pulling calves and now that I've got to this stage I feel I don't need to do that. I know a lot of the vets and a lot of the Ag. Department think I'm mad, but I don't have to get the vet very often because of my method and my 'open gate' philosophy. I think a cow can look after its calf better than I can. If she can move from one paddock if the wind's blowing or the rain or the sleet is coming in some direction, she'll take her calf and go beyond those trees over there. I've got windbreaks in most of the paddocks and this is what she does.

I'm into preventative health by putting what has been depleted out of their system into dishes around the paddocks—dishes in tyres so they don't knock them over. They calve stress-free.

I will not have dogs chase my cattle. Some of the agents want to round them up but I say, 'No, I'll get them into the yards for you, or into the lane', so they make allowances. They come half an hour later and I have them in the lane and we just walk them up nice and quietly. They're all quiet; I can get out of my ute and walk all around them, bull and all, and tell him how nice he is, and he responds.

You're into an alternative lifestyle for your cattle.

Yes, I would say that. But let's be fair to other farmers; if they're young they have to move in an intensive farming method with each and every blade of grass to get the money to meet their commitments. I'm freehold and that takes a lot of the pressure off me: all I do is keep upgrading my farm.

111

*Do you go to farm open days and things like that and courses that
the Agricultural Department runs?*

I did the Beef Management Course for twelve months,
which was marvellous. There were seventeen guys to start
with—a few of them dropped out—and three females, and
we all got so fond of one another that we met for months
after at a restaurant just to say 'Where are you at now?' It
was great, but I wasn't interested in a lot of it. I still went
back to my way of keeping books; I was a bit lost. It was
an accredited course and I could have got a job if anybody
wanted to employ me. I passed with flying colours and all
that sort of thing but, no, I do it my way. I live my life my
way, I can't help myself. It's something to do with being
close to nature and respecting everything on this earth and
it seems to pay off with animal health, my health and so
many things.

*You're in your early seventies now. Is there anything that you can't
do, or you don't do?*

There are a lot of things I can't do; actually, I'm very
ignorant of a lot of things and I have to get a bit of help
now. I can't service my ute but I can service my tractor. I've
got an old Nuffield and I can change the oil and put in new
filters and things like that because I did a course. Those
courses are marvellous: they build up confidence.

I had two guys come here one time in the 'eighties trying
to flog me one of the latest tractors with all the computer
systems and goodness knows what. I thought about it for a
while but I haven't got the work for it even though I cut
my own hay. I have all my own haymaking machinery. I go
on the mower, I cut it, and then I have somebody come in

to rake ahead of me and then I bale. But then I use contractors to cart it. I'm into square bales still because it suits me. I've been cutting my own hay for fourteen years or more now, and yet, it's a funny thing, I used to always go on the rake for my husband and I used to say to him occasionally, 'Let me go on the baler', but he'd say, 'Oh, no, no, this is too complicated'. The fellows around here laugh because I twiddle with knobs—God only knows what they're about but I twiddle with them—and I get the results because I just tune into what I'm doing. I'm very careful of my machinery because I pay for it if it breaks down.

Why do square bales suit you?

I had to take that step forward to get newer machinery to be able to move them about. A lot of people are going back to square bales now, especially on the smaller farms, because you stack up three round bales one on top of the other, if you're shedding them, and they take a lot of handling. It's very dangerous; they can drop on top of you if you don't watch yourself. Not only that, I think hay in square bales is better quality than round bales left out under trees and things because you lose about a third if you don't shed them and they're out in the weather.

Looking back, through the 'seventies it was get big or get out. We were milking cows and growing potatoes, my son who had disappeared overseas when he was about twenty was away for about three-and-a-half years and we were getting to the stage of wanting him to get back to dairying if he was going to take over. We thought we'd better hang in because the poor little devil would be so broke if he came back and what was he going to do. Anyway, he arrived home all right and then informed us he wouldn't be milking cows. He got a job down at Frankston Research Station and because he was always peering over the shoulders of PhD people, reading all their stuff, they said, 'Why don't you go back to school if this is what you want to do?' and he said, 'Okay, I will'. So he went back to school and got I don't how how many straight As which took him into a Melbourne university and he's a corporate lawyer now.

But getting back to the 'get big or get out', my husband thought he'd had a good year in potatoes, so he'd put in two irrigation systems, one on each farm, but I don't use it here. I kept one down on the other farm but I let the registration go because I put in a big tank. He used to breed dogs too; he was a good cattledog man, but I'm not into all that. I do it differently. I put in a big tank for a reserve of water to feed all the troughs and I used to help the fellows that did it by driving the tractor while they ran the underground pipes through. But I use my irrigation down there to fill the tank that fills the troughs. Just as well I did have it because with this drought it's been marvellous. I've filled it twice now.

So you've got your own methods of irrigating.

It's not really irrigating, is it? It's just filling the trough. I just use the old pipes from the irrigation system out of the big diesel engine to pump up water into the tank to keep the supply up.

You're very involved with women's groups and things around here. What brought you into that?

Even before I did a few skilling courses at McMillan Rural College they said they were trying to put skilling courses for women into place and would I help them. They wanted to know what my needs were so I said, 'Well, I suppose pulling a calf, say; fixing a fence; fertilisers; how to recognise weeds from good grasses'. They were whacking these things on this whiteboard and then they said something about driving a tractor, and I said, 'Oh, I know how to drive a tractor so I don't want that one'. 'But other women might' they said, and I said, 'Yes'. Then they said, 'Do you want a job?' I thought I had enough to do but even back then I was into empowering women—I think I've been in it all my life. That's the thread that keeps me going a lot in another dimension, to empower women to take control of their lives, to be responsible for themselves and to grow up. So I did, and it was great.

I used to help the tutor up there with courses and he was quite chauvinist but then he changed. One day he came over to me and said, 'Muriel, I'd sooner teach a group of women than men, because with men if one makes a fool of himself they'll all ridicule him and he's alone, but if a woman makes a mistake they'll all support her because they're all in the same boat, pretty weak!' Would you believe that's what the view is! But guys have got to be competitive. It's a pretty hard, brutal world for men, actually, and when I say I support women and want to empower them, I don't want to do it at the expense of fellows. But they have too much power and women haven't enough and we have to release a lot of this power. It's moving along now, of course, so they're balancing up the imbalance, which is good.

Tell me about the women's group you go to.

It's a continuation of Women on Farms. All we do is meet, we go round to a farm a month and anyone can put up ideas. We are non-hierarchical, we are co-operative and if any woman has anything to offer we don't care whether she's got one acre or a thousand acres, and we let them all know that, because some of them are a bit tentative, with not much confidence. They're growing very quickly and they're not frightened to put their ideas forth and we listen. Some of them we bag, 'That's a rotten idea!' or whatever, but we're going from strength to strength, which is good.

We go onto a property—we've been on alpacas, emus, ostriches, dairy farms, rotolacs with five or six hundred cows. We've been down to a Simmental stud, we talk to vets and they tell us about all sorts of things to educate us and give us insights into what's going on. I'm not impressed with a lot of the stuff. They push the barriers too far with too big-framed animals and they cause the female to break down in the birthing area.

Is it a discussion group where you discuss things like education and the concerns of country women?

Not really, because there's a big range of women out there. Some haven't moved along and some have moved along very quickly, so we've got to be careful because some are stuck in all the different places where I was stuck in life.

Do you see changes?

Yes, mighty changes! Some of the women at first were under the influence of their husbands but now they've moved out of the shadows into the sunshine a bit. You can see in their faces that they've moved along a bit, the penny has started to drop and they're taking a bit more control of their own lives. But we're not political, really. Why do I say that? Well they're all so busy with their own affairs on a personal level.

I get phone calls from all over the place saying, 'Come to a meeting' but I cannot go to meetings and run this project so I have to get my priorities in order. What do I want to do? Well, I don't really want to get out there because that's not really me, sitting around at meetings and just talking, this is really me, on the farm, doing all these horrible jobs.

You look very fit. What do you see your future being on the farm?

To be quite honest, I live in the present. At seventy-three years of age I wouldn't say I'd have a great long future so I live in the moment, and my moments are so full that it's wonderful. I'm really living about six lives in the moment. I seem to get around a lot of things. I try to read about the things I'm interested in—there's a lot of literature that comes through that I should be reading, but I don't.

I'm moving ahead, somewhere ahead, I don't know where because I'm interested in women developing and growing and taking their place in life with full responsibility for themselves in a lot of areas. That's not at the expense of fellows—I'm always saying this—because I've got a son and I love him and I had a husband and they were all stuck, like a lot of women are stuck.

But you're moving through?

I'm moving through. I've walked out of the shadows into the sunshine. Actually, that day I was telling you about when I walked that path, I walked along a path out of the shadows, into the sunshine and into myself as a person. That was the most rewarding thing I've ever, ever done.

You're also challenging age a bit.

Yes, but I'm not actually challenging it because I recognise you've got to die and you're not going to function 100% like when you were young. I accept all that, but I'm going to fully live until I do die because I love life. I've lost all my religious leanings and I've tapped into life. The closest I can get to the meaning of life is the life force and that's a

WOMEN OF THE LAND

mystery. There's a life force of all the species and it all comes from the one source. That's a wonderful feeling, that life force that invigorates and enlivens you, and I recognise it and I respect it.

You don't think as you lie in bed in the morning, well, I'm seventy-three years old and now it's my turn to take things a bit easy?

Never, never, never! No, for the simple reason that I talk to so many women in the town and I can look into their lives, women much younger than I am—say, fifty-one, fifty-two—and they're bored out of their brain. They're not really fully living. They've got to be racing around. They live their lives around shopping centres trying to fill up the day, or playing Bingo—fancy that, now, sitting playing Bingo. I'd be bored stiff.

ESTHER PRICE

*E*sther Price is one of the new breed of young rural women.
Relying on a computer, fax machine and of course, a telephone she manages to run her own business at home on the farm,
and care for two young children. Esther is a journalist contributing
to rural publications and working on her own promotions business.
She designs brochures advertising various sheep and cattle studs
and when time permits she enjoys working on the farm which is
near Kojonup in Western Australia.

I can remember telling Mum and Dad when I was about six
or seven that I was going to run their farm. I was going to
live in their ram paddock, actually—that's where I was
going to build my house.

What do you like about farm life?

Probably the people, more than anything. The community-mindedness of country people is the thing I like most, I think, about the country.

You've managed to combine what most people do in the city with farming life, and you're really quite remote here; you're 300 kilometres at least from Perth and very much in the middle of nowhere. Tell me about your work.

I've always wanted to combine rural living with something that would keep me challenged and occupied. Journalism never really crossed my mind until I was in Year 11 or 12, and that was probably when I thought, okay, maybe I can do rural journalism; to me that was the ideal career option to achieve what I wanted to achieve. I was fortunate to get a cadetship with *Western Farmer* so I went there straight from school and I did twelve months with *Western Farmer*, then I was offered a job with *Elders Weekly* which was at that stage a rival newspaper. I worked there for a couple of years and then on to *The Countryman*, but all the time, probably for the last year of my work for the papers, I was aiming at going out on my own and having my own business and being my own boss, which is what I did. So in 1989 I started my own business and it's been the best thing I've ever done; I've really enjoyed it.

Obviously I'm a journalist, so that's the primary role, but I guess I've specialised in rural publicity where I work for various companies in a rural capacity as their promotions person. I combine writing stories and taking photographs. I do a lot of work for individual studs, both merino studs and beef cattle studs, in a promotional capacity, and I have a sufficient understanding of livestock to know what I'm talking about, so they're not talking to just a journalist, they're talking to somebody who knows their industry, which is important, I think. I've got a computer with basic work processing software, a fax machine and a good camera that does all that I need to do with my photographic work. I don't do anything elaborate like develop my own photographs, I send all that away. I use couriers when I need to, and I guess basically I just need to be that little more organised because I can't just ring a courier at the call of a button. My jobs need to be a bit more organised than maybe a Perth-based journalist where you've got a deadline that you can adhere to at a lot less notice.

What about travel? Do you have to do much of that?

Travel's probably the thing I've missed most since I've had the kids. I was always on the road before and often interstate as well with my work, but now since I've had the kids I've just completely rearranged the business and instead of me going to people, people come to me. Since the second baby arrived I've cut it down a little bit and I'm really only working a couple of days a week full-time now and then just the times I can snatch in between when I haven't got a nanny looking after the kids.

Do you regret that?

Oh, no, because the kids are great and they're only going to be little for a little while. When they're at school I'm sure I'll be more mobile. But I don't think I miss out, really: I'll be having my couple of trips away this year I have no doubt, but certainly not to the extent that I was beforehand.

How much do you have to do with the farm?

Regrettably, probably not as much since the second baby's been here because if I'm not in the office I'm doing things for them or about the house. But up until Patrick, a lot. I really enjoy the cattle and I like to know which calves are which and who's by what—you know, all the breeding of all the various cattle. I do all the bookwork for them and I certainly know what's going on.

What sort of a woman's network is there around here?

I'm probably not the right person to ask, because if there is one I'm probably not part of it. The local girls have a play group which I go along to every second Tuesday. It's a roving play group and we just go to each other's farms and have a cup of tea and a biscuit and the kids have a play. And there are play groups in town and more sporting organisations really.

You get a bit busy for that, do you?

I've just got other priorities. I'm not very good at being in women's clubs. I guess my industry is so male that to be honest, I enjoy men's company and that's part of the reason I enjoy the work I do. It's a different level of discussion, I guess.

Did you have to break any ground with that, for them to accept that you did actually know what you were talking about?

Oh, yes, sure. I was seventeen and a half when I started work and going out on the stock round with the stock agents, yes, sure, I was as green as grass. But I've never been afraid to ask questions and I really loved what I was doing and I suppose that obviously showed. I guess I was a quick learner. I was never conscious that I was a woman in a man's field, never, and I've always expected to be part of it, and I guess I am now, well and truly.

So if you weren't conscious of it you didn't expect them to be, either.

No. On the odd occasion someone would come up to me and say, 'Do you realise you're the only woman in this bar?', or something, and then I might think, oh, wow, so I am! But it's never been an issue with me, and I don't make a thing of it and I don't expect them to. I've always had their respect, but it's not something that's ever played on my mind very much.

Your own children are growing up out here. What do you hope and plan for them?

Firstly, happiness and health, of course. You couldn't want more than that, really.

What about schooling and that sort of thing in the future? What kind of arrangements can you make when you're living in a place like this?

Certainly if we can afford it we'd like to send them away to a private school in their final years of high school. There are two very good primary schools in Kojonup, one Catholic and one state school, and we haven't yet decided which way we'll go with that. But there are plenty of options. There's up to Year 10 high school in Kojonup and further afield in Katanning there's through to Year 12.

Has the farm been your husband's or your own family's, or did you just come here as new people?

My husband's from Kojonup; his family has a big farming operation on the other side of town, but we don't own this farm. We worked for a couple at Yarloop—we actually lived with them at Yarloop in the first couple of years of our marriage—and they bought this property three years ago and we moved here then. So we're here as managers.

Does that mean you can't do exactly what you want with the cattle?

Oh, they're terrific to work for. It's like an extended family, really, so we have a very free rein, and generally speaking it's a big happy family where we all agree anyhow, so it's not really an issue, it's all quite harmonious.

And is there a chance of buying a farm if you don't actually own one from birth?

To be honest, if I had lots of lots of money I'd buy one, but I'd never buy one thinking I was going to make a profit out of it. The businesswoman in me would say there'd be better things to do with my money if I wanted to make some, but by the same token I'd never want to live anywhere else other than on a farm. So this, I guess, is the ideal compromise: having that regular pay packet working for somebody else but having the lifestyle and the industry that you enjoy.

Managers must be increasing. Families on farms seem to be moving out and big companies taking over. Is this a coming trend?

Yes, I'm sure it will be. I'm sure you'll see a lot more of it, probably not so much in Kojonup which is a very established old family area.

A lot of families, I think, feel that people who are just managers don't put the same kind of emotional and physical effort into a farm as they would if it were their family farm. I wonder if you'd like to comment on that?

Certainly not in our case. If we didn't work this farm like it was our own I don't think we'd be doing the right job. We refer to it as our farm, or our place, or our cattle, or our house, although we know it's not, and if we didn't have that attitude I don't think we'd be doing the right job for the people who own it. No, we throw everything into this. It's our life, as far as we're concerned.

So you don't see that as a coming problem with managers?

Probably not everybody's in the same fortunate situation that we are with the owners of this property. Good managers are hard to come by and I guess I'd like to think we're a little different in that way, but that's a lot to do with the people we work for.

Sometimes I ask farmers about their social life and they look vaguely out the window and say, 'Well, we don't have time; there's all these animals to look after'.

Social life ... yes, well just at the moment it's not at its best, but that's probably more to do with a couple of kids and no ready access to grandmothers for babysitting and that sort of thing. But Kojonup's great for that family-type socialising and we see a lot of our neighbours in the immediate community rather than actually in town. Then, of course, there's all the sporting things that we're both quite involved with. Life before kids was more social for us but I'm sure it will get back to being a bit more social. We probably don't get away as much as we'd like; we don't get to Perth or Albany, but when we do we certainly make the most of it.

CLARE McSHANE

F or Clare McShane, producing knitted garments from wool produced on the property was almost a hobby. That is until the price of wool bottomed while her five sons were all at boarding school. Clare and Alan then began to look at ways of adding value to the fine wool they produced at Lemont in the Midlands of Tasmania. Clare now runs a thriving mail-order business selling the knitwear she designs. This has given a new focus and financial vitality to the farm and also provided employment for knitters in the surrounding countryside.

My family moved to Tasmania when I was a teenager and I attended school in both Sydney and in Hobart. Then I was at Teachers College in Hobart and I was sent to Oatlands, which is our nearest town here, as a teacher. I was going overseas, but I didn't get there. I only got as far as

126

26 kilometres out of Oatlands, which is where we are now, because I married. I left teaching and had five kids fairly quickly—five boys. I did relief teaching for some years and I taught some HSC subjects in Domestic Science—which I'm not trained in. I'm a Primary trained teacher.

Our property is about 6000 acres. We normally run about eleven and a half thousand sheep, and some cattle. At the moment we're in a drought area so we've had to drop our stocking rate right down. But we winter eleven and a half thousand fine wool, Saxon-Merino/Corriedale-cross sheep which produce the wool for the knitwear.

What did you know about sheep when you first came here?

Absolutely nothing. I knew a lot about wool and yarn and knitting and handicrafts and that sort of thing, but my knowledge of farming was pretty well nil.

And how did you begin to learn?

Well, you become part of the business because all of a sudden you're needed to go down and race sheep off or you're moving stock from one area to another. You just absorb it because that's your life.

Could you ride a horse, drive a tractor, that sort of thing, when you came here?

No, I had driven a tractor when I was about fourteen. But that had been about it.

Did it take you long, then, to become part of this property, part of the workforce of the property?

When I was married, my husband—one of six brothers—was in a big family partnership and all the brothers tended to help each other so the women weren't always out there in the workforce as much as other farming families.

It wasn't till we became our own entity, which was in 1983 when the family partnership split very amicably because of the needs of other brothers and grownup sons and daughters, that I really became the other half. It's you and your husband and all your young kids then, and it's up to you to do it all. I've lamb-marked and I've cooked for shearers for years and done all those sort of things.

The original property my husband grew up on is 'Stonehenge' which is thirteen miles east of here. They built up a large family holding through hard work and entrepreneurial skill, and when it was split up, this was the property that we were on and so this is where we stayed.

Are your sons at school still or are they working on the farm?

The eldest son is at Duntroon, the second son is at university doing commerce and he's very interested in the knitwear. The third son is home; he left school at the end of last year. He's having one to two years here before he goes off to Ag. college somewhere. And Michael and William, they're twins in Year 11, don't know what they want to do. But they've all worked from eight or nine when they would work part-time in the shearing sheds. By the time they were ten they would be doing a rouseabout full day, working on the board. They've just always been part of it.

Because there's five and three quarter years between the five boys, all of a sudden the first one went off and the second one went off and when Michael and William went I had time on my hands and I was looking for something to do. I had started machine knitting as a hobby but I'd always knitted, all my life.

Machine knitting was great because you can knit quickly and get a garment done in a couple of hours instead of a couple of weeks. I was looking for good machine knitting wool, which is really quite hard to source, and, when wool was at its peak, I went to Coates Patons. They offered to process one bale and I started off with one other knitter. I asked one of the girls I was taking in an Adult Ed. class would she be interested in learning, and that's how we started.

Once I started I realised people out there were wanting what we were making, and, obviously, you put on another knitter and you get another machine and you put on another knitter . . . to the extent that we're now up to a workforce of thirty-five.

Initially we started selling to local craft shops and that sort of thing but after a while when we started increasing production, we had to find other ways to sell. We've been through Sydney and Melbourne with a suitcase full of jumpers, which is very demoralising, but it's very good experience.

How do you mean you've been through Sydney with a suitcase?

You fly to Sydney with a suitcase full of jumpers and you knock on people's doors, retailers, and ask them if they're interested in your product. And they either are or they're not. And they have a look. It's a very good way to learn. Not very pleasant but it's a good way to learn.

You've got a wholesale and mail order business. You've just had catalogues printed. What is it about the jumpers that you manufacture that is different from the ones at big department stores?

The ones made for big department stores are made offshore and they're certainly made of wool, but one doesn't know quite what sort of wool has been used. They are made in a big factory, they're not always terribly well put together.

What we offer here is that we knit exactly what people want, we've got a large range of colours, we've got a large range of sizes, and we also take specific measurements. So, someone with short arms or long arms or whatever can come to us and we can give them exactly what they want.

The quality of the wool is extremely high, they're very soft garments, they wear very very well and they hold their shape. So, you're buying quality at an affordable price.

And do you think that people are becoming conscious of wool? Most of the stuff you see in department stores—especially in women's clothing—tends to be acrylic.

Certainly the mass market is still acrylic-oriented not wool-oriented, but the niche that we sell into has a pretty good understanding of wool. It's pure wool and it's hand-done. Effectively, it's niche-marketing.

At shearing time each fleece is chosen for the knitwear, and it gets put into certain bales which go up to Coates Patons where it's processed into yarn to our specifications. It comes back here, we then work out our designs and sizes. We send out the appropriate wool to the appropriate knitter—one knitter knits one jumper; it's not a big factory, it's a specific order. It comes back to us, we check it and then it goes out to the linker who puts it together. It comes back in, we check it, we finish it off and then it's dispatched to wherever it's meant to go.

The jumpers are more expensive than the ones you get in most department stores, but are you finding that people are prepared to pay for that sort of quality?

Well, they're all hand-done and hand-picked from day

one, so, you're getting the best quality that we can give you. I don't think our jumpers are expensive for what you're getting. Certainly in the niche-market we're in, people are very aware of the quality. We also get a lot of people that come back year after year: once they've bought one they'll come back and buy another, which indicates that our garments are standing the test of time.

We went to the UK in 1991 because the cottage industry system is used extensively there and we couldn't find a lot of information here on how it worked. In the UK we were able to find out that they were using lots of things we had done and we were able to refine a lot of our processes—it all comes down to a system that works. One of our biggest negative aspects is our isolation here, and we have to turn that around and use it to our advantage. We use all the technology that's available—we've got Faxes and modems and computers and all the rest of it.

We've just put in a big production planning system which we had specifically written for us in Melbourne. All our manual systems now are being computerised, so instead of filling out great order books and linker books and knitter books, it is all logged into the computer.

Is any of the yarn that you manufacture used for knitters who want to knit things for themselves?

No, we've kept all our yarn just for the knitwear. It's probably some of the best yarn you'll ever get, and we decided that we'd keep it as an exclusive line just for the knitwear. At some stage we will get to a finite level. At the moment we're not there, but one of these days—and it won't be that far away—we'll get to be able to use all our wool here.

Is there a danger of getting too big and therefore having to cut corners and that sort of thing?

I suppose there is if we're not careful, but we're monitoring that all the time. All of a sudden you'll get a big surge and you've got to change systems so that you can cope, but because we're monitoring it all the time we're making sure that we can cope as we go along. We're working to a business plan, we've got goals and we know where we're going now, as opposed to when we started when we had no idea whatsoever.

If you were able to use all the wool that you produce on this property, could you use wool from the next property ... a bit like vineyards do, so that you don't ever quite get the wine from a specific place any more?

When we get to a point where we're using all the wool on this place we'll have to reassess, but it would have to go through certain standards. It has to be similar sorts of wool, it has to be hand-picked, it has to be fleece-wool only. We have to have control over that side of it from day one—as we do now—because otherwise we can't guarantee the product at the end of the line and we can never compromise our quality. We're never going to be the biggest company, but we can certainly be the best.

I have visions of people knitting all over Tasmania, saving the Tasmanian economy.

Well, who knows? Wouldn't it be nice?

Is this enterprise here going to be enough for you, you're not going to branch out into anything else?

No, this fills every waking moment. I wake up in the

morning and I think business and I go to bed at night thinking business. I enjoy it and it's been my choice to do what I've done. We also are looking to build the business for the boys because it can run in conjunction with the farming enterprise which won't give more than one son a living. The knitwear can certainly give two or three extra sons a living.

That's a big problem isn't it, with country people ... to provide some sort of living for sons who want to stay on the land?

It's very difficult, especially when you get many years of really bad wool prices, and then on top of that you get drought which really knocks you for a six, and then the interest rates keep going up. You're going back all the time, all your costs are increasing. They've got to really want to farm, and it won't hurt them to see the tough times, but it's going to be much tougher down the track, I think.

Do you ever think that you should persuade them to not farm, to take on something else?

We've always encouraged our boys to look at other avenues, and we've always suggested strongly that they do something as well as farm—get either a profession or an apprenticeship or a trade or something so you've got something to fall back on because when tough times come and you've got certain pressures on you it can be really very demoralising.

They've all been educated to the best of our ability and the three that have left school have done very well. They all look at doing other things so they've got something behind them, but who knows what's out there? It isn't getting any easier.

DEBORAH THIELE

*D*eborah Thiele has had a few firsts in her life. She was the *first female Agricultural Science Senior in the South Australian Education Department and one of the first women to be permitted to attend the prestigious Roseworthy Agricultural College. Her most recent achievement was to win the inaugural ABC award for the national Rural Woman of the Year. Although in her early working life, Deborah was advancing rapidly in the teaching profession, when she married Anton, a sheep farmer, her farming background reclaimed her. She is now joint manager/ owner of their farm at Loxton in the east of South Australia and is responsible for marketing the wool, lambs and the older sheep. She is also very interested in genetics and wool fibre and is active in a number of farming committees.*

I was brought up at Waikerie, which is an irrigation area

along the River Murray, in South Australia. I was one of three children—I'm the eldest—and I have a sister and a younger brother. We lived on what's termed a block: when the settlements were originally set out each unit of land was a sort of a rectangular shape and it was called a block. On these blocks they grew a variety of stoned fruit and citrus and vines and so on, but, over the years that I was growing up, my father moved out from what we call fruit salad type farming into large specialised citrus growing, to the point where he ran his own properties and managed the properties of others. I can remember him working extremely hard at that to make a success of it.

When I was in Year 11 or 12 I had to do a research project, and I did an analysis of the benefits of large-scale agriculture—the 'getting bigger' syndrome—which Dad was being extremely successful at. I guess I showed an interest at that stage. As kids, we earned our pocket money cutting apricots and picking oranges but the biggest influence was probably that as a family we were very involved with water skiing and the river.

We were a close family but we were also given lots of opportunity to spread our wings, to try things differently and were given responsibility and encouragement. It's interesting that, even this far down the track, when I was talking to my parents about the qualities that they admire in their children, they said, 'Well, all three of you have courage', and I thought: well, that's interesting, because if we have courage it's because we were given the courage to have a go and not to fear success, nor to fear failure. We've all had our ups and downs, but we've all just kept going and now my brother is a pilot with QANTAS and is living in Brisbane with his family, my sister lives in Saskatoon, Saskatchewan and she's a recognised artist in Canada, and then I did the various things that I've done in my life and am the only one that's back anywhere near Waikerie.

You mentioned that the river had been a big influence in your life.

We've got river water running in our veins. We spent a lot of our lives by the river and in the river. The river water as an irrigation scheme was vitally important to our very existence, so I've always just loved the water. And when I was teaching I always tried to get teaching appointments that were near water. At Port Augusta I went sailing at Kadina, so from water skiing I guess more the focus now is on sailing. I owned a boat for a number of years, and we've changed up to one that's a catamaran, that'll take the whole family out, but I just love it near water and I guess I always try to go camping or in some way be near it. And I love the land. I guess I'm a very tactile person—I like how things smell or don't smell—and things like turned earth and rain on stubble to me are nice smells. I don't like the smell of cities. As soon as I get out of the city I wind the windows down and let the air blow through.

When you were at school those last few years, deciding what you wanted to do with your life, was farming on the agenda?

At school we were encouraged to succeed and to put the work in, and a significant thing there was that although Mum had gone away to school, ours wasn't a financial position where we could. So, we were very lucky, I think, in that Waikerie High School when we were going there had excellent teachers who just encouraged things like sport, debating, chess, art and anything and everything. We were really encouraged to follow our best. The teachers were terrific. I have met people from Waikerie High School in good positions all around here. Our state member of parliament is from Waikerie High School; our federal member of parliament went to Waikerie High School; I went into Workcover at top level to talk about farm issues and the lass was one I had been to school with; I went across the river to talk to the bank manager and when I said, 'You must be one of the very few rural female bank managers in this state', I found she came from Waikerie High. It was that sort of tradition of excellence.

When I was at school I guess I tended towards taking on responsibility, so in my final year I was a prefect and a house captain, and I was also involved with boys. I can remember the pressure being put on me by my boyfriend at the time to stay in town—the inevitable 'get married, settle down' type of thing—and my parents were dead-set against it. There was no way that any of us was allowed to stay at home. We had to get out and make our way in the world. It wasn't ever said in a forceful way but simply implied and encouraged. So all three of us gained our tertiary education by gaining scholarships, and we all went on to tertiary institutions.

You were at Roseworthy when there weren't many girls there.

That's an interesting thing. When I left school, Roseworthy wasn't a choice for girls. It was all male and that was the way it was geared to be. But in 1973 it opened its doors to women. In the meantime, I had followed my nose and gone into teaching—I enjoyed teaching—and I had done a science teaching qualification. So I was out teaching science quite happily, right around the state.

The 'seventies were really good for farming. You had lovely margins there. Money and profitability were terms synonymous with farming in the 'seventies, and a lot of ag. science teachers got a little bit of ground together and quit teaching because they could do better farming. So the department had a huge shortage of ag. science teachers and made it possible for you to apply for a release time scholarship—that's what it was called. So I went back in 1981 to Roseworthy Agricultural College on a release time scholarship and they paid my full teaching wage for me to do a full year's postgraduate year in agriculture. After that I owed them a year's service anywhere they cared to send me, teaching agricultural science.

Even in 1983, if you were in the older buildings and went into the Ladies, the first thing you saw was a urinal! I thought, hang on a minute, I'm in the wrong place. So I'd whip back out again. No. 'Ladies' was the sign on the door. And then if you checked out the old buildings, somebody had obviously got a whole heap of these 'Ladies' and 'Gents' labels and put 'Ladies' on each alternate loo. It was the only way they could handle it.

In those days I was the only female in my course. They were gradually making inroads into Roseworthy but now, in 1995, when you go to Roseworthy there are girls in every course. They're in every subject range, and more in number.

How were you regarded in the 1980s at Roseworthy?

There were girls already there, so that wasn't unusual in itself, but the class itself were boys who'd been through with very few females, particularly in things like farm management, and I guess I was older than the general run of students there, so I was different in that regard. I still joined in and got along quite well, but I found that they would tend to try and take the mickey out of me if they could. At one stage we were out moving some sheep and the guys said to me, 'Nip over across those two fences there and run around the back there and bring the sheep forward, and we'll get them on either side from here', and I thought, oh well, OK. So I started to hare out and I came up against this fence and it was making a funny noise—a sort of 'zing zing zing-a-zing'. I thought, hullo, this is an electric fence. (We don't have fences on citrus blocks.) And there the guys were—you could see them all bunched up, waiting for me to touch this fence so they could laugh themselves sick. But I didn't. I went around through the gate and so on. They were terribly disappointed.

Three or four practicals later we had these young bulls in the crush and we had to measure them to see if they were good bulls or not—check out their vital equipment. And one of the things was to measure the diameter of the testicles. The lecturer holds out this piece of string and he says, 'OK, who's going to be the first to do this?' I looked at them all, and I thought, this is probably a bit too close to home. So I grabbed the piece of string and I said, 'OK fellers, I'll go first. But I think I need'—and I rubbed my hands together to warm them up like a doctor—'to have some practice first', and they all looked suitably squeamish (laughs) and it was, sort of tit for tat. I think to have a sense of humour and a willingness to have a go, and to stand up for yourself are basic principles for life. And we were all great friends at the end and got on fabulously.

After you'd done your course, you taught in high schools?

Yes. The first school I went to from there was Kadina Memorial High School, which was in the heart of the York Peninsula, a very traditional agricultural area in South Australia. I had a terrific time there. I joined the Ag. Bureau, and I can remember at the Ag. Bureau meeting they had to discuss whether they would allow me to join because they'd never had a woman joining. They actually discussed it while I was there, and they were to-ing and fro-ing about the whole kit and caboodle, and finally this old guy who must have been a very well-respected farmer in the district stood up and said, 'I think it'd be a good idea, because it'll just stop the bloody swearing'. And they all laughed. He didn't realise that he'd inadvertently sworn in the same sentence, and they laughed their heads off and said, 'Terrific, sounds like you need her', and I was in like Flynn.

They were marvellous. I could ask them any questions and they'd show me and I'd go out to their properties and I learnt a great deal from them. I also learnt a great deal from the kids in my classes who were off farms. I enjoyed the amount I learnt as much as the amount that I gave them in the academic sense. Often as not, I'd be reading the book five minutes before I gave the lesson, and some of them might have known it and some of them mightn't, but that's what most teachers do at some stage, I reckon.

We had a case where one of the female students in the class, who was a farm lass, wanted to do work experience with a stock firm, and we had a great deal of trouble. The counsellor, the principal, all of us were involved in trying to get this lass work experience with a stock firm. But after I received the ABC award, I was asked to speak to all the state managers from a stock firm. And I said to them, 'How many of you have had females doing work experience in your offices?' All but two—so that's about twenty-eight out of the thirty—put their hands up. I went on to say, 'How many of you had them doing saleyard work and going out and visiting farmers?' and I think I might have got one hand. But the fact is we're in a process of evolution and it's a long way from where I can remember with the female student at Kadina.

Your mother was also a farmer's wife. Do you ever talk to her about the differences in both your lifestyles?

Mum and I are really close and we talk about all sorts of things. I can remember when Mum had to be out there picking mandarins and we'd be playing around under the shade of the trees. It was something she preferred not to do. Whereas out there working sheep is something I prefer to do. The point to make is that women in agriculture have such diversity.

It's very important to have a stable family life, so that when you come in and you've been working really hard there's a meal on the table, there's some clean clothes the next day, there's at least a halfway decent warm, inviting house in the middle of winter to walk into. Those things make for being able to carry out a successful family farm enterprise as much as being willing to go out there and run around for hours on a tractor. Somebody has to do all those jobs, and how you divvy them up is up to each individual. There are, of course, personal preferences in any family for certain sorts of jobs.

Do you see farming very much more now as a team effort for family members?

Yes, and the last five years have been very interesting sociological years. Where there are strong farm families— that is, the ties are strong, they are a good partnership, there is mutual respect and responsibilities and so on—they've come together and they have survived the tough times. Where there are any cracks in that, where there is any feeling of 'I do more than you', or 'The money situation is your fault', or any feeling of guilt or whatever, when the pressure's on the cracks open wider. I think the divorces, the marriage split-ups, some of those sorts of things, are some of the sad aspects of the pressure of the last five years.

But I think there are stronger farm family units that have emerged as well.

What's the key to reconciling those difficulties within families?

Mutual respect, I think. Everybody has something to give, even our children, being as young as six and seven. Just the fact that they get themselves ready for school is terrific. They are pulling their weight in doing those things. Alex has his own 'eggie' enterprise and so I get eggs and he looks after his chooks and I respect the way that he does it. When I go over I might clean the trough out left to right and he does it right to left—so what? But you're respecting all members of the family and there's respect for your partner and for what they can contribute to that enterprise.

I sometimes think that city kids find it very difficult to find something to do that is actually contributing to a lifestyle, because in the city there aren't the small tasks that a young child can do on a farm. Do you think that makes a difference to country kids?

The thing I think is different, urban to rural, is that out here our workplace is our home and our home is our workplace, so when we go out and we're going to do a line of fencing, we might be doing that during the holidays or on a weekend as well. And when we do, and we know that the children are going to be with us, we pack a picnic lunch and various other bits and pieces and we make it an outing and we do it together. We'll be going along this fence line and Alex and Lottie will be dragging the hammer with them, or something like that, to help. So we can do those sorts of activities together. When it comes to shearing time they'll race home, change into their other gear and come in and sweep the floorboards. Just to have somebody on the end of the handle getting the dags out the way contributes to our ability to do that job more effectively.

In our discussions about what we'll do with the farm, Alex is determined to turn the whole farm onto solar power. He's a solar energy buff and we have all sorts of inventions around the place. He can already see one of the paddocks with these huge panels, driving all bits and pieces. So I guess the kids are a part of what we do, and that enables them to contribute in that sense. It's very difficult for a child where mum or dad go off to work. They can't be a part of that other work; it's the other time. So, when they come home it's family time or leisure time. And unless the family has a leisure activity together it's a dividing of the ways. I think that's probably more the crux of it.

Tell me about your own work on the farm.

It varies. I'm an outdoors person—that's why I was quite keen to teach ag. science, because I got out and about and I wasn't stuck in a classroom all the time. I like the sheep and the genetics of sheep and, in fact, when we were first married, Anton was very happy about that, because as far as he's concerned sheep are weed-eaters, and if you get a bit of money for the wool, that's great. He loves cropping and we crop large areas. But I could really get stuck into the sheep and I feel a personal sense of pride with what has evolved from those early days, and I enjoy things like classing the wool. I work out when the rams go in or out and the type of rams. I get a sheep classer in that helps. I enjoy the marketing of it and the whole thing. I also particularly like the office work. I like mucking around with figures and gross margins and analyses and stuff like that, which also means I'll go along as the family member who is part of a trading group, and I'll do buying deals, marketing of the wheat and learning more about that. They're the things that interest me, the market issues, purchase issues, dollars and cents and cash flows and all that sort of thing.

When it comes to the grain, I'm particularly interested in varieties. When I went through uni and teachers' college, I leaned towards the study of genetics and varieties and sheep characteristics—things like that appeal to me. But it's also great satisfaction to deliver something you've grown throughout the year to the silo. So, when I can, when our truck isn't broken down like it was last harvest so we had to contract cart, I'll cart the wheat to the silo while Anton's on the header. We'll take turns driving the tractor at seeding time because I think we both enjoy being out there. It's a long day, but it's also nice to have a break back home. So we divvy up the jobs like that. But most of the cropping aspect, I would say, is Anton's domain.

Of course, I know nothing about mechanics. I'll check the oil and if it's where it's meant to be on the dipstick, that's fine; I'll grease where I'm told to grease; and I'll check the water (laughs) ... and that's the limit of my knowledge. When you look at the amount of machinery, the tractors and the headers and the bits and pieces, that's Anton's area of expertise. He is a whiz with those things so parts and maintenance and whether things get fixed or not fixed and how they do and what we buy are all his area of responsibility. We divvy up things mainly to areas of interest, and there are others that we both know have to be done, so we just do them.

You must see some positives and negatives in rural life.

Yes. I like rural life, but mouse plague is definitely a negative. I had never actually been living on a farm in a family situation with a mouse plague, and so I couldn't remember the other one that was in the 'eighties. You have mice all through everything in the house. You go to put on your best jumper and the next thing you know the mice have been in there too, so you have to wash everything and clean it all out. You wash continuously. The morning job was to empty traps. We had twenty traps in the house, even though we'd stuffed up all the holes and places where they could get in.

We have rainwater on the house, so we rigged up this thing and my job was to nip up to the rainwater tank and scoop the mice out. Then we thought, we can't do this all the time, so what we did was get a really big, thick, anchor rope that was hanging around from when we used to have a bigger boat and put it down into the tank and then out over the other side. We figured if the mice went in and decided to go for a swim, they could climb out again (laughs). So we reduced the numbers that way. But they bred up from a paddock that had been destroyed by the weather. There was plenty of grain on the ground, and they moved like a wave. As we were seeding they ate it out behind us, so we got nothing from where they had actually been. We had to then bait in. We form what we call a death strip and we bait along that strip—we didn't actually bait in the crop. So, with a mouse plague—I mean, where do you run to? I didn't even have young babies, but there were people around who did. And there were friends who were up the mid-north where the school had those ceilings that are straw. The mice got in there and then died and the kids'd be doing their work, and these maggots would be dropping out of the ceiling onto their books. And the smell! So they had to close the school, strip it out and replace the ceilings with ordinary ceilings.

You'd drive along the road and they would separate like a wave as you drove along—all these little figures running off in front of your headlights.

But then I go for morning walks whenever I can, and I go along and see thirty different varieties of birds and the trees and the space and the limitless horizon. We'll often go for picnics in our scrub, just on our place—more so in winter than in summer—and you'll sit there on top of a hill in the middle of the scrub with the birds around you, having this lovely picnic in your own little bit of scrub.

And also, if we have a party, nobody tells us to turn the music down, because nobody can hear it other than us. We can have great parties.

So, it's just the space, and the sense of freedom, the sense of spaciousness that I love about it.

What about the films, plays, music—that sort of thing?

We do down to Adelaide to see plays and films. They have these specials for a weekend in hotels, perhaps in Adelaide, and you'll get a deal that includes movies or something. We also take the kids to the pictures when we're on holiday in Adelaide. I must admit I saw more plays when I was single and close to the city, and our life seems so full now that we probably haven't got time, but a lot of good things come up to the Chaffey Theatre at Renmark, so we'll go up there. And there's a very strong arts community in the Riverland so lots of things do come this way. Our kids have seen orchestras and plays and films ... it's a matter of making the effort to go and see those things. I bet if the same question was asked of a lot of city people they'd say 'Oh, no, we don't get there'.

There's been a lot of talk recently about city and country, and some city people seem to have a very stereotyped picture of people who live in the country. Do you find that?

All our friends who are in the city were also once in the

country—and relatives the same. I guess nowadays the fact that the numbers of people are increasing in the city and they're reducing in the country means that less and less city people have the opportunity to visit the country. In the old days you always had some relative who was in the country somewhere and so you'd go off to gran's or you'd go off to your uncle's or something and get some sort of experience and feel for the way of life. Whereas most country people have relatives now who are in the city, so most of them experience the city, and hence you've got that drifting apart.

Kids from cities also often used to get jobs in the country when they were quite young, just as a way of growing up, and those jobs are not there any more, are they?

There are a hell of a lot of kids who come up here fruit-picking during the fruit-picking season but we're much more mechanised these days.

Do you have a pattern to your day?

No (laughs) there's no pattern around here. When the kids were little and I was teaching, the pattern would be one of me going off to teaching and back. But when you're on the farm, you could think that your day's going to be pretty normal—an 'average' day—when you'll get up and go and do this thing and that thing—and the next thing you know, the sheep are out on the road and the fence is broken. Okay, there goes that typical day. You're off doing that. Or suddenly you see this great big wet patch on the ground, and you say, 'Oh, no, the pipe's burst'. So the next thing, you're being a plumber. Yet when it's seeding time or its harvest time there's a typical day in that you get up and you get going and you do that job and it goes all day and you're back again. But it's an ever-changing kaleidoscope of activity, and that's probably the thing I like about it. There is no such thing as a typical day, so it's never boring.

What would you say are your main achievements on the land?

Looking back I think there are some formative experiences that I consider achievements, that have contributed to the confidence I have for how I approach things. One of those was going back and gaining this ag. science qualification and teaching ag. science. I think my agriculture science teaching career is an achievement and it's given me a thirst for knowledge about agriculture and a tremendous interest in agriculture as an industry that I think is terrific. It's viable, it's productive and it requires guts, determination and brains to be good at it. It brings out a lot of the best things in people, as I see it. And then, on top of that, after I had done my year at Kadina, I did something that I was determined to do before I settled down. I put a backpack on and I had a round-the-world ticket where I just went out by myself, to see the world.

Back in 1977 when I was teaching here at Loxton for a year, I met a Scottish Young Farmer exchangee, and at the end of that year I went to Scotland and stayed on this farm between Aberdeen and Inverness. That was a big adventure. I landed there in the middle of winter on a Scottish farm with these Highland cattle, and my job in the morning was to chip the ice off the trough. And although the offer was there to stay much longer, it was just too cold, but it started me thinking, God, there's more of a world out there.

When I went for this trip my sister was in Canada and I stayed with her, I went back to England and Scotland, then I spent three or four months working on a kibbutz in Israel. That was one of the biggest experiences of my life, working on this kibbutz in Israel, in a culture under constant threat. Also, I saw my first beggar overseas—on a bridge in London—and the impression is still with me of seeing a person begging for money on a bridge in London, of all places.

And then you get into that Muslim culture, though you don't want to get too close to it as a single travelling woman, then in a country like Israel you can see the variety of life working on a kibbutz. The children were separated—it was a traditional sort of thing because back in the 'fifties and 'sixties it was highly likely that their parents would be killed, so they separated and brought the children up as the future of Israel. They didn't have families like we know them.

A lot of friends came over and we did a variety of travelling and saw a fair bit of Europe, France and the Mediterranean and everything. And then I came back to Australia by choice. And I came in saying, 'This is the lucky country. This is a place it is worth contributing to, making better, because, by golly it's got a lot of things going for it and it's the best place in the world'.

Before that I was one of those who thought everything else is better than Australia. I wasn't even going to put an Australian flag on my backpack—oh, none of that. But by the time I'd been through America and been told, 'Oh, you're English, are you?', I got so fed up that I walked into Australia House in London and the first thing I did was buy a jar of Vegemite and an Australian flag. Like everybody else I put it on my backpack and it opened doors, it really did.

So you came back determined to do what you could for this country?

Not the great 'I'll do something for Australia' sort of thing—I was just in my twenties—but it was a matter of coming back and not any more looking over the fence, the national fence if you like, thinking the grass is greener on the other side. Instead, having been out there and done it, I was saying, 'Gee, the grass is green here'.

I get really annoyed with people who knock Australia and who aren't prepared to go out and do something for themselves, because the opportunities are here. You only have to see other countries and the situations they live in to realise how much we have going for us. So, it was an attitudinal change that then reflected itself in how I went on teaching, and got a little more ambitious in terms of my teaching. I applied for a senior's position, to run a faculty, and I wrote education materials and stuff like that. I got stuck into things a bit more and, in fact, Anton and I met as he was asking me about travelling overseas. He had built up his farms, and he thought, right, well now I'll go and do some travelling. He never really got there, so it'll be great if we can get there together.

After we were married and, say, in the last nine years, the achievements have really flowed from my involvement with our family farm as a family and as a business enterprise. So my achievements are that we are still here; we are still farming. The year after we got married was the first year of the Export Enhancement Program, so the wheat prices plummeted; then came deregulation of the domestic wheat market; then the floor fell out of the wool price; then there was a mouse plague, and then there was a drought. Now, if anybody's still there after those first years of marriage—that's an achievement.

The other thing was I got so mad about all these things when I understood the realities of our enterprise that I said, 'Crumbs! Look at this legislation; that is so ridiculous.' And so I got involved with the Farmers' Federation. That's another avenue of achievement. I have worked my way through to where I now hold positions of influence and authority within that organisation as a section chairman of community services, as a governing councillor and a member of the executive.

I don't go for 'firsts'—it just evolves—but I was the first female zone chairman that they had for the South Australian Farmers' Federation. Then, of course, the Rural Woman of the Year award was an achievement—one that just came by dint of other things that I've achieved. I haven't ever set out to achieve things, life just evolves, one thing rolls on from the other and as you go for one thing you tend to end up doing the next thing.

What difference has the award made to your lifestyle?

It's made it busier. It was the inaugural award, so I feel a responsibility to see that I do the best I can by the award and by all those women who are thrilled about its very existence. I think it's terrific of the ABC to do it. I do as many speaking engagements as I can. But I have a priority—that I speak about women or women in agriculture or agriculture. I've had other requests for various things and if they fit in, fine—if they don't, I'd give the priority to those elements I think the award is about. The second thing is I'm travelling from one side of this country to the other, and I do need some time home with my family just to catch my breath and to contribute back to it, because we still have to make a living on our farm.

RUTH PATERSON

*R*uth Paterson, Tasmania's Rural Woman of the Year in *1994, is credited with organising the biggest* AGFEST *that state has ever seen. Eleven per cent of the total population attended. She was also the first woman in Australia to chair an agricultural field day Committee. Since winning the Award she has taken up a job with the Department of Primary Industry to encourage a rural women's network and advise the Government of issues that effect rural women. Her energy and enthusiasm were obvious when I met her at the farm she and husband Phillip own at Oaks, not far from Launceston in Tasmania.*

My great-grandfather, grandfather and father were all agricultural contractors to this district for a period of over eighty years. They emigrated from Cornwall in the late 1800s; they were farmers in Cornwall and they were farmers here.

After the Second World War they realised that much of the machinery used previously was all being sold off for scrap, so my father, Jack, and his two younger brothers set about collecting one of every piece of machinery that had worked in the state and the basis of that collection makes up Pearn's Steam World, which is on the Bass Highway at Westbury. They've donated that to the local municipality. Since then it's been added to greatly and it attracts interstate and overseas visitors daily.

Was your father a contractor when you were growing up?

Yes, he was. I'm the youngest of three girls, the third daughter and the last chance of a boy! I had a fairly traditional upbringing; the women in our family have always worked extremely hard on the land but twenty years ago, when I left school, to take agriculture as a career was not really the done thing, nor was it encouraged. So when they reached retiring age they gave contracting away.

And what did you have in mind?

I wanted desperately to work at home as I did during the holidays and after school but, as I said, it just wasn't traditional, so I went off to Launceston and worked in the insurance industry until my marriage. Since then Phillip and I have been farming here for about fourteen years.

Did it ever occur to you to do an ag. science degree of some sort?

No, I guess I just accepted that that's how it was. Five years later things really changed: I had friends that went off to do ag. science but at that stage I felt it was just too late for me, and it wasn't until I got involved with AGFEST, which is the field day here in this state, that I really started to be ambitious. I see nothing wrong with ambition or setting goals. I love agriculture. I'm a fifth generation Tasmanian farmer and extremely proud of that, and I suddenly had this ambition to try to do something for agriculture in this stage.

Going back a bit—your father was a contractor, which is not really a farmer, is it?

He did have his own property of about 500 acres in partnership with his brothers and they went off contracting to support the farm.

I was born and bred on a dairy farm at Hagley. Dad was the agricultural contractor in the district. Phillip was a dairy farmer and we now farm our own 300 acres here at the District of Oaks, which is between Carrick and Bracknell in the northern midlands of Tasmania. We farm vegetables, poppies, a lot of grass seed, and we fatten lambs and cattle.

We're lucky to live in an area of the state where we can diversify into other things. I know in the Midlands it's sheep and sheep only, but here we can do a little bit of everything. Perhaps that's what's kept us afloat—one thing's down and the other thing's up.

The array of things going through this farm must make it quite interesting.

Very interesting! Fairly busy and fairly hard on the overdraft at times. Traditionally this has been a dairying area but now it's considered to be fairly dry for dairying: you have to put a lot of work into irrigation, so we went to a cash cropping mode. I don't know how long we'll keep doing that because at the moment cash cropping has a fairly low profit margin, but I work off the property now and that's off-farm income.

Before you got your job in Launceston what sort of things did you do on the farm?

Just about everything. I like the livestock side of it and I drive the tractor. I always say that I get the buys' jobs. Phillip makes the managerial decisions but I have input to them and we work as a team, and a very good team. There's an old saying that behind every good man there's an even better woman; well, it's in reverse here: I'm the one that's been off the property and in the limelight and I've been able to do all those things because he's here supporting me every inch of the way.

Tell me about AGFEST, how it works and what it is.

AGFEST is run in this state by the Rural Youth Organisation of Tasmania, whose age group is fifteen to thirty years of age. The AGFEST Committee is made up of members, or past members like myself, of that organisation. There's a committee of thirty young rural people with an average age of twenty-four. Back in the early 'eighties Rural Youth in the state was funded by the Department of Agriculture and when things started to get cut, that funding was one of the first things that went. They had to find their own means of support so they set about organising this field day. I don't think that first committee realised the monster they have created because now, thirteen years later, it attracts about 11 per cent of the state's population and about 400 exhibitors. They have their own 200-acre property which has its own power grid underneath and facilities like toilets and office accommodation, and it's now a very, very important part of this state's economy. It's responsible for over $12 000 000, conservatively, to the economy as a whole in spin-offs such as transport, food, accommodation, or whatever.

Luckily for me it's only one kilometre to the site. I was chairman of that committee for two years after being involved for about seven or eight years, and I don't think I could have contributed had I not been just around the corner. It required a lot of time, anywhere between twenty and 150 hours of voluntary time per week.

About 75 per cent of farmers come, which is very good, and last year we got 52 500 people. There's no other field day in Australia that can boast that they get 11 per cent of their state's population and there is no other Rural Youth Organisation in Australia that is as self-funding and as successful as the one here in Tasmania.

We're still very machinery based and very strongly agriculturally based. We have rather a large craft area and some people ask what that has to do with agriculture, but there's a lot of farming women in there who have diversified into off-farm income by getting a start in displaying their wares at AGFEST. And we cover the fine food area, machinery, just anything that is agriculture.

Do you find people coming from the city as well?

A big percentage comes from the city and this year the committee have a big push into the interstate and overseas market. We feel that if someone wants to buy something Tasmanian they'll come to AGFEST to do it.

Do they have AGFESTs everywhere?

There's one in Queensland but this is the only field day in this state.

You're the first woman to chair an AGFEST committee and the first woman to chair an Australia-wide field day. Can I ask you what's involved in actually organising this sort of huge event?

I didn't take it on because I wanted to be the first woman; I took it on because I felt I really had something to offer and it certainly was a big challenge. I think it was the biggest personal growth and development crash course challenge anyone could ever have. You're trying to keep together thirty young people and you have to organise everything from the food to the toilet paper and keep them all working together and put a typical rural aspect on things.

Have you had to look after things like transport and food and all that sort of thing while people are down here?

No, our catering's all done by community groups so that's direct income straight back into the community; I think there's about seventeen of them and last year they averaged about $7000 profit. No, it's just a matter of organising all the facilities and the advertising and the PA and making sure that we've got enough caterers, but not actually the work-ings of who serves what.

Is the main aim of the thing to teach young people about various aspects of farming?

Definitely. It's about seeing what agriculture is really about and educating people. Rural Youth intend to move into home hosting so that people in the city can stay with people in the country. So often with the multi-national com-panies that we deal with, decisions are made by people in front of a computer in an office block in high-rise Sydney and they forget the very basic point of people. The decision probably works when they press the button at the end but it doesn't always work for the people, and I think that's probably where we're going wrong as a society. We're forgetting people, we're forgetting basic communication and we're forgetting that it takes teamwork between both of those for things to work and work properly.

Have you any examples of things going wrong?

I'm also involved with counselling in this state and so often the problems that arise between families are a lack of communication between generations or between family members. Everyone's getting stressed out but if they had only sat down round the dinner table and talked through their problems and had their say and understood how each other felt, then the problem probably wouldn't have arisen in the first place.

Going back to those people pressing buttons in high-rise buildings in the city, are you really contemplating bringing them to the country and perhaps giving them a weekend picking pumpkins or chasing sheep round a paddock (both laugh)?

I think if you have a crop fail or your best dairy cow dies or whatever, people can say to you, 'Oh, that's hard luck, that's bad', then they go off about their duties because, as I know from experience, their pay is going to be there the next fortnight. But until you've actually felt the pain of your best dairy cow dying or your crop failing and no income— the actual pain and feeling it—you don't really understand.

As far as I'm concerned, rural Australia is the roots of this country, we're the ones that are still in touch with nature for everything we do. We're controlled by Mother Nature's little whims, be they flood, fire or drought. The industries and the towns all make up the leaves and the branches of the tree, but I often wonder, if they keep on exposing the roots to high interest rates and low commodity prices and we have something like this drought we're experiencing at the moment which exposes those roots even further, how are the leaves and branches going to survive?

In this state primary production is worth thirty-five per cent of the GNP and about thirty-three per cent of direct employment so it is extremely important to the state's economy. I doubt whether we get that in return.

I guess Tasmania is small enough for people in the towns to drive through the countryside to get to anywhere quite readily, whereas people in Sydney or Melbourne can live their whole lives without seeing even a cow. Have you got any thoughts on how this city/ country gap of understanding can be bridged?

I guess it's education, and education starts with the very young, getting into schools and teaching them from a young age the importance of agriculture. I think city people still see us as a bunch of whingers who drive their Mercs to town in their tweed suits and their Stetsons. Well, we're a long way off that. We're out here struggling against the elements seventeen hours a day, seven days a week, to live, for many, below the poverty line, and I don't think that we, as agriculturalists, can continue to do that.

In Europe during the war they nearly starved and Europe now looks after its farmers. I don't want to get into the subsidies or anything like that, I think that's non-productive, but there's an attitude there that must be changed. Look at the work Landcare did. Ten years ago Landcare was the greenie, radical hobby farmer, and now if farmers and mainstream community groups aren't into some form of Landcare they're not in the race.

Most farmers don't want to mine their ground; they want to look after it and they want it to be sustainable, but they can't afford to do it. So I think if the city people want good clean water, they're going to have to help us pay to get it, and if they don't want poor old Fred to chop down the tree, that's fine—but don't just send Fred on the dole, pay for the tree and let him have the opportunity to be a person with some pride and a living also.

It's a difficult thing for people who live in cities and who are lucky enough to be employed at all and who get regular pay packets whatever happens, to appreciate that out here pay packets are sometimes infrequent and sometimes non-existent.

Exactly. You rely on the weather and these days commodity prices have very small margins so it just takes one mistake, just one, and you're in trouble. Farmers of the 'nineties have to be planners, they have to be innovators, they have to be well educated and certainly very good managers, and I guess some will fall by the wayside during this drought be it through their own fault or not. But we've got to look after our agriculturalists or else the country will starve. They can import it all but are they going to get as good quality and as fresh? As I said, Europe starved, so is that what we want to head for, too? Is that what it takes before we change something around?

What sort of opportunities do you see out there in terms of marketing some of the stuff you're growing?

Marketing is the key to it all. I mean, we can compete on world markets. When you look at a lot of our competitors who are suffering such problems as acid rain and soaring pollution, we are producing a very good quality product here, but we no longer can do it with small margins. Some companies seem to be going for the big quantities, but is it better to go for the more gourmet market, tell someone it's good and back it up by being good, so then they're prepared to pay that extra bit more?

We're growing squash. I haven't the technical term here for them but they're for the Japanese market and they have to be a certain size and a certain age and they can only have one blemish on them. They're picked and packed and done up very nicely for the Japanese market and I think they use them to make chips.

So there are odd niche markets, I guess, that you can supply if you know about them.

Yes, that's it, but our costs in Australia are just incredible. There's a big potato war here in Tasmania at the moment and we're told that they can produce them just as cheaply in America, so we should be able to, too. But the Americans can get their tractor parts for a fraction of the cost, their diesels for a fraction of the cost, their fertilisers for a fraction of the cost. We're so heavily taxed here, it's hardly a level playing field when you're paying more for what it takes. My nephew is here from England at the moment and he gets a similar price for his lowest grade potatoes, but prices for all his machinery and so on are so much less and prices for his other commodities are so much higher that he can afford to juggle things a little bit. He gets up some mornings and says, 'This is a really strange country. I don't know why you bother'.

Why do you bother?

Because it's in the blood. I think it has to be in the blood and you have to love it. There's a certain feeling when you get up in the morning and wonder what today's challenge is going to be, to see the product that you've grown and nurtured going down the lane in the back of a truck to get a good price. There's a certain amount of pride in that.

What happens on a morning like this morning when you wake up and an early frost has blackened the tops of the corn?

You get the fire going pretty quickly before breakfast (laughs) and you hope and pray that you can get the rest of the crop done. As I said, that's the chance, that's Mother Nature and that's what farming's about. I guess if it wasn't in our blood we'd probably all go to the casino and blow our money, make just as much profit and have a lot more fun! (laughs) But that's farming.

Your two daughters are at an age when, I guess, they're starting to think of what career they might go after. What are you telling them?

That they can be whatever they want to be. I think that's the beauty of living in the 'nineties, especially as a woman; you can be whatever you want to be and have the confidence to do it. Isabel at this stage wants to be a nurse or a radiographer, which I think is fine, and Stephanie hasn't made up her mind yet. But I'll support them to be whatever they want to be, and if they want to come home I'll encourage them to get some sort of tertiary qualification first.

Can you see great changes happening in the rural sector?

I think so. I don't think we can get any lower now. We've bottomed out, so it can only get better, and I think agriculturalists are prepared to stand up and fight now. I'm involved with Women in Agriculture which in this state is only about six months old, and there is a real, positive feeling that we must stand together and change. In the past, I guess, we've blindly left it to governments and bureaucrats to tell us what to do and expected them to provide the goods. Well, in the 'nineties that's not going to happen; you're going to have to get out there and get it for yourself and do it and do it well.

What does that involve?

Education and training. Women in Ag's about training and having the confidence to get up there and get involved with agricultural politics and business. I think in the past we've let the husbands go off to the field days and the meetings, but now they've got too much pressure to be able to leave the property and go off to a meeting so those organisations have gradually had less and less people to draw on, and if women can take up some of those roles then it's all the better. For agriculture, business and politics to continue, to perceive that only the men are the farmers means they're missing out on 100 per cent of their client base.

Do you see that women have special things to contribute to those sorts of committees?

I think so. I think we look at things differently. I know in running AGFEST I tended to look at things differently from the way perhaps the boys had done beforehand. We're usually better organised—you have to be to run a house and work outside and, perhaps, work off the farm too. I think by tradition women are the nurturers and the protectors of their family and in nature there is no greater instinct than a mother protecting her young. So if women are out there protecting their farms and their families and trying to re-invigorate the rural communities they usually hang on to the death.

What's the acceptance like when you go to some of these meetings because your husbands can't go?

I don't think the men mind at all but, although I knew I
was confident enough to go and that I knew as much as
everyone else there, it took me a long time in myself to feel
comfortable. I felt internally a little bit inadequate, but by
being involved with AGFEST and now the Rural Woman of
the Year Award I'm confident in myself. I think that's what
the Rural Women's movement is about, just teaching that
extra bit of confidence. I always use the four Ps: in business
you have to be positive, you have to be professional, you
have to be passionate about your cause, and the last one is,
you have to be patient. If you look up the Oxford
Dictionary, patience is calm endurance under pain, weari-
ness or provocation, and don't women know about that!

So you're able to pass some of this on to other women.

That's what I'm trying to do, yes. I'm trying to let them
see the opportunities and, by attending a function with
other women, to realise that someone else is suffering the
same things—being out at all hours of the night putting the
tarp on the header, or when the sheep have escaped into
the garden or the oat paddock yet again, all those little day-
to-day problems you have on farms. You're not alone and
you can share that and work on it and build a good bond
and good confidence.

*Has being Tasmanian winner of the Rural Woman of the Year
Award made any difference to your life in the last year?*

A fair bit of difference. When I came home from that
award there were bottles of champagne and chocolates at
my back door and about thirty or forty messages on the
answering machine, and that didn't stop for weeks. I got
cards and letters from people from all over Australia. So it
means being recognised in supermarkets and it means I've

RUTH PATERSON

opened Shows and community groups. I do about two speaking engagements a month which I really enjoy, because that gives me the opportunity to speak to people, both country and city, about issues affecting rural Australia in the 'nineties and about teamwork and about standing up and doing something to change things.

I've got something to say and I've got the opportunity now to say it (laughs). I've been chased by political parties and all sorts of things and I don't think I'm anywhere near ready for that, but it's been a wonderful opportunity; it's opened doors that previously mightn't have been shut but would have needed a full CV to get through. It's been a big confidence boost, although I still find it fairly embarrassing sometimes (laughs). Someone said to me once, 'Oh, Ruth, you're a role model for other women', and I thought, who, me? But perhaps I am. Anyone given opportunities can achieve: it's just that I've had those opportunities and not everybody else has. I hope they get them.

MAISIE HODGETTS

*M*aisie Hodgetts was brought up on a dairy farm in Scotland and came to live permanently in Australia with her husband and three children in 1973. They settled on a small farm near Denmark in the south of Western Australia and began building up a Hereford stud. Tragically, Maisie's husband drowned three years later, before the farm was properly established but she made the difficult decision to stay in Australia, to try to make a go of the farm by herself.

What made you come to Australia?

We thought there would be more opportunities for children.

My husband was out here before to look at farms and he looked at this one and the couple at that stage didn't know if they wanted to sell or not. We were interested and they promised they would let us have first chance to buy it.

Tell us about the land when you first moved on to it.

It was reasonably good. We had quite a bit of bush but pasture was OK. We found out that to get really good pasture you have to give plenty of fertiliser.

The house was an old weatherboard asbestos home—but it was home and it was comfortable. We liked it very much.

We'd come from dairy farming and started on beef farming here so there was no comparison. We had to start from scratch learning how to go about beef farming and whatever else we had to do in connection with the farm.

We were in a walk-in, walk-out situation so we took over the herd that was already there and started off cleaning it up. We wanted to have a Hereford stud so we concentrated mainly on Herefords.

Were the cattle Herefords? How did you start?

We did it very gradually. Most of the commercial herd were right and we wanted to have a stud just in a small way. We started going out buying good cattle and a decent bull. It was a couple of years before we really got going— they were expensive. After two years we had to stop because cattle prices crashed—money wasn't available.

My husband went out and got work and I stayed home with the kids and did the necessary jobs on the farm. Every-thing as far as our cattle was concerned, improving our stud, was brought to a halt. That was for the first two years and then in the January of the third year we were in Australia my husband had an accident and he was drowned.

Cattle prices were pretty low at that time but I'd got to look at reducing everything. We'd got some sheep and some pigs in the meantime. I got rid of the sheep and kept on the pigs for a year and the cattle to a manageable size. The stud went by the way because I couldn't cope. Apart from the farm I had the kids—Jamie was eight and Ross hadn't started school and Janice is in between. She was seven. Ross started school that year and I didn't really want to carry on at the farm at that stage. I would gladly have gone but you can't just stop and take off. After a year I saw things really differently and I'd such a lot of good friends and people helping me I just couldn't do it. So I thought, well, I've got two sons and one day that farm will be theirs and there will be something for them. But so far nothing has happened.

So that's what kept you going, was it?

That's what kept me going. I was always getting plenty of helping hands and that part of it was very good.

Did you know much about having pigs?

I hadn't had anything to do with pigs on my farm life but my husband had pigs in his early farming career and I really enjoyed the pigs. I was sorry I had to part with them because they are very easy to handle and they were breeding sows. You know, you get attached to the animals.

What were the things you had to do to make the farm so that you could manage it?

Just reduce my cattle, and I let out 200 acres of land to my neighbour and then I could handle it. We had about seventy breeders and their offspring and I always run a few steers.

It must have been fairly hairy from time to time.

It was. You have lots of times for decision making. Probably that was my worst thing, having to make decisions about what we were going to do next, but we got there.

Your kids were a bit young to help in that sort of decision making.

Yes. I did always include them in anything that was done. When we talked about what cows we were going to sell or what cattle had to go or whatever we were doing, I always included them because I thought that would be a good thing for them in the future. If they have an understanding of what we are doing then they know how to go about it.

My neighbour Les Smith was very good and he still keeps an eye on us. He is a man of seventy-two and he is a wonderful neighbour.

I learned a great deal in the first few years because I had always left it all to my husband. I went along with him when we were doing things. I was the housewife doing the cooking and washing and looking after the kids. I didn't really take a serious part in the farm side of it but after you know you've got to, you do it.

What did you learn very quickly?

Just about how to manage the cows. You've got several paddocks and you can only leave them in one for so long— a week or ten days—then you move the lot. You're feeding out, and we just had small square bales in those days and I had a tractor and trailer. Of course calving time is a very important time. You just have to be able to go out in the morning and check them—they come first—and make sure they have a live calf. If there are no problems you're right. If there were I got my neighbour or the vet. But the vet in those days was from Albany, and pretty expensive, so most of the time we didn't worry about the vet.

Could you drive a tractor before your husband died?

Yes I'd learned that. I drove a tractor before we were married.

Did you have any formal training to help you with running the farm?

No, but I think being born on a farm—even though it was a dairy farm—gives you a fair bit of common sense with animals. You notice if one is off colour, you know what's going on in the farm. It's a natural instinct.

What did the bank managers say?

We had problems with banks because we didn't have any money after we'd bought all these expensive cattle. And money was short—that's when my husband went out to work. The bank wouldn't loan us any money, but we got a loan from Rural Reconstruction at about four-and-a-half per cent. We diversified as I said—sheep and pigs, which were doing better than cattle were doing.

After your husband died?

I had an insurance policy and I was able to clean my feet so I didn't owe anybody anything. I never needed to go to the bank manager or anything. That saved my day. It was great to get up in the morning and think, well, I don't owe anybody anything, and that's been my policy from that day—never to get in debt. I've got a nice home now. I sold land to get the home but I thought, my kids are not on the farm and I've always wanted a nice home; I don't want to buy land and I don't use this hundred acres which was leased to my neighbour. We put it on the market and got a good price. We started from there and I've been in here two years now and it's lovely.

I like my old home too. I go down and I see my trees and all the bits that I've done to that place. The trees are just starting to grow here and it's coming.

Is anyone in your old home?

Yes, my neighbour who helped me all along. His son got married and they had nowhere to go so he and his wife rented, but that is finished on Sunday. They are moving out so I am looking for someone else. I've heard the young vet in town is looking for a place.

Before my husband died I'd got part-time domestic work at the hospital. I went back to work there in 1986 and I'm still working there, just doing casual. When they need me I go in and that's good because you get away from the farm, you get mixing with people. You've got conversation, that part is very good, and a little bit of money. If I want to buy a new table or some chairs or whatever I've got some money there.

It could be a bit lonely up here.

Yes, if you didn't go out. I've got a friend now, a gentleman friend and he is the secretary of the Lions and I'm a Lions Lady so I got out to the Lions functions.

You've done quite a few innovative things with the property over the years.

We started up with a new breed a few years ago. My brother-in-law in Albury is the manager for ABS Breeders and he does the embryo transplants. I was asking about having something different from the ordinary Hereford/ Angus and he came up with this breed called Gelvie. We didn't know how to go about it but he said, well, look, when there's some more embryos I'll let you know. There was a phone call a few days later to say he'd got fourteen embryos and had somebody for seven, so would I be happy to take the other seven. I said, Oh yes, I'll have a go. They're quite expensive but why not branch out to something? We had it all done in Busselton. We had the recipient cows and we got three out of the seven which apparently is very good. When they arrived we had two heifers and a bull. The bull's been with the cows, this is his second year, and he's doing excellently. And the two heifers have produced this year for the first time and we have two new little bulls. I would like two heifers but still we've got two bulls and they're lovely.

Sounds as though you're working towards another stud?

That would be really interesting. They're all registered now. You know, if I find I've got some more money, perhaps I'll buy a couple of heifers, and that will boost them.

Are you contemplating getting some more embryos?

If I was advised to, I'd have a go again.

Are there any of those sorts of cattle around this area?

Not many in Western Australia.

What's the advantage?

Good lean meat which is what the housewife wants. They are very easy when it comes to calving, they make good mums and they are easy to handle which, for me, is the best thing.

What will you do with the two little bulls?

We'll keep one and sell one.

Do people cross breed them around here?

I know somebody who does. I'll take him to Kojonup if he looks good—bigger sale and more people. Otherwise I'll take him to Albany because they have a bull sale once a year there.

How long do you think it takes to build up a sizeable herd?

A long time. I just want it as an interest, a paying hobby. I don't want a great big Gelvie herd. I want to always have my commercial cattle.

This place is a living, but is it more than that?

I couldn't see myself being anywhere else. People say, don't you ever want to go back to Scotland. I would like to go back for a few weeks, but I haven't been back yet. Every year I promise I'll go, but you can't walk off a farm, you've got to be sure there is someone who'll look after your farm.

I have a sister and two brothers in Scotland. My sister has been out, she came out in 1980. I promised to go back in ten years but I didn't do it.

Have you travelled much in Australia?

I've been over East to my brother-in-law, and I went to Ross's march-out in Wagga Wagga. I've been up to Karratha. My daughter was working at a road house which has since been destroyed.

You must look around and think how much you've achieved. When your husband died you didn't have a lot.

We didn't, no, but I look at the place and I think, gee, is this really mine? I can't visualise that it's mine. I always talk about it being ours. I sometimes think it would be nice if

one of the kids came back one day and wanted to farm.
Jamie might. He's doing enrolled nursing now. I'm glad
they've gone and done something else because farming is
like anything else: it has its bad, sticky moments and there's
not much money in it. If they've got something else they
can turn their hand to they would never have to be fully
dependent and that's a great thing.

What do you think, looking back on your life?

We have had happy times. I can remember when we
came out to Australia it was wonderful. It was hot weather
and we'd jump into the car and go to the beach and think
nothing about it. It was wonderful. And I thought what a
big difference from dairying where all you saw was cows
morning and night. It seemed such a wonderful way of life.
And now I've got plenty of friends and really have some
nice times, not going to concerts and shows and things like
that, but family gatherings and little groups in town. It's
really good.

*A lot of people looking at your life story would think you were
very brave, that you had done something quite extraordinary.*

Well, people have been good and if I rang anyone and
asked for help they would be there. I try to do what I can,
I like to be independent. It's wonderful to think you have
neighbours and all you've to do is ring them up and they
will be there.

You kept going, but did you have any option?

I didn't in the first year because of probate. I was told,
for your own interest, stay. It was very hard. I had my
mother-in-law, she came but it wasn't the best thing. The
children were very small and I was always on the farm and

granny was there when they came off the bus and granny got all the praise and all the notes and all the stories that happened at school and I felt so jealous of her. She was the one ... the kids were hers and I was the person who came in at night. It was good that she was there because they really needed somebody. So I had to make up my mind for both our sakes, because she was a nice lady and we got on really well, that she would have to have her own home, which she did. She went off to Perth and I had to rearrange my working on the farm so that I was there when they came off the school bus, even if it was only for ten minutes to make them a drink and hear what happened at school. It was good.

If you had left the farm the probate would have been higher, is that right?

That's right. If we had gone then the farm would have been sold at a good price. You get a valuer in to give you a price on your farm then probate step in and I thought, why do that? Try and avoid it.

I guess the first year after your husband died would have been fairly terrible.

Yes, you're so bitter. I used to think, well, why did it happen to me? If only we hadn't gone swimming ... and all the things that go through your mind. If I went shopping (it was the 150th Year's celebrations in Albany that year) there would be so much going on in the street and people would be laughing and singing and here was me. I was so broken-hearted, I couldn't lift myself at all. But time is a great healer. You never forget, but it does heal.

How long did it take you to feel that even without him this was home and you could build something here?

After twelve months you see things really differently and I was determined then that we would hang onto the farm no matter what. My husband had bought forty-five Angus cows and they were beautiful and the first year I only had the one bull and he couldn't cope with all these animals. After the first year we realised about twelve of them were not in calf and we had to get rid of them. None of them made a hundred dollars, you wouldn't believe it. I thought, oh, dear, we gave them away, but that was the price at the time. We had no choice.

Did you sell that full Angus herd all at once?

No, eleven went and as they got older we just gradually sold them off, they were lovely animals.

It's the animals that you like on the farm is it?

Oh yes, that's my life. Every day I go out and they are calving and it's wonderful to see what transpires in a day. I would just like to improve what we've got. Look after the farm as it is and make improvements each year.

How much longer do you think you will go on doing that?

I've already slowed down. That's why I got on the bike today.

SUE HOLT

*T*anunda, Tolleys and Hardy's and Yalumba ... the names
are familiar to anyone who likes Australian wines. I passed
them on my way through the Barossa Valley—its Teutonic tidiness
still in evidence—to see Sue Holt at Eden Valley just south of
Angaston in South Australia.

Sue runs a Poll Hereford Stud on the land once owned by her
great-grandfather. She says her roots are deep in the soil just like
the old gum trees that have been part of that land for many
generations.

I was born here and I thought I had a pretty good childhood—I ran wild until I was twelve. We had correspondence lessons and I guess because of petrol and cars and
things we didn't really mix too much with the community.
We made our own fun with our pets.

177

I can remember being very offended when I was five years old. I hadn't started school and my great-aunt Rose said to me, 'What are you going to do when you grow up?' and I said, 'I'm going to be a farmer'. She said 'Little girls aren't farmers.' With that I got off her knee, slightly offended, and thought: my dad's a farmer, why can't I be a farmer? I hadn't realised that there was a gender difference. I thought I was just a human being like everybody else.

There were three of us here and we just made our own fun. We used to annoy Dad by trying to be with him when he was getting sheep in, and in the shearing shed. You couldn't miss shearing—that was the best time of the year.

Everything came to a screaming halt when I got sent to Adelaide to school. That was the most traumatic time of my life I think. I was homesick for five years and that's a real grief feeling. I couldn't wait to get home for a couple of years. Then one of my friends said, There's a job at the medical school for three months. Would you like to try it? I thought that'd be all right—just three months. So I went down to town. I still didn't like being in Adelaide, but I did enjoy being in the medical school. I guess that was a background for what I'm doing now—injecting animals and sewing them up and pulling calves out of cows and helping ewes lamb because I was working with animals down there.

Looking back at that rather sad period at school which you had, did it do you any good at all? Did you get anything from it?

I suppose you do. I suppose you make friends that you keep for life. Perhaps if I hadn't gone down there and met this friend who had a job at the medical school I wouldn't have met my husband and that would have been a tragedy. But I envy my nieces who went to Scotch College where they had an ag. course they could do and I think if I'd had a school that had had an ag. course I would have been a lot happier, because I just so much missed country things like pets. I used to smuggle the school cat into my bed at night in the dormitory which didn't go down too well, but gee, I missed my animals. And I missed open areas. It just seemed so strange to be locked up in the city. Oh, and sport—I enjoyed my hockey and tennis, and I did enjoy the actual learning but I could have done it just as well here, I think, at the local school. So we sent our lads to the local school to make up for it.

Have you ever done any formal ag. training?

Not formally. But we certainly go to every farming seminar and lecture and field day and everything else that we can get to. We're doing property planning now and I think if you want to stay in the game you've got to keep up. It doesn't matter how old you are you've got to keep going to these things, trying to learn the latest technology et cetera.

This farm that you're on now used to belong to some of your ancestors—some of your grandparents. What does it mean to you to look out the window and see those big old gumtrees out there?

I suppose it's a sort of a spiritual feeling, I don't know. But you think—gosh, your grandfather and your great-grandfather actually saw these trees, walked past them, saw this land as it was then, and I guess it's something that the Aboriginal people talk about. I think it is a spiritual feeling. You certainly feel that your roots are really deep down here.

Because we're so close to the city with the high land prices compared to productivity we should sell up, we should move out. But I don't know if I could. I think I'd probably curl up and die like a snail with salt on it. To leave it would be very hard. The first ancestor to take this land up was Angus. When he came out he took up about 28 000 acres in this area and he had tenant farmers on some of it—probably about eighty acres per farm. There are little cottage sites all over the place and they actually planted wheat. There also were timber fellers—thankfully they didn't take too much timber from here—and they used to collect wattle bark.

The actual process of growing wheat crashed here because of the climate—I think they got rust as well—then it reverted back to broader acres and, about 1860, my paternal great-grandfather took it on and that's where it's been ever since. I'm the last of the family here. All the others have left the Barossa and gone to the south-east or Queensland or wherever, or died. So I'm the last lonely little one. But I think we'll stick it out. It's probably better to do what you know than to try and move out and start again.

It must have been pretty unusual for people at that time to leave these big stands of trees still standing.

There were copper mines east of here where there were a lot of blue gums and peppermints and things, and they're pretty well cleaned out. And also the she-oaks were cut down for feed in the 1914 drought—stock feed. And on the range west of us a lot of the timber was taken for boilers for the wineries—and I guess, too, for building fences. At least now, with Landcare, they are starting to replant, so that big bare area hopefully in another thirty or forty years will have more trees on it. But it's not a very good sign of what some people did in the past with the land blow. It's very fragile land up there and in the drought it'll blow, or wash, so we really need the trees back. The enthusiasm of farmers to get into Landcare, to do something for the land, to have their farms sustainable in the future is tremendous. Although I just don't know, the way things are going, how sustainable agriculture is in feeding these extra people that are coming on earth every year—ninety-five million of them. The land degradation, despite Landcare, is incredible. It's almost obscene the land that's going out of production under cities and under roads. We're losing fertile land under concrete.

And how do you feel when you see that sort of thing going on?

Despair, I think. I'm looking very much long-term—not just in the next year or decade or hundred years—and if they want a hundred and ten million people in Australia by the year 2090, what are we going to feed them on, if we've covered all our fertile land with housing, cities, roads et cetera? I think it's a tragedy for the future. If people are critical of what our ancestors did to this land we're also going to get it in the neck very much for what we're doing now and for ignorance of the future, for ignorance of development making big money now, using up this tremendously fertile land—not that we've got much in Australia—and just taking it out of production forever. Once you've got concrete and you've got houses, it takes a lot to bulldoze them down and plough up the land again.

Let's put the cities, for instance, where the multi-function polis is going to be. You can design high-density city living in a way that's pleasant to live in. You don't have to stick people in twenty-storey-high blocks of concrete. Surely we've got architects out there who can do that, who can make pleasant living inner city areas for people. Let's put our cities on land which is very low productivity and let's save our good land. A lot of Adelaide is built on beautiful deep, rich soil that hardly even needs fertilising. It's gone for good now. All the vegie growers are being pushed out further and now they're getting into trouble with salinity, with lowering of the water tables. We just don't think! It's about time we started thinking for the future if we want to have sustainable agriculture and sustainable people.

How does Landcare actually work?

It seems to work from the grassroots, I think, which is probably more important than working from the top down. Groups of farmers will get together and say, Look, we've got a problem here. We've got this salinity creeping in; we've got this dreadful erosion; we've got fertility disappearing down the creeks; how about doing something about it? And I guess that's how it starts. That's how ours started. We've got patches of salinity here. Our little group started as an offshoot of a local ag. bureau, and we've got a very strong group now. We seemed to want to conquer Rome in a day—we wanted to go out and do all these projects at once with about twelve members, which was a bit difficult. But I think we've settled down now. We're starting to get into catchment management; we're looking at acid soils—we're trying to do trials on that. We're looking at pasture productivity, because if you've got good pastures then your land isn't going to drift or wash. City people, as well, should be as enthusiastic about Landcare as they are about Saturday afternoon footie, because it's in their interests. It's their food, it's their life that's being affected if we can't produce the food for them. It is a very important thing.

We're actually trying to set up a communication network which will get information into the city on what happens out here—where the food comes from, basically. And because people depend on farmers to provide their food—if there's no farmers there's no food—then it's in their interest to support Landcare, perhaps through donations. (There is a Landcare fund being set up.) And they say that for every farmer there are twenty jobs created, either supplying his needs or handling his farm outputs. So it definitely is in the city person's interest to be aware of and support Landcare.

A lot of city people are involved in Trees for Life, in which they propagate trees which go out to farms. Some of the school children come out and they'll help plant trees and get involved, which is good. They're getting involved in Water Watch and Salt Watch and all this sort of thing, but I would just like to see a lot more.

Country people seem not to like going to the city, apart from for essentials. But city people love coming to the country, yet they have very little understanding or respect for it.

They certainly like to get out to weekends away in the country and you can't blame them for that. But they really only see farms or something that they're driving past to go to another destination. They might see a tractor going round and round, or a mob of sheep being mustered, but they don't think any further than that.

It's quite interesting. A friend of mine has a Bed and Breakfast here, just up the road from us, and when she had some people come from Sydney to look at it they said, 'We can't stay here—it's too quiet'. The town's ten minutes away, I think, and they couldn't quite cope with that. I felt sorry for them, actually, because this is where life is. You can talk about the city with the nightclubs and all that stuff, but this is where reality is, and quiet. I think a lot of city people would really appreciate some peace and quiet but these people were so used to being in town they couldn't deal with it.

After you left school and worked in Adelaide, how did you get back to farming?

I couldn't stand Adelaide and when we got married and looked for a small farm to buy, we actually bought one that's just two kilometres down the road from here—where our son's living. We still farm it—it's got a vineyard on it.

And then you inherited this place when your parents died.

It was left to the three girls—I've got two other sisters— and Johnny and I bought one sister's share and the other sister's still in because we'd run out of money. So she's got a one-third share on two-thirds and then Johnny and I've also got the other farm. We run commercial cattle. Dad had always had Herefords but I took their horns off by mainly putting Poll Hereford bulls over them. And my sister's got her Angas herd here which I look after. We run sheep, we do a little bit of prime land production, but it's mainly wool, and we've got a vineyard as well. And I've got my Poll Hereford stud.

I do a bit of everything. I run the stud and Johnny looks after the sheep, but I do the wool-classing. And since the wool crash we've tried to do everything ourselves, so I do the wool-classing and the cooking, which is a bit difficult at times, especially if you come up here at five to twelve and the crockpot hasn't been turned on and the meal's not cooked.

I love the tractor work and we share ploughing and seeding, haymaking, baling—all that sort of thing. I can do fencing. We pull bores. I like the stuff I can do. I used to be able to crutch sheep, but they're getting a bit heavy for me, or I'm getting a bit weaker in my old age. But I'm totally involved in everything that happens on the place.

At one stage your husband got quite ill, didn't he? How did that affect what you did?

When my parents died, he was still working off-farm, and there was no point coming home because the farm was left to the three girls and there wasn't any income. So I ran it on my own. Mum was still alive then but she wasn't too well and when she died I did everything myself because he wasn't home. On weekends he'd help with the heavy jobs, but I put fences up—in those days I could get strainer posts in holes but I use the tractor now.

When he got ill it was pretty tough because he was that sick that I couldn't even discuss things with him. If there were some flyblown sheep out in the paddock I had to quietly get them in and do them myself. He couldn't even cope with knowing they were out there. And I was doing the hay-carting with the bale loader. I'd get twenty bales on the truck, then I'd stop and stack them, and then I'd load up another twenty bales and stop and stack them. It's a bit wearing, but I did it. I think I was absolutely in a mental vacuum—totally exhausted. The only thing that kept me going was every now and then, when it got too much, I'd pick up a cat and go for a walk in a paddock and just sit on a stump cuddling my cat—just to keep sane. Nobody could really do anything to help, it was just something you had to get over, and I guess I was pretty worried about him being that sick, because he couldn't even walk from the house to the woolshed. I can remember one shearing, he'd go down and he'd sit on a chair and he'd just cut the skin pieces off bits of wool—that's all he had the energy for. It was pretty worrying; however, we got there. He was out of action for about five years.

You're part of the Beef Improvement Society. Tell me about that.

Beef Improvement Association was set up to help producers improve their product, learn more about their
product and there are groups interstate. One started recently
in the south-east and I thought, well, crumbs, South Australia's got a lot of cattle, so I chatted around the place and
found there were other people interested in joining. And
another chap whose brother is in the IA interstate was really
keen so we set up a group here. Basically, we try and set
up a couple of field days a year on beef production, whether
it's bull selection, how to care for cows and calves, nutrition
or whatever. I really think that a lot of beef producers don't
know enough about what we're producing; when you see
or hear them talking they really need to learn a lot more,
and if they want to survive in the industry they've got to
learn because beef's being hammered by chicken people
who've got their act together.

We've had an American speaker come over, we had a
seminar last year and we had quite a few people turn up for
that. I feel very strongly that we've really got to get it right
because our markets are getting a lot tighter with their specifications and it's no longer a matter of just throwing a bull out
in the paddock with a cow and selling the offspring. It's more
complicated than that. You can almost computer design your
herd now, so we've really got to get it right. Genetics play a
big part. With Breed-Plan you can actually have estimated per-
formance of progeny of bulls and cows, and the more progeny
they've got the higher the accuracy of their predicted per-
formance. In that way you can computer-design your herd by
picking cows with low birth weight; by picking bulls with high
600-day weight or whatever.

We're only a very small stud and it costs a lot to do all
these things. We have a chap come out, scan our cattle for
fat and eye muscle area. We have a vet check our bulls

before selling to make sure they're sound for breeding. We are part of Breed-Plan. That isn't cheap, and you'd think perhaps for a stud this size it might be stupid, that you'd be better off just pocketing that money instead of spending it, but I think we're looking long-term. I want this stud to be something that people are going to respect and want to come to for their cattle because they'll know how they're going to perform. We won't make any money for a while yet, because we'll be putting it into sourcing genetics from round the world to try and get the sort of cattle we think will make money for clients.

Your grandfather or great-grandfather led a very different sort of life on this same land.

Yes, it's interesting. On Dad's side, my great-grandfather started off in Scotland and I think what happened there was that the landlords wanted to take over the small farmers and put sheep there. So they lost their farming area. So he and all his brothers emigrated. He worked his way over here as a ship's baker and he became a police trooper, initially. Then he came back to Angaston and started buying up land. He had land everywhere, I wish he still had, but this is the last bit that's left of the land he originally had.

CAROLYN LYONS

*Carolyn Lyons lives at Tooraweenah, west of Gulargambone
in New South Wales where they still give directions in
miles. I managed to lose my way on the pot-holed and sandy back
roads where passersby were non existent. Eventually I came across
a man on a horse with a mob of cattle who was able to direct
me—in miles of course—to the Lyons property, only an hour late.
Carolyn has lived in the country all her life and farming is just
part of what she does. Community concerns occupy a lot of her
time, recently distributing food sent by concerned city people.*

We were on a property out of Nyngan called Illyria as children. There were three of us, my elder brother, elder sister
and myself, and my mother and father. We did all the things
there that all kids learn—we rode horses—and very, very
rarely got off the place. We had governesses and we used

188

to try to get rid of them—shotguns in the back, carpet snake in the bedroom, all sorts of terrible things, but we always got rid of them; we went through a lot!

You did, or they did?

Oh, well, they didn't stay very long; we made sure of that (laughs). We had a siding a mile and a half through the scrub and we used to walk them through the scrub and put them on the train!

Memories of childhood! We were smoking. The rabbiters used to come out from town and try to handle the rabbits with myxomatosis plagues and things like that and we used to bribe them to bring the smokes out for us. Dad caught on and wouldn't allow them to bring any more so we used to take the middles out of the cushions, wrap them up and go up into the shed. I burnt the shed down, smoking—about five years of age I was! That was a big memory, sitting up in the back of the bales, and then she caught alight.

The whole thing burnt down?

Oh, yes, we lost the lot. And then we had an old Jersey cow we used to ride. She was called Kangaroo (laughs)—I don't know why we called her Kangaroo, but we used to ride her. Then I can remember the first horses we had. We used to do all the stock work and then we went bad in the drought and had to leave. I do remember the transition. I remember the loss. I don't think Mummy was at all sad to leave; it was a very, very hard life we used to have. We rarely went to town. We had a grandmother not far away and that was our big visit, probably a couple of times a year.

We came to the city and were sent to boarding school. I was at boarding school for ten years.

*Do you see a great deal of difference between the life that you're
living here and the life your mother lived on a property?*

Yes, I do. My mother was there as a woman to have
children, to provide food and nurturing and nothing else.
Mother didn't really do much gardening, she never went
on a horse or anything like that, never worked out in a
paddock, never went into the office—none of those things.
It just wasn't that era. Mummy was quite old when she
had me; she was forty-something and I was the baby. But
no, their lifestyle was totally and utterly different and much
more limiting, much lonelier, much more isolated. In fact,
I don't know how they survived, although she drove a car
and was an independent woman in her own way, but we
lived a long way from anywhere. I often wonder how the
women out west survived; they were very stoic women.

We had the party line [phone] and the siding wasn't that
far from us so we used to see the train go through and
you'd meet people on the siding for a yarn or whatever.
And, of course, we saw our neighbours. I remember Auntie
Marge was one and then we had neighbours over on the
other side and their families are still around. They visited
and we visited, but we didn't seem to go much farther
than that.

I don't know what Mummy did with her life, I honestly
don't know how she survived, because she came from a
very well-to-do family of six girls and one son. They lived
on the railway line near the siding, but their father travelled extensively and had large properties in New South
Wales and Queensland and they lived a very good life.
They had holidays six weeks of the year: they went to
Sydney and their father set them up at this dreary hotel
and they were taken to lunch and afternoon tea. So how

she came back to marry and breed and live and survive, I'll never know. Great ladies!

Did you ever think when you were growing up that you would spend your adult life on a farm?

I didn't know any differently, I suppose, so I probably thought I would be going back there. But we had ten years of boarding school and only saw our parents probably once a term—once every three months—and you became involved with being a girl and being part of a school where there was a certain ethic and ethos and way of life that completely covered you. I remember not ever thinking that I would get married and not thinking much about where I would go if I did. I think I probably thought that I'd get on the road to life and things would happen.

What did you do when you left school?

I was given three months to learn shorthand and typing and business management, the whole thing in one, and then I became a secretary at a very large firm of solicitors in Sydney. Not very long afterwards I ended up as secretary to the senior partner, who's still a great friend of mine. I was there for some time. I was never very good as a secretary and I don't know how I managed to stay there (laughs). I really had two jobs because I decided that I must extend myself and do better, and I moved then to work with another very big firm in the Stock Exchange and became secretary to the general manager there. I had a lot of fun in those two positions and met a lot of wonderful people who are still my friends today.

Then I went abroad. It was meant to be for fun, but it wasn't, because I had to take my mother who was going blind and they said that they could save her sight. Prior to coming back I rang HIM and asked him would he like to marry me because I thought it was about time I married him (laughs) and he said, yes, he thought it was a good idea too. We got married four or five months after I came back, so I've been out here for nearly thirty years now.

Did you find him in the Stock Exchange or in the lawyers' office?

We were once at the same party but I didn't even know him. He remembers the party vividly but I don't. And then I was involved in the management of a function in Sydney and someone had told him that if he wanted a ticket to the ball to ring this girl in Pymble, which was where we lived. So this fellow introduced himself and said that he'd been given my name and number and could he have a ticket? I said yes, I would leave the ticket at the front door of the ballroom and he could pick it up there. So he arrived and gave me, I think, £50, because the boys had all come from the country at Easter-time with 'the cheque' and they'd go through 'the cheque' and come home and have nothing for the rest of the year.

This one had the cash and nothing less, so I said, 'Well, I don't have any change so I'll have to leave it for you at the Australia Hotel', which was then in the centre of town. The agreement was arrived at and the following morning when I was at work I got a phone call to say that he would take me to lunch, so we arranged to meet for lunch and thirty years later, to this day, he still remembers what I wore! We met and it was all very nice and just after sweets had been served he stood up and said, 'Well, I'm going now'. I said, 'Oh, but you haven't finished your sweets!' (laughs), and he said, 'Well, I still have to go because I'm going to catch the plane to Bourke'. And he did and I didn't see him for twelve months. He got up and went to Bourke because he had a job as a jackeroo there.

He came back twelve months later and rang me up again and that went on for a little while, so it was a very considered decision!

So you moved out here to this property as a young married woman?

Yes, we moved to a cottage of six squares and I had three children in that cottage: there were five of us in six squares and it was a great character builder, I suppose I could say. I had three very sick children in that cottage so I learnt a lot about life and living and growing up very, very quickly.

The property belonged to your husband's parents, I guess.

Yes, they lived in this homestead.

How did you fit in with that? Did you have access to family discussions on properties and things?

No, when we were first married even my husband didn't have access to those discussions: my father-in-law ran the show and made the moves and the decisions and we all had to jump. I think it was a bit of a shock because I wouldn't jump (laughs). I can remember once in my very early married days going to town and coming back and being met at the gate with, 'Where have you been? You don't leave this place without my permission'. So I drove off again just to prove a point (laughs).

A few things happened like that until they realised that I wasn't going to be told what to do or how to do it. Even just working in the yards I was told that women didn't work in the yards and I wasn't to do it, but I used to work in the yards until I was eight and a half months pregnant—I had to go to Sydney then. It didn't worry me; that was my life and I was going to throw myself into it.

But we got over all those problems and my father-in-law and I became very great friends.

But your own father hadn't prevented girls from doing stock work?

No, as children we were very much a part of the work force. Whatever the season was, whether it was marking or lambing or mustering or shearing, we were very much involved. It was part of our life. You don't disassociate when you're living on the spot, so I found it hard that it wasn't acceptable as a young woman to be involved with the day-to-day things. I was always involved.

Did it take a while for your point of view to prevail?

I think we had about three real humdingers, and after that we were right (laughs). We were great mates, actually.

Tell me a bit about the property: what you grow here ...

It's not considered a large property, it's only small for this area, but we do consider it's in the right corner. We get the good rains and we have a diversification of soil types which allows us to graze and grow grain crops.

We don't have any sheep: we went out of sheep about fifteen years ago, which was my husband's decision. He is certainly, and is known to be, a very good manager. He seems to think ahead six months and plans ahead and has that gut feeling that a lot of the bush people do, and it's worked for him. So we have no sheep now; we have cattle and cropping and we diversify in the crops. If, for instance, we need to put some more nitrogen back in the soil we'll put a certain crop in, or we might lay fallow for twelve months and start in another area. We're not big farmers by any means, not only because the acreage is small but because our real love and interest is cattle. We have a Hereford commercial group but we haven't gone into the studs: we buy stud bulls to put over our Herefords.

Then a couple of years ago we were in France and we became interested in Salers which are the oldest breed in France. We did quite a lot of homework on them and we have Salers on the ground at the moment. What we did was put the Salers over the Hereford heifers because we were guaranteed then to have ease of calving: the Salers are very good mothers and very good milkers and they're long and rangy because they're used to the mountain tops of France. They came from the Massif Central, which is very mountainous and rangy, so it gave us lift off the ground, it gave us good calving, it gave us good milking, good mothers, and it worked very well. We've been doing that for several years now, only across the heifers. Then last year we decided to branch out and see what we could do by introducing a Charolais bull over the first cross Hereford-Salers, and they are quite something!

A League of Nations! I heard at your award that you were interested in French sailors (both laugh).

Yes, it took quite some time to explain to them.

Why this cross-breeding that you're doing?

Well, you develop what you've got. It's no good just sticking with what you want because you like it and you're used to it; you have to look ahead and see what the market is dictating, and that's what we've done. We're looking for hybrid vigour so that you're putting the best of both breeds into one drop and you're getting a better animal. But that better animal should also be able to provide what the market is looking for in these days, which is marbling and depth of fat. As you know, we're a country that's gone into lean meat so you don't need the big, heavy, fatty piece of steak any more. We're very much involved in looking to that other end of our interest, which is the market and the international market. In fact, we're just at the precipice of developing a Coonamble beef feedlot and marketing co-operative, so it's very exciting. We've been working for four years, and when I say we, it's really Tom, my husband, but I do all the work so I know what's going on with him.

We are at the stage now of an environmental impact study being done. We've had money released and there's been a tremendous amount of work done, and it's really rather exciting. And that, again, is going to generate activity in the beef industry and the feedlotting industry and the abattoirs and the export industry from this region. A 20 000 head feedlot is really going to generate some interest, some work, some money into this region and, as I say, we're just on the precipice at the moment.

Perhaps you would explain a feedlot.

A feedlot is where you take a selected group of cattle, usually steers, and you put them into a certain area and feed them a certain amount of grain and/or fodder in order to get them to gain weight within a certain amount of time. The normal time for a feedlot to finish an article would be about ninety days and then they range through the different markets. You can have the export market or you can have the home market. You bring them up, let them grow out, feed them up and get them into the different markets and therefore you're getting money for your produce but you're providing what the market is demanding, and that's a big industry now.

It sounds like the top end of the market, as well.

It is. They know what the market's demanding, you see, and they produce to that. We might put ours, as we did, through a feedlot here: we might go for sixty days and get them to a certain stage and feed them cotton hull, which is one of the new interesting things (thank God, we haven't used any cotton trash). You feed them up and then you sell them to a feed lot and they take them on and feed them up to another stage and age and then they sell off too, so it's a matter of being pretty assured of what sort of money you're going to get so you can really program and budget. As long as the market stays and as long as the market's being read you can handle it from your end as a producer, but in order to do that you have to be aware: you have to read, you have to get around and talk to people, and that's rather exciting because you really are on the top end of the market; you're riding the waves with it.

It takes time to join animals and get a calf on the ground and then watch it grow through but if you could see these, they're beautiful. I call them Wild Mink—they're just magnificent looking things and they've got the right structure.

What sort of effect have the overseas crises had on you, like the cotton one a few months ago, and every now and again the problem with hamburger mince in the United States or whatever?

It's devastating, devastating. For instance, this morning we heard that one of our friends who's an excellent manager and has done all the right things has lost $200 000 because of the helix. Four hundred steers were fed during the drought and he's been found with helix in them. He's lost a fortune just overnight.

So what does he do with those animals? Are they just shot?

I think they have to be eliminated: they certainly can't be sold on the normal market. Somebody said that there was a breakthrough where, if they grow them out, they might be able to clear it, but they wouldn't be able to be sold for the consumer at this stage. So your budget's up the creek.

What's your main responsibility on the farm?

I was going to say to make sure that the books balance, but they never do! But that's not my fault: the figures are there, it's just that the costs are exorbitant. I do all the books and all the management of the office and if there's stock work to be done I do that. My husband was away in Korea with this beef co-operative and I ran the place. The drought had just started in with a vengeance and I had to muster everything on the place and bring stuff back from agistment and truck them down south, and wean, and cull, and sell, and everything. So if I have to turn my hand to anything I do, it doesn't matter what it is.

I don't ride now because I had a very bad accident just before I was married. He promised when I'd stopped breeding I could but he didn't keep his promise (laughs). Also, my sons have grown up and they've taken over a lot of the work that I used to do. I think that's great in some ways but I really do miss being out in the paddock. You know, you move a mob of cattle from one paddock to the other and you know why you've done it and you see the progress and it's all a means to an end, and now, because I'm not needed out there, I don't see that transition and I don't see that change, and I miss it.

I don't miss the heat and I'm useless at lifting, so I'm pretty useless altogether, but I can muster and draft and cull and I have an eye for stock, which I've developed, I suppose, since I was a child. So I'm useful, but getting less useful.

You were involved in a droving trip some time ago?

Several years ago now. Because we had a weed on our place in Queensland that was killing the cattle, we had to evacuate 28 000 acres and we had 1000 calving cows on the road. My two sons and another man took off with them. I'm really pleased I wasn't there at the beginning and I'm only just now hearing some of the stories. I think I would have died if I had known what was happening.

They left here with trucks and things. Our drove was nineteen horses and twenty-two dogs and a galah called Pete. I was very anxious that the boys didn't become rough and uncouth if they didn't have anything of home. I thought that if they had a galah they would have to look after him, nurture him, so I made them take Pete with them. Pete would come into camp every night while they played the guitar; Pete was terrific.

One night we came into camp it poured rain and we were in a bit of a gully and we got washed out. The horses went across the creek and the truck rose and we couldn't find Pete. But he came back eventually and we pulled up at another place and one of the boys bought a dog, for God's sake. They used to shoot them just as quickly as they bought them because they were useless and you couldn't have a useless dog with calving cows. Anyway, he bought this useless dog and the dog ate Pete. We all cried. The stockmen cried and the boys cried, everybody cried, a very sad loss.

The drove was a great family affair but we had no water, we had no electricity. I was not on the road for all five months but the kids were. It was a great experience because it was so tough and so hard and yet invigorating and wonderful. We slept under the trees and people used to bring us things. Somebody brought us wonderful rock melons and watermelons that he'd grown.

My son became the best damper cook in the west. He had his eighteenth birthday on the drove. He gave a party himself and every stockman from everywhere came to that camp. Thank God I wasn't there! It was an experience that they will never forget and will always be a great part of the base of their life because they needed great strength and great ability to manage. They were only young boys and they had to manage ringers who were punch drunks, stampedes, mad horses, going in and out of towns.

I remember going to the Roma picnics and I had this black and white hat, gorgeous beautiful straw, and for the whole drove, every time we got into the Ute everyone had to say, 'Watch out for Mum's hat, watch out for Mum's hat'.

When we got to Roma I went to the hotel and said our sons were coming in later and the clerk looked me up and down because I was in droving outfit, hat and boots, and he said, 'I don't think you're booked in here, Madam'. Anyway, I got over that one. I got dressed up with stockings and high heels and went down and said 'I am the Madam you wouldn't have.'

So you and husband came and went from the drove?

Yes, because we had to run this place too. They had to stay with it but we had others come and go.

At one camp, on the first night, my son came up and he said, 'Now Mum, no women around here. We just shower in the creek. But we bought a bit of tin and we've put some holes in it and this is what you do.' He had the iron on the ground and a piece of hessian around and he said, 'Strip off, come out of the room, put your foot on the corrugated iron step and pull the bucket upside down and that is your shower. Right?' I stripped off and walked outside the door and I heard, 'Git back to camp, garn, git back to camp', and I thought, 'Oh the ringer—the ringer's come back'. Anyway, I yelled out to see if anyone was there but there was no movement and I was stuck. I had to stand on the corrugated iron in the middle of the scrub and nothing happened then I suddenly saw Pete the Galah. As well as all the swear words he had picked up the sentence, 'Git back to camp!'.

But we got the cattle back home. We lost a lot of calves, it put us back five years in our calving but we got them back home and there was great excitement.

You've also developed other interests or other commitments. Why did you start moving into community work?

I've always been involved in the community. My children went to school here—seventy-eight miles a day, and I took up remedial teaching, just as a volunteer. I became involved with the P & F and then I took up with the day care centre and was involved in that as a volunteer. I used to get the kids to go up and talk to the oldies: I believe in that, children and oldies, it's very important.

A lot of people give up that community involvement once their children leave school, but you haven't done that.

I'd go nuts, and I don't think I have the right to do that. It would be really nice to go from one chaise longue to another with a good book, I'd really enjoy that, but I just think I've been given so much I've got to give a lot back.

So your life on this property has been a good one?

Well, yes, I think I've been terribly lucky. I've got two arms and two legs and two eyes and a lot of people don't; I have a marriage which I can see now is extraordinary and for which I'm extremely grateful and which I never ever take for granted; four beautiful kids, although I nearly lost three of them through illness when they were babies—I spent nine years at the kids' Camperdown Hospital with very, very sick children.

One got encephalitis; she was very ill for a very long time, and another one got salmonella which is para-typhoid dysentery and he was very ill for a long time, another one was deaf and another one was born with twenty-three holes in her heart. I'm very lucky, though. I saw children die beside mine and mine are still alive, and I just feel I owe a lot, I really do.

I'm just wondering if the fact that you've had a lot of health problems with your kids and have had to battle has made you sympathetic to other people and therefore you've gone into community work, or has it been a philosophy of yours, that you should help other people?

I suppose it's just the way I tick more than anything else. It's part of my upbringing, part of my family ethos. Even with the things I'm involved with now people say, 'Oh, it's because your son's sick that you're doing it', but it never even entered my head that that was the case. I was asked on behalf of someone who was sick to help them so I went in and batted for them, and it just so happened that my son was sick, too. But that wasn't the reason I did it.

The drought has been making things difficult here for people and you were involved in that drought relief. Tell me about people giving things to the country.

The city interest was precipitated by the media, by people being shown to be in drought, in need, emotionally upset, lacking finance, with dying stock and empty tanks. People saw this and thought, What can I put in there? What can I do? People started to come from all angles to give support and to show interest. It was fantastic. It's the first time I've known that linkage to be so strong.

What incident made you aware that city people were giving to the country?

It was obvious through the media. Every second night in our loungeroom we were watching drought and a lot of what I was watching I was also part of, so I knew what was going on. The media was the conduit and very, very effective. People started to consider what was going on and see what they could do to help.

And how did that help manifest itself?

In so many varying ways, precipitated by great care and need but not necessarily by great thought, causing quite a lot of problems at the receiving end. In many instances people were giving what they felt was good.

There are two sides to every story and I'll give you one: I have an elderly woman who tells me she had twelve children. She rang me and asked for help because there was nothing in her fridge. No-one was coming home, they'd all grown up and gone away. She has one boy left and he's not making any money, her husband's gone and she had nothing in her fridge for Christmas. She said it would be lovely just to open the fridge at Christmas-time and find something in there.

This woman had cattle and she needed money to feed them. She'd had cattle all her life and, in fact, one day when one of the calves got out she went out under the fence to get it back to its mother, and that's where she had one of her children. She brought it back with her in her arms. That was the sort of woman she was and the sort of life she led.

She received a jar of very expensive Christian Dior face cream from a woman in Sydney. It was put into a parcel that got to her and she rang me to tell me about it: it was the most exciting thing. She said, 'I've never had anything like that in my life. I get up every morning and I put this stuff all over my face and I feel good!'. I'm sure she must be very old and most people would say, 'What an absolute waste, how ridiculous. That wasn't her need. She needed to keep the cattle alive and have something in the fridge.' But look at the good it did her. So I'm not going to denigrate anybody for sending anything or giving anything, because in some instances what appeared to be irrelevant was totally important to a recipient.

People sent Weetbix, people sent perfume and people sent underpants, people sent a lot of tatty old clothes which upset the people who received them—they took them out and burnt them. I've had a couple of calls about that. People received cheques from Farmhand which made an enormous difference to their lives. One woman rang me from Canberra and was very arrogant and very annoyed because she'd asked and asked for two children for the holidays and she hadn't got them (laughs).

So the help was very uneven.

It was, yes. It was not coordinated.

Did anyone ever come to people in the country and say, 'Look, what do you need, how much of it do you need, and in what way can we help you?'

I'm sure that happened in some places. I seemed to be very involved here at many different levels and I was actually never asked that question. I was told what was going to be given or what was going to be done and it was up to me to do something with it: whether it was a Christmas present or a Weetbix parcel or a cheque or a jar of cream, it was up to me. It might be interesting to note, too, that it was very hard for me to know exactly to whom to give things, because it's a vast area and a lot of people who were in great need were certainly not going to come forward and say, 'I need'. They did towards the end of '94 because it was becoming a very public thing to do and almost acceptable. I say almost, because in a lot of cases it's still not acceptable. Someone says, 'We've always survived out here and we'll survive again, and nobody's going to give me welfare, and my father did this and I'm too proud to take that; don't come near me', and then he goes back inside and belts up the wife. That happens. Don't let anyone know we're hurting.

I don't think there's fault only on one side, if we're going to call it fault. I think it's really lack of experience and lack of basic knowledge and commonsense about how to attack a crisis.

What do you do when somebody rings up and says, 'We're sending you up a truckload of Weetbix' or a truckload of Weetbix and baked beans? How do you deal with that?

First of all I ask them not to do it. I ask them to turn it into money which is very much easier to distribute. The other side of that coin is that it allows the recipient to decide what their need is. If I say to you, 'I think you need a glass of water', and what you actually need is a loaf of bread, I'm taking your independence away, I'm taking your pride away, I'm taking what little you have left and telling you what you need. I have no right to do that. So first of all I'd say, 'Please don't send the food; please send money and allow people to decide for themselves what they need'.

And all the stuff coming into town, of course, has its effect on the local shopkeepers, I suppose.

Yes. There were a lot of strained people in relation to that. Again, it's a lack of thought because, as I said to one very big company's PR person, 'It's a wonderful thing you're doing, putting all this tinned food in bins, but please can you just visualise what it's like when the truck arrives in town and the driver opens the back of the truck and says, "Well, here you are, this is all for you darling cockies". Do you really think that people are going to open their doors and come out and say, "Thank you, I'll have a tin of spaghetti"? They're not.'

And then you look at the grocer and he says, 'I've got all that here. I've bought it all to provide it for this town and I've got to stay in business if this town is to survive'.

You've learnt a lot from this drought?

Yes, and don't you always? Whatever crisis presents we learn a lot. We suffer a lot but we learn a lot; we know what not to do next time. But also a lot of good comes out: a lot of people come to the fore who would never have had the opportunity to be seen or to give of their particular ability, or to satisfy their need to give to another, to care. It's very hard to see when you're living a drought, but there is a balance.

JULIE WILLIAMS

*J*ulie Williams has lived all her life in a country town where most of her close relations and many of her friends were on farms. She obtained a Diploma in Agriculture and while working with the Women on Farms groups published the influential report 'The Invisible Farmer—a Report on Australian farm women' for the Commonwealth Department of Primary Industry and Energy. Currently Julie has a job at the Ellinbank Research station near Warragul in Victoria.

Although I lived in a town, Warrnambool, in the south-west of Victoria, both my parents were from the dairying areas around there. Family members had come out in the 1860s so there were a lot of fringe relatives who were on dairying properties but my father worked in a machinery business, and worked mainly with dairyfarmers, fixing and selling dairy-related machinery, haymaking equipment, that sort of thing. I ended up going to agricultural college and doing a diploma in agriculture. I worked in different areas of agriculture for a short while before having a family, and then got back into it in the last six or seven years.

Have you ever been a farmer?

No, I've only ever worked on farms. I've done a bit of relief milking, that sort of thing—working as a farmhand on dairy farms and working as the wife of a stockman. We nearly went on to share-farming at one stage, and we would have liked to have gone into dairying, but we've ended up working *with* the farmer instead.

At the moment I'm working on a project with the Department of Agriculture working with dairying discussion groups. It's a statewide project and I'm coordinating the southern part of the state which is all of Gippsland and the south-west. It's giving farmers within the discussion groups leadership training so that they can take on the bigger role of running the groups themselves. This project's come partly from the Target Ten Project, a very big dairying project. Part of it is to put farmers through a three-day course on pasture management, and then run the group of people in the course as a discussion group for the following twelve months. After that time most groups want to continue as a discussion group, but they can broaden their interest base past your management. The extension staff and the factory staff involved in running the groups initially aren't able to continue running all the groups because they are building up new groups all the time. So from the Department's point of view we want to help groups to continue in the long term so it's my role to give them some leadership training and to form a bit of a network so they can see what's going on in other areas and get new information to their own groups.

Why was a discussion group necessary?

There's a great range of reasons why farmers enjoy going to discussion groups. It's a good way for people to compare notes on what they're doing on their own farms, but it's a bit of a social reason too, because farmers are often on their own all the time. From the Department of Agriculture's point of view it's a good way to see a group of people at the same time and often people are more likely to change their attitude towards a farming practice if they can see other people that have done it or go to farms where it's being carried out. The discussion group format reinforces a lot of the new information that's being taken on by people.

Do you get men and women coming to these groups?

Yes, it varies a bit. If it's mostly a male group, then it's a bit trickier for the women to come along unless they're fairly confident themselves. But there are a lot of groups which have a good spread of couples who are heavily involved. Often it depends on whether the family has young children and whether the woman in the partnership has other obligations which are seen as higher priorities. But we do encourage all members of the family—whether it's owners and sharefarmers—all those involved in the farm, to come along to the discussion group day.

Who sets the agenda?

With the Target Ten Pasture Management courses and subsequent discussion groups the first twelve months is set by the extension staff because they're based around pasture management issues. But, leading on from there, or with any other dairy discussion groups that are formed by factory or other farmers, the topics they cover depend purely on what interests them at the time. That's one of the reasons we hope the farmers will take it on as their own role, because it gives them more scope to direct the discussion group in areas where they want information.

Is it mainly industry-related stuff, or do you get family and social issues being discussed as well?

Mostly they're to do with dairy farm management, although there is a bit more interest now in things like time management, how to handle stress, more of a whole life approach to dairyfarming. That's being encouraged by the Target Ten Project too. They're really encouraging people to look at the whole picture and not just profitability.

Is there any resistance to you as a woman coordinating the groups?

Well I'm oblivious to it if there is (laughs). Over the years of working with, initially, mostly male farmers, I haven't had any trouble but I'm fairly confident and I can see that there can be problems for women involved in agricultural industries if they feel overwhelmed or inhibited by dominance of men.

So you think that confidence, or self-esteem, is probably the key to being able to perform in that kind of arena?

I think it is very much part of it. I was involved with Women on Farms skills courses four or five years ago, and part of the reason for those courses was that there were quite a lot of women who were keen to learn but felt inhibited in the basically male groups that the courses were being run with. So, we ran them as women's courses for them to gain a bit more self-confidence and then go and join the mainstream educational courses that are being offered in agriculture.

Are you involved in the Women on Farms or any of those discussion groups that are going on at the moment?

I keep an eye on what's going on. I'm not involved so heavily any more, the first priority is the Target Ten discussion groups because that's where the pressure is. But we're certainly trying to involve any other discussion groups, as long as they're basically dairying folk, to become involved in the leadership training that we're doing. There's a women's group in the South Gippsland area and they had some people come along to the leadership days too. As far as the leadership of groups goes, it seems to be a role that the women within the group are quite happy to take on. Once they're confident and they're part of that group the women have better communication skills often, and are more confident in taking on the roles of running a group. So it seems to be quite a good involvement in some ways.

Do you think women will have a different sort of influence on the agendas of the meetings and the discussions that take place?

Women seem often to be more interested in safety issues, with chemicals or tractor safety and perhaps with more environmental issues. That's why it's good to have a spread of men and women so you cover all areas.

It seems to be a tough life for them out there, I've been talking to some of them and things are not getting any easier.

No. There are reducing margins between the income and the costs, and there's a huge area of information they need to cover—the finances and nutrition and pasture growth, animal health—it's a huge knowledge base that a farmer needs to run a good business. But they seem to be pretty positive and doing a really good job.

I guess most of these farmers wouldn't have had really formal training, or even a great knowledge of these sorts of things, from their fathers or their families?

I think the pasture management courses being run through Target Ten have been really good, because even if people have had some formal qualifications, the pasture management courses have really gone to the basics of grass growth, and given everyone a good background. The ones who are really keen to learn are often people who have come from a different industry and don't have any blinkers on. They really look for any information they can get.

When you look at your long-term future, do you see it in this sort of area, or are you itching to put these things into practice?

I enjoy my weekends (laughs) and doing a bit of travelling or camping or whatever. I enjoy working with people and I think I probably do a better job at that than actually implementing it. That's a bit awesome—getting out there on a farm and making things work. I feel I've got a role in helping the farmers source information and link them up with resources that are available so they can do a good job themselves.

And it takes you out in the countryside—doesn't keep you in offices all the time?

Oh, it's good being able to travel around. I've found it really interesting even within Gippsland, going to South Gippsland and sharing information on what's going on in the West Gippsland area. They're really interested to know what's going on down here.

YVONNE ARMSTRONG

Yvonne Armstrong was just finishing a long day in the packing shed when I visited her farm near Orange in New South Wales. Pallets of freshly picked apples were stacked around the huge shed and a machine that resembled a car wash was dousing the fruit destined for cold storage. But the sorting and packing machines were quiet and the pickers had gone home as we sat down to talk about the demanding cycle of fruit harvesting that keeps her, her husband Cliff and some of their children on the go most of the year.

I was brought up at Camden just outside Sydney. I spent thirteen years there. We had a grape vineyard, more or less as a hobby: my stepfather was a public servant and he was in retirement, so it really wasn't a business venture. He became ill and we moved to Sydney in 1955 and there I

213

finished my education and went nursing. I stayed in Sydney until I got married to my husband in 1962, and that's when I was introduced to the apple orchard and found there was a bit more to growing fruit than taking it off a tree and putting it in a box.

The orchard was established in 1916 by my husband's father. He came here and bought the land as virgin bush and virtually cleared it with a pick and shovel and a few horses and chains and just planted acre by acre. Being undulating and fairly hilly it was quite a task and something that would be rather daunting when you look at today's methods.

We've got 200 acres of cherries, nectarines, plums and apples and we're going more into the newer varieties of all the fruits that we grow.

Does that mean replanting all the time?

We have a management system in place where we dig out a block, rest a block and plant a block, so it's a three-year operation to get a block of trees in, and that's all varieties of fruit we grow.

Did you know much about growing fruit when you came out here?

Nothing at all (laughs)! Not a thing. As I say, I came more or less from a medical background and so, apart from the grapes, I knew absolutely nothing about horticulture at all.

I found the first year very difficult. I'd lived in an institution with a lot of people around and I found that country life was a bit dull after the city life. I'd lived right in Sydney, not far from Kings Cross. I'd nursed at Sydney Hospital and at a nursing home at Darling Point and down at Woolloomooloo where the Eye Hospital is now, so it was a completely different lifestyle from what I was used to. I always had a love and a feeling for the country and I particularly liked

Orange before I met my husband. I thought Orange was a very beautiful city and I still hold those views.

I resigned from nursing and my husband told me he was going to put me on a throne and look after me, but it certainly didn't work out that way. It's been a hard slog right from the day we were married, and life on the farm has got harder and harder as the years progressed to keep up with technology. To keep in business you've just got to keep up, and that takes a lot of work and a lot of effort and a lot of management skills.

How do you do that? How do you learn these new techniques?

A lot of times it's gut feeling. Both my husband and I are involved with the industry so I suppose we've got a front seat on where it's going. We travel a lot to see what other people are doing. We visit other people, we visit other districts and so we're learning all the time. Every year holds a new challenge for us, so it is a real challenge just to survive.

Apples had a very bad time a few years ago, didn't they, when the English market dropped out? Were you involved in it then?

No, Tasmania suffered in those days because they were exporting. We had the domestic market of Sydney and we were able to meet the demand that was down there, so we haven't been involved that much in exporting, although I was involved two or three years ago in trying to get an export company off the ground, which we've done. The Orange district has formed an Orange Export Co-operative and we're hoping to export more and more fruit from this district, mainly to South-East Asia. We find that that's where the potential is—Taiwan and Singapore, Malaysia, Indonesia: I think that's where the future of our industry lies for us. We're certainly producing far too much for the domestic market so we've got to look and grow what our customers want overseas, put a quality assurance system into place and try to have a national approach rather than a regional approach. I'm still one of the directors of the Orange Export Co-operative and that involves mainly organising and trying to get more and more growers interested, trying to improve the quality of the fruit not only for ourselves but for the district. It's encouraging growers to plant the better varieties rather than what they've been planting for the last twenty or thirty years, and trying to move them as much as we can, interviewing prospective buyers, talking to people, visiting other countries. There's quite a lot involved but I think we've got to look a bit further than just the region; we've got to look at it as national if we're going to be at all successful.

Does the Asian consumer want the same sort of apple as the Australian one?

They're looking for a sweet apple and they like certain varieties of Red Delicious; they like the Fuji, the Royal Gala. These are the varieties we can grow really successfully, and we've got to have quality and be price competitive as well, so we have to be very efficient in how we operate to try to satisfy their needs.

The art of apple growing is no longer just picking it off the tree and sticking it in a box, is it? Could you give me a brief run-down of the cycle once the apple comes off the tree?

We start picking in late February, early March, and that goes through until about the end of April normally, with different varieties coming in at different times. We start off with the Royal Galas. Jonathans have just about seen their day: although there's a few still grown around the different regions this is an apple that will probably die out and the Royal Galas will take their place. It is a very good tasting apple. The Red Delicious, I think, will be here for many years. There's been massive plantings around Australia and we've got a certain look, but they're improving all the time, too: the colour's getting better, the taste is getting better, the size is getting better.

We're growing more economically than we used to; we're going in for more intensive plantings, smaller trees so that we don't need to use ladders, and producing a better quality piece of fruit.

Usually they're picked by hand and put into bins. The bins are then brought into the shed and dipped for long storage into CA (Controlled Atmosphere). We've got modern technology now where we can keep fruit for six to nine months in nearly the same condition as when it's picked off the tree.

We're also using less and less chemicals in growing the fruit. We're on integrated pest management programs so that instead of using full-strength sprays we're using half-strength and probably less of them. We're monitoring our orchards a lot more than we used to so that we're only using the sprays that are absolutely necessary, and hopefully we can try to bring back the ecology around the area so that the natural environment will control our pests rather than using chemicals all the time.

I mentioned the Controlled Atmosphere. What is picked is not dipped straight away; it's taken from the tree and probably put into cool storage for a short period—just chilled so that it takes the heat out of the fruit. It then goes over the grader where it's washed, it's waxed if required, and also stickered for our premium fruit. We sticker our fruit because we're proud of what we grow, so people that see stickered fruit should know that the growers are proud of what they're producing and normally it should be of good quality.

We pack every week and what's packed during the week goes to market the following week so it's always fresh; it's never stored for any length of time once it's packed. This is the Sydney and Flemington markets at the moment. We are joining a national company which is called the Apple and Pear Corporation Pty Ltd. It's only a new company, a lot of growers getting together and marketing under one Australian brand which will eventually be a one-desk selling operation both for the domestic and the export markets. The advantage is that we will have long, consistent lines. It will be packed by product description so that we can go direct to supermarket and say, 'What do you want? How do you want your fruit packed?' and we pack to what they want. That will give us a better average price. It will give them probably a cheaper price but a product that they're looking for, and it will go straight to their warehouses so the cool chain of the fruit won't alter and the consumer then will get a lot better product at the end.

What's your role in all this? What part of the orchard is your responsibility?

I manage the packing shed. We're going into a quality assurance system there which means that we document everything we do so that if there's a problem we've got a trace back to where that problem comes from, and also to try to put up a quality product to our customers.

We haven't got a big operation. We only pack our own fruit and we have about six or seven people working there. We have about three packers and three people to service them normally. It's not a modern packing shed by any means but we're looking at the top end of the market so it's hand packed so that we can put up a good article.

Do you liaise with buyers?

Not at the moment. My husband does most of the selling but the bulk of it goes to the Sydney market and we have an agent in Sydney who sells the bulk of our fruit. That will change. I think there are big changes in the marketplace. We're certainly producing far too much; the supply is greater than the demand which means depressed prices, and as we get more and more the quality goes up and up and a lot bigger percentage goes into processing because of that. Perfectly good fruit with just a small blemish will go to juice, or to peelers, or to processing because the market demands perfect fruit.

You've obviously learnt an awful lot since you came here as a young married woman.

I've been on the orchard now for thirty-three years and I've probably physically worked and done the books for the last twenty-five, so, yes, I have learnt a lot. I've also travelled a lot around Australia and overseas, so I've learnt what other people do and tried to take the best of all worlds for ourselves.

When you started was it usual for women to work in the orchards and in the packing sheds like that? You're taking a management role, aren't you?

It's still not usual. Possibly I'm unique in the sense that I've always strived for equality between the sexes, probably because of my background. I was brought up as the only girl in a family of four brothers with Victorian-era parents, as I always referred to them, where the male was the bread-winner and it didn't really matter whether the women got an education or not and, of course, that went right against my grain, so I've fought for equality between the sexes and that women get the same opportunity as men.

When you first went to these meetings and on these boards were people prepared to listen to you?

No, but I made sure that they did (laughs), by just forcing my way and being outspoken, being controversial. Eventually they started to listen to me and now I'm accepted. I felt I knew what I was talking about. Whether other people felt the same I'll let them decide, but I felt I had an opinion that was worth voicing so I voiced it. Whether I was right or wrong I guess is irrelevant.

Did you ever get rebuffed?

Yes, but I gave it back. Anyone that tried to humiliate me or put me down certainly never ever attempted it the second time around. I became very used to it. I expected it and I knew how to defend myself against it, and eventually I think I have been accepted by males in the industry.

What do you think that women bring to the industry that perhaps men don't?

Women bring a lot of commonsense; they're better organised; they certainly think a lot differently to men; they can cut corners and still be efficient. I think if there's a long way and a short way to go a man will always go the long way and the women will always take the shortest cut. I think women utilise their time a lot more efficiently than men do. I think the pressure's on them. Men think they've got a business to run. Women have a business to run, too, but they can look after children, they can run a house, they put food on the table, and it's all expected of them and never a thought that maybe they haven't got the time to do all these things; it was just expected of them and it still is. You've got to be thinking of a million things at once and yet be able to get through them all.

What's it like having your house within about six or ten feet of a packing shed, with all the demands and worries that are waiting there for you as soon as you walk out the door?

It's certainly got its advantages but it's also got its disadvantages. The disadvantages are that you have no privacy—although I've got a jungle right round my house to have a little bit but it's not all that effective. The advantages are that I can race in at three o'clock and put on a leg of lamb or something for tea, and if I have visitors I can entertain them in my home, which is important. I can make a cup of tea—I have a lot of important people come and I can entertain them in the manner that they expect. It has its advantages but it has its disadvantages in that you don't get a minute to yourself.

If you wake up at three o'clock in the morning with a memory of something that should be done and hasn't been done, are you tempted to go and do it?

No, I cut completely off. Once I get inside I forget about the shed completely but I've always got too many other things to do inside.

Can you ever get away? Do you have holidays?

Yes, we get away. We're very involved. My husband's the New South Wales representative of the Apple and Pear Growers Association. He's the state chairman of the New

South Wales Apple and Pear Growers and he's also the local chairman of the New South Wales Farmers fruit section of Orange. I'm virtually on the same committees. I'm the publicity officer for both the local and the state branches. I take an active role: I've been a delegate to conferences at the national and state levels. I find I get frustrated that very few women take a role. When I go to meetings I'm usually the only woman there and that disappoints me a little bit, but I try to encourage other women and they just don't seem at all interested. A lot of them are working: they've got their own job working outside the farm gate which might account for the problems we have with women in the organisation.

How much is this a family affair?

It's a family affair in that I have my son working for me. I've got two sons. One's not interested; he's got his own business and is running his own affairs, which I don't hold against him. This is a very demanding industry to be in and it's a lot of hard work, and if he can find a job that's not so demanding and hard, good luck to him!

What goes on in the cycle of the harvesting of the different sorts of fruit you have here?

We start with Royal Galas: they come in at the end of February and that's when we start off with our apples, then we pick our Delicious, then we've got our Fujis, Braeburns, Granny Smiths and, last but not least, the Pink Lady which is an Australian-bred apple developed in Western Australia. I don't think this district is really suitable for Pink Lady. Our climate is temperate and they like a warmer climate so there's not that many Pink Lady trees planted in this district and it won't be a major variety for the area. The apples go through to December and in the second week of December we start our cherries; they go through till Christmas and about Australia Day in January we start our stone fruit—we have mainly nectarines and a few plums. That takes us through to the middle of March and then the whole cycle starts again.

Do you ever wish you could go away and leave it all? It must be very exhausting having a relentless circle of demands.

Yes, I'd sell out tomorrow! I get very tired. I think there's too many heartaches in this industry: you can get wiped out in half a minute with hail; you're relying so much on the weather; you're relying on pickers to harvest your crop, if you can get enough pickers in time so the quality of your fruit doesn't deteriorate before it's picked. There's just so many challenges. The rewards can be there. It's a very intensive industry: you can make a lot of money but you can also lose a heck of a lot.

DIANA BEAL

*D*iana Beal is a farming academic. She moved from the Canberra and Brisbane bureaucracy to some land near Toowoomba. For around twenty years she worked as a farmer on her own land while carting hay for other farmers, at the same time adding to her academic qualifications. She is now a lecturer at the School of Accounting and Finance at the University of Southern Queensland. Part of her job is to run courses for farmers on managing their accounts. She continues to farm in her spare time assisted by her eighty-four-year-old mother, Enid.

I spent my first twenty-eight or twenty-nine years in Brisbane but my mother came from a station property. I did economics at university, as my first degree, and when I graduated as an economist I found in the late 'sixties that nobody particularly wanted female economists because you couldn't send a female economist to the bush. (I don't know what would happen to her, but something obviously would.) So the market for female economists wasn't exactly strong and I ended up going to Canberra where I worked for the old Bureau of Ag. Economics for about a year, which was about as much of Canberra as I could stand.

I came back to Brisbane and the only job I could get was as a base grade clerk in the Auditor General's Department, which I didn't like very much. So I thought if my fate was that I was going to be an auditor, I'd better get qualified in that. I went back to university at night and did a commerce degree, so I've got an accounting background as well. But, happily, after about a year in the Auditor General's Department, I was able to get across to the Department of Primary Industries in Brisbane, and I was much happier in that job.

It was a funny sort of a catch-all job but it really was looking at environmental stuff. I'd always been interested in natural things but in that job I was dealing with natural things and the environment and actually being paid for it, which was rather nice. So in the DPI I used to pick up quite a lot of farming science and it came to me one day that I really didn't want to be a government servant any more—I wanted to go farming.

My mother and father were quite compliant in this— which was nice of them—and so we looked around and decided that the Downs was where we wanted to be, so we found a farm on the Downs.

When you put your knowledge to practice, what did you find out you really knew?

It was a great big learning curve. We bought a place that was reasonably small but that we could finance reasonably easily. We could have gone for the bigger risk and the bigger return by going for a bigger place and getting a big loan, but that doesn't sit with my character too well. So we went for the small place which we could finance and we grew lucerne hay on the creek flats, with irrigation, and cattle on the ridges. It's not a place where you'd make a fortune, but it's not a place where you go broke either.

For twenty years it was my livelihood. Very early on I found that you couldn't trust hay contractors to come when you needed them and if they didn't come when it was the optimum time to do things, then you lost the crop. So we put money into buying the equipment, and that's fairly expensive, so to make the best use of it I became a hay-making contractor, toddling out all around the district and making hay for people. We built that up to be a fairly reasonable sort of business. But after twenty years or so of doing that sort of thing, you find your back goes, and then you think to yourself there must be more to life than continual back pain.

Did the local people think you were a little bit strange doing this sort of work?

I guess so (laughs). There probably aren't too many female hay-making contractors around the place.

After you'd given up the hay contracting, was the farm a goer then, without that sort of income?

It depends on how much income you need. Certainly there's not a big income on small farms, but then the opportunity came up to do some part-time tutoring at the local university, so I thought I might as well have a go at it—even though my degrees were getting reasonably old by then. But the first year stuff was OK and I managed to pick it up again. I've obviously been on a fairly steep learning curve there as well. Then I got interested in family history, and that's been very good because with my outlook on things I thought I ought to learn something about it, so I found there was a graduate diploma in local and applied history, which includes family history, at the UNE in Armidale. I did that as a part-time course for two years and got the graduate diploma and that got me back into academe.

From there I got interested in landscape history and that tied in with my work with the local Landcare committee in Rosalie Shire which was formed very early in the Queensland history of Landcare committees.

What was the impetus to set up the Landcare committee here?

There was a push by the state government to get Landcare going. They wanted it to be seen to be a grassroots movement yet there wasn't much movement around the grassroots. At that stage they had to push things along a bit and the first meeting here in this shire was called by the shire clerk to try to get something rolling. After we formed the committee it rolled, and in those early days we were probably one of the more successful committees because we managed to get hold of money pretty easily. We developed skills in putting in submissions and we got some good projects going. In fact, our salinity project, dry land salinity, is probably one of the most documented and most seen dry land salinity projects in Queensland.

Is the land round here particularly badly degraded?

That depends on your point of view. In my view, yes, but I think you'll find it is in most areas in Australia that have had a history of settlement over a reasonable time. It really depends on your value judgments. If you were willing to take a forgiving sort of attitude you'd say, 'Oh no, there's not too much degradation', but if you take a realistic one, in my view anyway—yes, there is. This area has had land cultivated since about the 1850s which makes it a pretty old area in terms of Australian history. It was settled by squatters from the 1840s onwards, and they were actually growing lucerne here on the land that we own from the 1850s onwards. It's a pretty long time for agricultural cultivation.

Dry land salinity is a big problem and that's caused by over-clearing of the ridges, so that the rainfall goes through the recharge areas and ridges and ends up down the valleys. If you've got some geological structure which forces the water to the surface and you don't have deep-rooted vegetation to soak it up, then you get salts brought up and you get salinity patches in the valleys. Lack of care of stream banks is another one and people still do it. They don't keep their cattle or animals away from the stream banks and so they overgraze those areas because they've often got a few trees left and they've got shelter. Having the animals overgraze those areas means that the banks get broken down and then you get erosion when the floods come down. There's a major problem on which not much has been done so far, woody weeds. This area was one of the major areas for the prickly pear invasion. That's been overcome and probably good things came from it in that there must have been a heck of a boost to the organic matter on the surface of the soil when the prickly pear all fell down with the cactoblastus. But what happened then, of course, is that nature abhors a vacuum, and if something goes, something else comes in, and what came in in this area was lantana and boxthorn which are a major problem. Boxthorn is an African prickly plant. In Africa they use it to keep the lions out of the corral, so you can imagine if it can keep lions out of your corral, then boxthorn is a pretty horrendous sort of plant. It's got very nasty prickles and I guess one of the ancillary problems with it is that it has a nice fleshy fruit, like a very small tomato, and the crows love them. So the crows pick the fruit, eat the fruit and go and sit on the fence-post and defecate and then you get a new boxthorn coming up underneath.

When you first started off trying to get a Landcare group going, how did that work? How do you enthuse people?

The only thing you can do is hold field days or things that you think will be of interest to people, advertise them as well as you can and hope for the best. And we've concentrated on salinity out at Brymaroo near Rosalie Plains and we've looked at woody weeds—we've had demonstration areas of how you should clear these things. The big problem is that you want to get rid of the woody weeds, but if it's an area where you've got some remnant vegetation you don't want to clear the remnant vegetation—or, at least, you shouldn't want to.

Another thing that we've done was a remnant vegetation survey. That was done by amateur botanists and our big problem with it was that we got the funding and we started off to do the project, but then we ended up with drought. The drought was so bad that the samples we'd send down to the Queensland herbarium to be identified were so atypical with the drought that it was difficult to actually identify them. That threw a bit of a spanner in the works but we have managed now to finish that project and we've got a fair idea of where the remnant vegetation is in the shire.

If you survey an area and decide that such and such has to be done, is each landholder responsible for carrying out that program on their area?

Landcare is a totally voluntary process at the moment. There are a number of mechanisms that are getting up but all you can do really is work on a voluntary system and put up demonstration sites showing various processes or methods and then hope that other people will take it up. There's now a second string to the Landcare bow in that integrated catchment management is coming along. I see that as trying to set sort of a macro-recipe in place, whereas Landcare is often looking at micro-problems: you've really got two thrusts at the same time.

There'll be laws soon to make you do things like that.

In the best interests of the country it may be that there should be laws, but our tradition of doing this is that it should be voluntary. There's a difference of opinion in society as to exactly what freehold means in terms of rights and responsibilities. Traditionally, of course, freehold meant that the landholder was free from serving the lord in the military manner, which is a bit different from what people now think freehold means. There's this thought around that I own the land freehold, and therefore I can do what I like with it. But there is a major, or an overall, responsibility which is higher than that: it says that the people, as a whole, own the land and those people who have freehold have only got tenure for their lifetime. If you think about that, it's a pretty important distinction from, say, 'I have the freehold and therefore I can do what I like with it'. That sort of attitude would be fine if you think you're going to live forever.

What about their family's lifetime, though?

A lot of people don't seem to think that. It's just 'I, I, I'. But there's enough evidence that philosophers and other people think that the land is different from other assets, and that the community really has the overall responsibility, regardless of who owns the tenure at the moment.

I guess one of the main jobs of the committee is educative?

It certainly is. And you've got two thrusts to that process: you're trying to educate the people that are there now— education of adults with all their hang-ups and their goals and so on—and you also try to get to the young in the schools and educate them for the next generation.

You'd think it would be fairly obvious that if the land wasn't producing what it used to produce, and obviously things weren't going well, some sort of course of action would have to be taken. Is it difficult to convince people that something needs to be done?

Yes and no. There are people who will tell you in a very bewildered tone of voice that the place is not as productive as it used to be and they don't know why. You just wonder how you can help them, because if they can't sit down and analyse what's gone wrong, or can't realise that they have to go out and ask somebody for advice on what's going wrong, well it's a bit hard to know what to do with them. But there are some really smart businessmen and very good land managers out there who understand the processes and they know that things are going wrong and they know that they have to fix things. But often it's a case of, do I sacrifice something now for the long-term gain, or do I hang onto the short term now, and even though it's disappearing incrementally, it's only a small amount each year, so it doesn't really matter all that much. Really ... it's short-term versus long-term thinking.

That I guess can be tied to finances and the economics of the place?

Definitely. You can't go round blaming people totally for being greedy and short-term in thinking. If you're only just getting enough money to put food on the table, well then you're obviously not thinking too much about the long term and how you can make things better, because you just cannot afford it.

Do you think you could describe how, in practical terms, people get rid of a patch of salinity on their property. I mean, if you had one here, what would you do?

Brymaroo—our big project on salinity—is a pretty good case study in that. It's on the plain just south-west of Rosalie Plains homestead and what we had there was a fairly well-defined catchment—a small one with a creek down the bottom—and there was an area of about sixty hectares which was totally salinised, meaning that in wettish periods you had water lying on the surface the whole time—it didn't dry up. There were mosses and bulrushes growing in that, which is very unusual in the Darling Downs, I can tell you. The soil was so salty that it had lost its structure and one of the big advantages of Darling Downs soil is its structure—it's a self-mulching soil, which means that when it dries off, on the surface you have a whole lot of crumbs about a quarter of an inch in diameter and that is a very, very valuable resource, because you get the ability for rainfall to permeate very easily—you don't have a sealing surface—and that is a big plus. Well, with the salt, the soil has lost its structure and it's virtually like sand at the seaside. It's just in small grains and on that area which was very, very badly salted we'd get wind erosion. So that just shows you how bad the structure was. The soil would just blow into little sandhills, little soil hills—and that was because it had lost all structure and it was down to very fine grains. So, when we first started there wasn't too much in the way of help in sorting out what the problem was and what we should do about it.

We thought, well, we know that this is caused by over-clearing of the ridges, so what we'll do is we'll put the trees back and see what happens. So we started on an ambitious planting program, and the idea was to plant 18 000 trees on the ridges, which are the recharge areas, and also at the toe slope which was where the basalt from the ridges actually met the valley floor, which was of sandstone-derived country. And we started that off. We thought, well, there's a limit to how much you can do each year, because obviously in this area you have to post-water the things; you can't just bung them in and say, 'Well, that's it—we've planted our trees'. It's the aftercare which is the big, big problem.

We thought each landholder could probably only do 200 trees and in that area we had about five or six landholders who were involved so, we were looking at basically a thousand trees a year. We started off doing that and after the first year we were actually propagating our own. We did that here on this place. At one stage we had 5000 trees in the backyard, which is a lot of trees to water, I can tell you—especially in a drought.

We thought the best way to spend the government funding we had was to do everything we could ourselves and only spend the money when we had to on buying planter bags and soil and so on. Obviously when you're propagating 5000 trees you actually need quite a few cubic metres of soil, you just don't go out into your garden and dig up a bit of soil. We had to buy soil, and buy bags and buy slow-release fertiliser. That was our first plan—that we would replant the trees, and then see what happened. Anyway, the DPI salinity research section got interested in our project and they came along and did quite a few test bores to look at where the saltiest patches were in the valley. They found that some of the groundwater was quite good in quality, so they hatched this scheme where if they put down bores and pumped the water up and used it for irrigation when the quality was good enough, then they would solve the problem, because you're going to lower your water table and you get an economic use from your water.

They went ahead and did that and we got some funding to put a test bore down to see what sort of flow could be maintained in an irrigation pumping situation and found that was OK. So, as a result of what started off to fix an area of salinity we've ended up with enhancing the amenity in that valley in that there are now a whole lot more trees than there ever were before. It's a better valley to live in, it's obviously a better valley for the wildlife, because there's a whole lot more trees there, and two of the landholders have got irrigation, where before they had none. All in all, it's been a wonderful outcome.

What does the soil look like now?

I haven't had a look at the very saltiest part just in the last little while, but I would imagine that it would take quite some years for that soil to come back to a reasonable cultivation soil. You need a number of years' rainfall to actually leach the salts back down into the subsoil again, and then your surface soil will be a much better quality.

Another thing that's happened in that valley is that CSIRO developed a salt-tolerant lucerne and we were lucky enough to get hold of some of that. A couple of the landholders have planted it, and what they've got is this salt-tolerant lucerne growing in this reasonably salty area, and because there's so much water about they've virtually got a self-watering crop, which is wonderful. We've had four years of drought which in our view for this area is the worst drought since European settlement—one hundred and fifty years. But the dairy farmers who have had this lucerne crop, which keeps coming up, get a crop of lucerne eighteen inches high in the middle of a drought—and they're not watering it—it just waters itself. It's wonderful.

Does the government allocate a certain amount of funding for all these things per year, is that how it works?

The funding comes mainly from the federal government, and there's an amount given for Landcare administered by the states. Those groups that want to do a project put in an application and, of course, as with all these things, you develop skills in putting in applications and that does impact on the outcome. If you get good at putting in applications you end up with more money than those people who aren't good at putting in applications—that's just the way it is.

You were chair of the local Landcare committee for a while?

I was chair for six years, two terms. I reckoned after that that any group is better off for a change in direction. I could have carried on, but it seemed to me that it'd be better for the group if I got out and let somebody else have a go.

Was there any worry about accepting your leadership?

It's always very difficult for a leader to know that, but it seemed to be OK. We didn't have any great arguments or discussions, and we seemed to be reasonably successful the way we were going. I guess in a leader you've got to have somebody who can think about what the problems are and perhaps a bit of lateral thinking in actually deciding that there is a problem. Because I was involved very early in the Landcare movement, I've been invited to go to other areas where they're trying to set up Landcare groups and one of the standard techniques is to call a public meeting and then ask people what they think the problems of the area are. Typically, the first reaction you get is, oh, we don't have any, and then you break them up into small groups of five or six people and give them a lump of butcher's paper and a pen and say, 'Here, write down what you think the problems are', and by the end of half an hour your butcher's paper is full and they're asking for more sheets of paper. So going from a situation where they said there weren't any problems, you end up with dozens.

It's a very different way of thinking, isn't it? You're actually training people to think of the land quite differently from the way they've thought of it before.

What you've got to realise is we should be only using the sustainable yield. It's just like our own finances: if you've got some capital behind you, you should be only using the sustainable yield of that capital if you want to keep it. If you don't want to keep it, fine—you can spend the capital. And it's the same with natural resources. If you feel there's a long term and that resources should be kept, either for yourself for the future or for future generations, then you shouldn't be running down the quality of the resource. What you should be doing is taking just the sustainable yield of the resource. And that probably is a different way of thinking, because if you look at the history of our land management in Australia, we certainly haven't kept to the sustainable yield, and the result of not keeping to that sustainable yield is land degradation, and that's everywhere.

So, I guess Landcare is a kind of philosophy and a movement. Is it growing quite quickly?

If you listen to the bureaucrats now involved with Landcare, they say it is. There are certainly an awful lot of Landcare groups and they're being formed virtually every week in Australia, which is good. The latest ABS (Australian Bureau of Statistics) information reckons that one person on every third farm is involved in Landcare. From talking to people I think there's a bit of a locality difference in that. The areas with the worst problems and the areas with the most viable farms seem to be the areas that have the best Landcare groups.

We've discovered here on the eastern Downs, even though there are some vital Landcare groups typically in those areas which have small farms, that the farmers are getting fairly old. The average age of farmers in Australia is supposed to be fifty-seven. Well, I would suspect on the eastern Downs the average age of farmers is quite a lot more than that. And often the kids have gone. The kids don't want the farm, they've seen that there's too much hard work for not enough money, and they've gone off to the city or elsewhere. So you've got a pair of elderly parents with no kids at home, probably a very quiet sort of lifestyle. The farm will keep them going, but they're not particularly interested in going out at night to meetings and so on. So, in those sorts of areas, where you've got elderly farmers— probably small farms—it's reasonably difficult to get vital Landcare groups up and running and keep them going.

Where does the scientific expertise come from? I guess you have to pull in a lot of that.

In Queensland the Department of Primary Industries. I guess in the other states the Department of Agriculture.

They're obviously right behind the movement, because what's happened in recent years in Queensland is that the state government has pulled resources away from DPI and there's a bit of a vacuum there. In fact, the Landcare groups, to a degree, have stepped into that vacuum. There are quite a few DPI officers funded through federal grants now, and it's Landcare money that's being used up to have DPI officers in districts.

Is the CSIRO helping with research and things like that?

It would depend on the project. We don't see much in the way of CSIRO work here, although I understand there's a mouse project going on on the central Downs which is obviously of vital interest to the farmers there. But in our particular neck of the woods, as far as I know there's no CSIRO work going on now.

The whole Landcare thing is very much a strong movement here. Are you going to stay involved to the extent that you are, or do you have other projects that you'd like to put your energy into?

No, I very much believe in Landcare and I'm very keen to help in that area. Even though I've stepped down as chairman, I'm still the treasurer of our group and when I get finished with my PhD studies I shall take a more active role than I have in these last two or three years. But there's a limit to how much you can do.

What about farming? Do you see yourself ever coming back to full-time farming, or farming being able to sustain you?

No, I don't. I think the area where this farm is has so much rural residential development around it that I think this area, as a farming area, is gone, really. You get so much rural residential you just cannot run a farm—no matter what size the farm is. If you've got paddocks, say, across a road, which means you've got to take cattle across the road, you'll find these suburban-type people want to drive through them at a million miles an hour, and that's not very good for the health of your calves. We have had calves hit by people in the past; it just doesn't matter to them. The cows can be there, you can be driving them—it's not as if you're just letting them stray all over the roads—you're definitely driving them from one paddock to another but these people will just speed through them. It's absolutely illogical. You wonder why they came to what's basically a country area if they want to behave like that.

Then, if you're undertaking a plant industry of some sort, at some stage or other you're going to have people complain if you're using sprays, even though we think we use our sprays very responsibly. We're always very careful to spray early in the morning when the wind is usually not up, and make sure that the wind's blowing in the right direction so that any drift goes to areas where it can't do any harm. We don't use very many sprays anyway. We're always amused at the way people go on as if farmers love getting on their tractor and spraying things. I think, to a man, they hate it; but when you have to spray things, you have to.

But there must be a limit to how long those normal processes of farming can go on when you've got houses all round you. Once houses start coming into an area, your farming is going to disappear inevitably.

I should ask why you like living out here, a little bit out of town and in a semi-rural setting, when you're not seriously farming at the moment. It's closer to live in town.

Good heavens. You don't think you'd go to town just because it's closer to anything, would you? When we first came here it was a totally rural area. There were three dairy farms up the road from us and I think only one wife out of all the farmers up the way worked in town, so in the morning we'd see her go off to town, and maybe during the day one or two other cars would go to town, as farmers went in to get parts and so on. And that was the sum of the day's traffic. And they'd come back again in the afternoon. So, probably four to six cars going past during the day was it. But in the past twenty years, things have changed quite considerably. There's only one farmer now up the valley beyond us—one dairy farm, rather. And there are two housing estates containing probably fifty houses—that's beyond us on what's basically a 'no through road'—plus quite a lot of houses around us on the other side. So we came to a farming area, and now it's no longer a farming area. We've been overtaken by other forces. But I still wouldn't go and live in town. I still like open spaces.

Even though I now work at the university full-time, we still farm in a sort of a way. We've still got cattle and we still make hay—and it's reasonably difficult to make hay when sometimes you've got to be at some other place at a particular time. Hay-makers have to adopt the philosophy that the hay comes first, because hay is very exacting in what it wants. If you're going to make good hay you have to do what the hay wants—not what you want. So that's a bit of a problem.

I'm busy trying to teach a young man how to make hay and it's an interesting experience for both of us, I think.

Your main work at the moment is teaching people how to run their accounts. I guess the old farming method, like most households, was to put all the bills in a shoebox and have a look at them at the end of the year.

At the university I started off as a tutor, and I was pleased they promoted me to lecturer, and I spend half my time as a lecturer in normal academic things. But also a couple of years ago we had a new Dean appointed to our faculty, and he came from Sydney—he lived under the Harbour Bridge, I presume in quite a nice apartment. But he was amazed that here we had a rural university that didn't seem to have much congress with the rural hinterland and he was keen to develop community associations. I'm not really quite sure how it all happened, but I'd always thought that, with my economics and commerce background and my farming experience, I should be able to help some people with their financial management and their financial recording. I remember thinking when I was 'just a farmer', that for about two or three thousand dollars a year, I could manage quite a few hours off the farm to help people. Of course, finding somebody who wanted to give me two or three thousand dollars a year to do this was reasonably difficult. But when the new Dean came along, somehow or other we hatched this scheme together that the Faculty of Commerce at the University of Southern Queensland would run a free scheme for farmers doing just exactly what I'd been thinking about all these years.

I don't know whether there was some sort of Machiavellian plot on my part, I don't really think so, but it came to pass that I now spend half my time going out to the farms of people who ask for help and show them how to do financial recording in a simple way designed for their particular enterprises. We show them a simple but effective system which allows them to take their accounts out of the shoebox—and they literally have them in shoeboxes or, if they're a big farm, an apple case. We take the accounts out of this very primitive form and put them in a book—a manual recording system. Obviously, the way things are going with computers, big places really should be computerised because it makes it a lot easier to do the recording. It also makes it a heck of a lot easier to do the sorts of things that are required in the way of decision support. If you've got to decide whether to grow this crop or that, or whether you should go into cattle or feed-lotting or whatever, and you use a computer to help make that decision, you're probably going to make a better decision because you can look at a whole lot of combinations a whole lot more easily than you would if you were doing it all manually.

Some people are overwhelmed with the amount of mail that comes and they just don't know what to do with it. It seems rather odd, but that's what happens. Some of them keep the junk mail and some of them throw out the accounts. So it's a matter of putting a process in place. Some people don't open their mail which, again, seems rather odd, but they just get overwhelmed by the flood of the stuff.

A proper office procedure is absolutely vital: open the mail when it comes and chuck out all the chaff that you don't need, and keep the good stuff, put the bills aside, have a bill paying day, and then get into the financial recording once you've paid them.

Who usually comes to these? Is it both husband and wife—or does one come more frequently than the other?

More wives keep books than male farmers, and we've had a majority of women who've asked for help. But there certainly have been a large number of male farmers as well. And we've had groups together—husband and wife.

Are they receptive to the idea of computers being useful things?

It depends on who you talk to. There's supposed to be

about twenty-five per cent of farms with computers, according to the computer industry, but many people in the computer industry will tell you that a lot of those computers aren't being used to the full potential.

That's a whole other course, is it?

That's one thing the DPI are doing. They are trying to get people to be more computer-proficient, which is good, because that's the way things should be going, I think.

What sort of differences do you see in a farm, once they get their finances under some sort of control?

I don't know that you see anything very major in the physical sense. If people understand what's happening, they may in fact go out of one crop and into another faster than they otherwise would. Basically what happens on farms which are not controlling their finances particularly well is that they send their information off to their accountant and it comes back probably six or eight months later—there's usually a terrible time lag which would drive me nuts if I had it. But when the final accounts come back—the balance sheet and the profit and loss account—many people can't read them. They have a quick look at them, sign them and if they have to send them back they send them back. If they don't they just file them and that's that. And they really haven't had any advantage from getting that information, because they are not using it. So, what you're hoping that you'd do with people taking more control of their finances is that they would be monitoring what's happening as it's happening, and that there would be some changes in terms of enterprises. You'd also hope that their accountant's bill was a bit smaller, which, again, is something you don't see in the physical assets, but it'd certainly make them feel a lot better (laughs).

In an area like this, have many of them got qualifications of any sort to run farms?

I suspect not. Probably the majority have only gone to school until age fifteen. Even now, many, many young people from farms think if they're going back on the farm they don't need an education because they're only going to be a farmer. Obviously that's the wrong way to think—farming is one of the areas where you need a lot of skills. You need a lot of physical skills and you need a lot of mental skills or business skills. It is certainly the wrong way to think, 'I'm just going to be a farmer, therefore I only need to go to the minimum amount of education'. When those people get to be thirty-five or forty, when they're dealing with their own kids who are trying to put the same story over, then you get a different attitude. They say, 'I wish I'd gone further myself because I know I need these things and I haven't got them'.

Schools aren't getting that message through? Local high schools and things should be able to influence that a bit?

You'd think so, although I don't know. I don't have any dealings with the high schools, but there's a possibility that the teachers in high schools aren't farming folk anyway—they're city people who are just at another posting and who aren't really thinking about where their students are going. I suspect that there isn't the weight being put on that push for a higher education.

How does the finance course make a difference to people?

I take lots of people up to the stage of bank reconciliation.

It is absolutely vital, if you're going to keep your own books, to do a bank reconciliation. In my view, if you don't do a bank reconciliation you might as well not even start, because it allows you to check that what you've done agrees with what the bank says, and, in terms of the tax man and your accountant, what the bank says is the truth. The bank statement is the document that is taken to be the correct record and so all records that the farmer keeps himself have to agree with that bank statement. Of course, the banks can make mistakes, and if you are keeping your own records properly, you might find that the bank has made a mistake. If you hadn't found it you could lose out. So, for you it's a check on the bank as well, but mainly it's a check to see that your records are correct. I've got lots of customers out there now doing bank reconciliations who weren't before, and they're certainly happier for it, because they feel that they are in control of things.

Does that give them more confidence to make adjustments and changes?

Yes. We've got a neighbour here, a dairy farmer, I've helped to get to that stage and he now feels that he has a much greater understanding of his finances. He feels a whole lot more confident about actually talking to bank managers, talking to his accountant, because he understands more about what's going on. Nowadays there's so little in it in terms of the farmer's terms of trade that he's got to make every post a winner. On the other hand, of course, you can't make every post a winner in the sense of using up your natural resources, so it's a fine line between using your natural resources well and with the long term in view, yet making enough out of the place so you survive.

LORRAINE HEWETT

*L*orraine Hewett left school at thirteen and yet many students taking Veterinary and Agriculture degrees in Perth owe their practical knowledge of artificial insemination to her tuition. She was able to observe the natural behaviour patterns of rams and used this knowledge to train an elite group able to perform in a wide range of farm environments. That was in the 1970s and 1980s. Now, while remaining involved in the farm that she and husband John own at York, about an hour's drive from Perth, Lorraine showed me her latest innovation—a wool fibre testing laboratory. This booming business has the latest computer and laser equipment.

When I was a year old my parents decided to make their go in the country. My father, being an aeroplane engineer, decided he would start his own garage, and they had a

246

garage and a shop on the side of the road. It used to be like the half-way house for truckies coming from the outer farming areas to Perth so we did very well and knew lots and lots of people, but as children we were fairly isolated because there just weren't any children around us.

It wasn't a town; it was just a roadside place. You'd call it the equivalent of one of the roadside places on the Nullarbor now, that's how isolated it was at that period. Of course, it's not like that now with so much more car travel. The road was gravel and we were fifteen miles from the nearest town, but we never ever went there.

My dad used to drop me down by my legs into the tops of big trucks to clean the motors or get things that he'd dropped because he couldn't get down. There's nothing I can't do, cleaning engines and on the mechanical side, but I refuse to do it on the farm any longer.

The school I went to had fifteen children. I went there just to Grade 7 and from there I had to go to a school fifteen miles away. We went about four miles by pushbike and then the bus would come down and pick us up from there. There was the school and a hall and a tennis club—a community area, if you like—and the schoolteacher lived with us because we lived on the road.

He took me to school when I was four, and consequently by the time I got to Year 10 or Third Year High and did my Junior I was only thirteen so I finished school a little bit earlier than I should have done. But at the time the teacher said to me, 'Lorraine, do you want to be a nurse?', and I said, 'No'; 'Do you want to be a schoolteacher?', and I said 'Oh, no', and he said, 'Well, you might as well leave school; there's nothing for you to do then'. So I said 'All right, I'll leave', and that's what I did.

If I'd wanted to be a nurse or a schoolteacher my parents

would have had to send me to a boarding school which they couldn't really afford. And it was way out of their league: it was not something they'd ever thought about because they'd grown up in the city and didn't think in terms of boarding school, and neither did I. All I wanted to do was get out and meet people.

I think my mum could see that I was trouble waiting to happen, which is how she put it (laughs). In November when we finished school a car came down from Perth with these three young guys and they wanted to know if I was allowed to go to the movies with them. Mum said, 'My goodness, my daughter, this is not going to happen here!'.

She had seen a job application for a governess in the newspaper and had rung and spoken to the owner's parents. They had rung the owner up and said, 'Look, this girl is very young; she's thirteen, just about to turn fourteen. How about giving her a try?'. You see, what she really needed was not a schoolteacher so much as somebody just to help with the children. She had a little baby of six weeks old and a two-year-old, a four-year-old and a five-year-old. I went down for an interview thinking, well, hey, this is me, I'm getting my first interview, and I got the job and Mum and Dad weren't anywhere near, I did it all on my own. It wasn't until years later that I found out that Mum had really initiated it all.

So I spent the next twelve months on a station north of Canarvon and that helped me; that gave me a year to grow up. Those poor people didn't have four kids, they had five when I look back at it, but they were very patient and very loving people and I had a very good year.

I came home for Christmas and my eldest brother had an accident on New Years Day and was killed. My younger brother was living in Sydney and he said to me, 'Do you want to come across?' and I said, 'Well, I haven't got the money', so I got a job looking after two little girls whose parents had a nightclub in Perth and they were fantastic to me as well. I stayed there for six months until I saved enough to go to Sydney.

I worked for Hordern Brothers in Sydney. I made some fantastic friends there and that's when I joined a group of singers. Horderns had their own choir and we had this fellow who used to direct us in plays. We put on things like 'Showboat' and I loved singing, absolutely loved it, and that's when I really knew that's where I wanted to live: I wanted to stay in Sydney and stay in that sort of environment.

But I came home. When my eldest brother died it sent Mum and Dad into a spin. He'd followed the stocks and shares and he'd made quite a lot of money. We were all bowled over. He had his own house and all sorts of bits and pieces and, of course, when he died the money was split up evenly amongst Mum, Dad, my brother and myself. Mine was held in trust, but Mum and Dad had this money and they decided that what they'd always wanted to do was have a farm. They thought they could retire on a farm— they didn't know anything about farming at all—and it was quite amazing, because they bought this little 900 acres or something out the back. It was just wet after wet, and Dad rang me up and said, 'If you're coming home for Christmas can you stay and help me at least put the crop in?' So while I was staying at home and putting in the crop and nearly dying of cold and overwork my girlfriend that I'd been to school with said, 'I want to go to a ball but Mum and Dad won't let me go because the fellows aren't really up to what they're wanting, but they'll let me go if you come along as a chaperone'. By this stage I was eighteen. So first of all we went to this little country dance—all there was was a hall out in the middle of nowhere with a tennis club, because you've always got a tennis club next to your hall—and they had a local band, and for some reason or other I was the only eligible girl there and I had the best night! There were about twenty-five guys who didn't have women with them; they'd come from York and around, and in amongst them was John, and one look and I knew! I never expected that to happen. I never, ever expected that I would fall in love so quickly, but I knew straight away that there was something special with him and ten weeks later we were engaged to be married.

So I never did go back. I was supposed to go to New Zealand on a singing tour that had been organised but I never did go back (laughs), only for visiting. That was the start then of a most exciting life, and I guess because John and I were both kids—I was eighteen and he was twenty-three—we sort of grew up together and grew with each other. To say it was full of romance is easy, easy pie. No, we worked hard at it. We knew that what we had was pretty special and it was worth the work. We lived on a family farm with his mother and father and two brothers and they were all living on the farm together, so it was a whole new concept. I was right down the bottom of the heap, I can tell you, so the best thing for me to do was to go out with John and his father and work. His father was just fantastic to me: he let me try everything. I can remember driving the car and he said to me 'How long have you had your licence?' Well, I didn't have one; I'd forgotten about that and they hadn't thought to even ask me. But, you know, you did things like that and you got away with it, and I didn't do it on purpose, I didn't do it to avoid having a licence, I just hadn't even thought about it.

But the love of farming was something that they had and you just couldn't help but feel it. (They still farm over there; John's mum is eighty-six and she's still on the farm with the eldest brother.) You couldn't get water to the place and also we didn't have the power; there was a thirty-two volt battery. When you're eighteen you don't care, it doesn't matter. We had two rooms on the side of their home, and that didn't matter either until I was pregnant with my third child and I said to John, 'This is it; we really must do something' and we moved out on our own.

The partnership had actually purchased this farm, as it had purchased others, and Dad felt that this farm would be the farm for John. John is the born and bred farmer in the family. The others are good farmers, don't get me wrong, but John just lives and eats and breathes it, and this was a really bad piece of country—beautiful country which had been very badly treated. I remember our first crop on this place: we got a bag an acre and at the same time we had nine bags an acre off the old place. We brought our sheep from the other property and we put them on this place at one an acre and they were still looking terrible.

It was some of the earliest crop country in Western Australia and, come what may, on the 12th of April they did their first dig-up and then they'd go back and plough it again, and they'd do it again, and they'd keep cultivating up to twelve cultivations. It didn't matter whether it had rained, what the weather was like or what the ground was like, they still went ahead and did it, and I think it was that over-use that was the problem. That allowed cape tulip to get away and the ground was pretty terrible, and that was a challenge then. We had something like eighty trials running on our place on sheep and wheat growing and pasture manipulation and things like that.

We were the first people to try what they called spray seeding. We sprayed it, killed the weeds and came along afterwards and just direct drilled into the ground. Sometimes we used to only have two-and-a-half hours between changing points on the drill, so it was full-on. You can imagine, the ground hadn't been ploughed and all we'd done was spray the weeds and we were direct drilling the seed into the ground which was as tough as Old Harry. Oh, it was dreadful! We'd get out there at two-thirty in the morning—John would come in and say, 'Come on, Lorrie, we've got to change points again', and we'd be out there and your knuckles would be bleeding and you'd be dripping—a drizzly rain would always come at that time, John and I used to have competitions how fast could we change a set of points. We always came out of it, it wasn't a problem in the end ...

We used to work round the clock. He and I would keep the tractor going round the clock; we did everything together. When he wasn't doing something I was, so that there was always someone with the kids or the kids were with us.

How did you see to do things at two-thirty in the morning?

I don't know; turn the ute lights on, I guess. There was a lot of moon out, too; there's a terrific amount of moon at seeding time. You only get a few really dark, dark nights, and it's not that it goes on for months. It doesn't take long to put in 1000 acres.

How long did you do that for?

Well, I'd been helping on the home farm until we came over here, so I don't think I really stopped till maybe seven or eight years ago. I kept it up for twenty-odd years.

The kids were generally always with us, we never left them anywhere on their own. The only time that I didn't have them with us was in the later period when we had the Kalannie place—the eldest brother went to Kalannie—and I had them with me all the time then because I was often on the farm on my own. I used to get girlfriends sometimes to come and stay with me at night time.

That was a big place: we were trying to develop new land up there. We'd been up there clearing and we had old wood fires and at that stage I was getting pregnant on and off, and the smell of the sandalwood—nearly all the wood up there was sandalwood at that time—made me so ill. I still can't bear the smell of it. Everybody would kill for it but I can't bear to even smell it now. I couldn't stop being sick so John's mother went up there and she looked after them and fed them while I came home and looked after things here.

Very often I started the cropping on my own down here until the boys arrived back. The first year that we were on our own totally, not in the partnership, John had a tree break off. He was pushing down trees and he knew that something wasn't quite right and, as he backed the tractor off, the limb came down and went through his leg. He was out of commission for a long time with that and not long after he burnt his legs when a drum exploded; he was cutting a drum open and it exploded and set fire to his legs. They were both freak accidents and John never had accidents. We'd had an insurance policy at the start and we thought, oh, he never hurts himself, and we'd only just cancelled it when we had these accidents.

So for twelve months I looked after the farm and that was the first time I decided that no matter what happened I would never want to run the farm on my own. I could do the sheep work but the cropping nearly wiped me out.

We just didn't have the money to employ anybody and we were doing minimal cultivation, which meant I really could do it, it wasn't over-heavy for me. But sometimes I'd stand in the shed and get my breath back and try to get a decent look on my face so when I came in I didn't look as exhausted as I felt.

How did you learn the techniques you weren't trained for?

John never stands still. In everything we do he's always looking to see how it can be made better. Sometimes it doesn't work that way but he's never afraid to try something new and he's never afraid to encourage me to do the same, so he's allowed me to step out. The Australian Merino Society was only young at the time we were starting on this huge AI (Artificial Insemination) program: we were inseminating 100 000 sheep throughout Australia, and the rams being selected were coming from the one property. The students were pretty good, and they said, 'Well, we'll train the rams if we can use your rams as feed trials'. So we used to get five or six times as many rams as we'd require, knowing full well that on the feed trials there would be ten per cent that would never be any use for at least a year because they were so starved. Then the better ones would come through and they'd be trained; there'd be a team of five or six or ten, however many were needed at the time, to be trained. On the Thursday afternoon they would feed the sheep for the last time and then the kids would go off for the weekend. John and I would go over on the weekends and we'd feed them. I'm a bit hot under the collar about animals and I'm inclined to spoil them. All our dogs are part of our family and our sheep ... we don't have sheep that are nasty, we don't have sheep that are rough and pushy, and because I was working with them any ram that turned or was nasty we would just cull it out regardless, because I generally had the children with me and we had to protect their safety.

One day I said, 'God, we must be able to find some other method of training these rams, I'd even do it, I don't mind'. So the next year when it came to ram training time I got this phone call asking was I serious about training the rams. I said of course I was, without even thinking at all. In two days down came a team of sixty of them and I just hadn't a clue. There were no books written about how to train rams. People had trained individual rams but they really hadn't thought in terms of sixty rams to be sent all over Australia: every eighteen days they were going to be on a new property with a new set of people.

Well, that started what was most probably the biggest learning period of my life and, I think, one of the most important periods for breeding in the sheep industry. This period of learning was phenomenal. I thought all I was going to do was train rams and I said to John, 'Whatever do I do?' and he said, 'God only knows. You're the one with the mouth (laughs). You're the one who said you'd have a go at it'.

So I had all the equipment and I thought, well, there are sixty absolutely top rams there and if they weren't all working, or as many as possible after the training, well then I would have failed at it.

I went up with a deck chair and a couple of apples and a small bag of lupins and a book and I just lay there. I had a forty-four gallon drum cut in half and I just dropped a few lupins in there. I'd run my hand through them and just eat my apple and read my book, taking absolutely no notice of them. I had a notepad and I'd write down the eartag number of any ram that came near me within that first day—I'd be up there for two to three hours because by this stage the kids were all at school. I thought, well, they'll be the first ones I'll work with because they're obviously not stressed out by me—and I found I had an affinity with them, they weren't nervous of me. I didn't realise that there are people who don't even need to make a sound yet the rams will tense: you can feel them draw themselves in, and they'll stand and not move or they'll scatter. Yet there are others— I'm one and there are lots of others that came into the sheds when I was working—and the rams never move at all. They just go on doing whatever they're doing, chewing the cud, or they'd come up.

So I thought, well, I'm going to need some sort of order with these rams, so I'd feed them and I did this for about four days, sitting up there in the deck chair. They learnt, of course, straight away, and the minute I walked into the sheepyards they'd come charging up. They knew I had the lupins, you see, and lupins are like gold, they just love them. So I'd sit there and let them chew and then they'd come over: they'd get curious because I was taking no notice of them, just eating an apple, and they'd come up and you'd get the odd one who'd want to eat the apple and then you'd get the odd one who'd start chewing at the paper and dribbling over my shoulder—yuk—but it worked.

By the end of the four days a quarter of those animals were quiet enough for me to actually put my hand out with the lupins and they'd eat out of my hand. So I thought, I'll take them inside and we'll have a dummy ewe in the ewe bail and we'll see if any of them are interested. We found out then that a ewe didn't need to be on heat: we thought we had to have a ewe on season for the ram to mount. Well, you don't; it just needs to stand. It's not the smell so much, it's the stance in which the ewe's there; she's restrained and if she stands when he comes up, he's going to be fine.

That was the actual training part and it was relatively easy. It got to a point where within the first two days I could take the AI rams and get them to mount the ewe and I could collect semen from them. I was collecting something like 3000 at least.

When you say a dummy ewe, you mean an ordinary ewe?

Just an ordinary ewe, but we collect the semen. We use an artificial vagina to deflect the penis. You don't have to touch the penis. Somebody said to me once that it's a bit tough on the ram and I said, 'Well, I can't think of one thing tough on the rams because I can make a pretty good AV (artificial vagina)', and they learnt that wherever I was going to be there was either the ewe or there were lupins; I was never going to let them down.

But it was not just training the rams, the rams were easy; they were adorable, they'd just do anything I wanted; it was training people to treat the ewes with quietness and gentleness; gentleness as much as anything; allowing them the opportunity to see what was happening to them rather than just rush them in, throw them over a fence and then get twenty-five per cent of ewes actually in lamb. We used to just put them in the race, leave them for a good ten minutes or half an hour, and then we would go along, just walking along gently going backwards, and rest on their backs so they felt like a ram was actually jumping, and you'd just poke the little doolackey in there and inseminate them. When we'd finished we'd just walk out the front; there'd be no hassle, no noise, we'd walk away from them, leave the door open and let them walk out on their own. We'd have a trail of lupins out to their paddock and it was amazing, we had eighty-five per cent lambing from our first 'shot in the dark'. We were just so rapt; it was better than we ever had with the old ewes, and all it was was this gentle training and gentle work with them.

Did you get any kudos from this?

Yes (laughs) ... I can't remember, actually. In the Australian Merino Society they talked a lot about Lorraine's SID method, the old 'shot in the dark method', so I guess, yes. I wasn't after any; I did all this for gratis because I really was having a damn good time and learning so much. It was like going to university but actually hands-on and having no limits, none at all, even down to how much were we going to dilute the semen, how much semen we could get from rams.

Kids were coming to me and saying, 'Look, I've got to do this to get my degree. Can I run a trial with you?' I was rapt in that because they had all this education as well and I had the physical, hands-on experience and they had the proper way of writing it up, and they had access to machinery that I'd never even seen. They had these machines that you could put the semen in and it would tell you how much dilutant you would mix with it. We'd been doing it visually for years and we found out after doing a trial—I think there were four of us involved in that trial—that the visual method was identical but, still, it was a means to an end; we still found some things happening.

You must have developed a method of training rams that didn't involve sitting in the deckchair with lupins.

Yes, eventually you didn't need to do that, but they did learn. It's amazing how, if you're confident and you're not worried, they pick it up and, as I said, I have an affinity with them. The rams would arrive fresh out of the paddocks and often I was training just about as many stud rams as well. People would bring their stud rams in and they were very, very quiet, very often just overweight, or under-exercised more than overweight because they'd been kept in pens ready for showing. They'd been to the York Show or the Sydney Royal Show, or whatever, and they'd been trucked over here, the poor things. We found out that semen production in rams is no different from humans. If you've got a guy who sits watching TV all day on the weekends and slobs down beer, doesn't do any exercise, he doesn't really produce the sperm that a man does who's out there physically keeping himself in good shape. It's exactly the same with the rams. The rams exercising would be fine. I worked out lots of methods: they'd come off the back of the trailer or the ute—or out of the back of a car, I might add, a number of them brought their rams to me in the back of their Land Cruisers—and I'd walk them up to the top of the hill. We've got a nice little steep hill at the back of our place, and if they couldn't make it to the top of the hill I knew there was no way that they would be able to work. I'd say, 'Well, you can either leave them here and I'll walk them up the hill for a few days, but even then your sperm count's going to be down on what it ought to be'.

But the wild ones, the ones that came from the AMS, they would do the most atrocious things to them. They'd be shorn and they'd bundle them on a truck and drop them here and they were wild, wild. I'd go in and there'd be sixty to eighty or a hundred of them in the pen and you'd have to find out which ones were going to work. It's amazing that there was always one amongst them that had a problem and it would set off the others. Without moving—it wouldn't bunt or fight—it would standover the others. I used to pen them in pens of five and you'd find a pen that wouldn't really work and you'd have to work your way through till you found the one that was causing that problem and then he would be out of the program. It's amazing, it's like a standover pecking order. He'd have these standover tactics and there was always one in every hundred like that.

In all the time we only ever had one really true-blue homosexual ram. He would never mount a ewe but he would mount the rams and he would bunt a ewe to get the ewes away, which was astounding.

You've obviously become quite an animal behaviour expert.

Yes, I guess I did. There was a lot of animal behaviour work done here with students. They wrote up bits and pieces from it. We found out that rams like young ewes in preference to old ewes; they do like pretty ewes in preference to ugly, fluffy, woolly ewes. You get a ewe that's particularly rough and coarse in its feel and looks untidy, and the rams will bypass that to go to a more attractive one. They do have likes and dislikes, there's no two ways about it. I mean, given no option, they still have to work with that ewe but they really prefer not to. It's quite amazing. But they do like the young blonde ones, too—typical! (laughs)

During that time there were trials and experiments going on and you had students coming out here. That's not bad for somebody who left school at thirteen! And you had to get the students trained as you had to get the rams trained.

The students were no different to the rams. Twenty-five per cent of them were pretty dedicated, they just wanted to know everything, and there were twenty-five per cent at the end who really were there just because it was a day out. Then there were those in the middle who were going to do whatever was expected of them eventually. But in all honesty, I only ever had one failure in all my students and it was an older man who really wasn't interested at all. He wasn't a farmer, he was a dentist who was just doing this course. He shouldn't have been in it. He wasn't interested at all.

I hope that the others enjoyed it as much as they certainly showed they did; when it came to examination time the proof was there. There were some phenomenal operators out of it and some incredibly interesting kids. The students were the highlight of my life. They were just so incredibly interesting ... and interested in everything. They brought up things I hadn't even thought about—they kept me on my toes (laughs)!

I often think the luckiest thing for me was that I wasn't a farmer's daughter so I had no preconceived ideas of what should be. So the things I've done are to me logical rather than the norm, because I didn't know what the norm was. I didn't realise there were restrictions; I didn't know there were places where women shouldn't go.

A lot of the things we did with rams was observing what they did in the paddocks. I used to say to people, 'When a ram puts his horned head down don't ever move away because that's a sign of aggression. If you watch them and a ram puts his head down the other puts his head down and they move back so they can come in. The first thing you do is step forward and he won't bunt you'. And it's dead right, he won't bunt you unless he's vicious and nasty in the first place. But the minute you step back ... it was just observing what they did, that's all it was.

I think the only disappointments I have had, and they're some of the reasons why I don't step forward about a lot of things now, have been criticism from men in the industry—very few of them, but all you need is one to really put a damper on things. I guess small-mindedness is in everything and it's no different in farming. Had I been a man I'm sure I'd have had no problems. Very often when I was invited as a guest speaker they would invite John and he would say, 'But I don't do the work, Lorraine does it'. 'Oh, well,' they'd say, 'do you think she would talk in front of us about such a thing?' It was amazing!

And when you did talk . . . ¿

I like to think that I blew their socks off (laughs). I can remember going to the University of New South Wales in Sydney. They had invited the Australian Merino Society to come on over and talk about what they were doing because we were new then. When it started the average age in the AMS was twenty-five. Apart from Jim Shepherd, who'd started the AMS, the rest of us were round about . . . well, John was twenty-five and I was only about twenty, so the whole group was pretty young and enthusiastic. All the professional people had been up. Jim Shepherd had spoken and the Director of the Australian Merino Society had spoken and it was all very serious. They had leaders in the industry, scientists, and Mr Faulkiner, and they were absolute gentlemen and the ladies were absolutely wonderful. I was as nervous as an old bitser when I got up on the stage. I knew all the names, I'd read all the books and these were all the people with studs that had been going for generations and generations.

Anyway, I had a fairly large handbag and I said, 'Well, I do the artificial insemination programs, I help write them up, we actually train the rams and, of course, any self-respecting artificial insemination person would have one of these in her handbag', and I brought out the artificial vagina and said, 'You'd all understand what this is!' They all burst into laughter and I could tell straight away that they were really interested in what I had to say. There wasn't one aggressor. You look around and you can feel if they really want to hear or if you're just there for ridicule, or you're the party trick. I've been invited to a few places where I was the party trick and I made sure that by the time I left I wasn't a party trick.

But that allowed me to relax and genuinely get into some really good stuff. And the questions they asked: they really knew what they were talking about. It was probably the most rewarding of all talks that I had ever been to and I realised then for the first time that what I was doing was important. Up till then I felt like I was a little farmer's girl from out the back of West Australia and I had nothing to offer. But I knew then that I did, because the questions they asked were relevant and they were exciting; they were on things that I really wanted to talk about. And they had things to add, and instead of it being me up on the stage, on my own, talking, it was a group situation where we were swapping ideas and things. I remember being asked out to different stations, different farms, to have a look at their programs to see whether there was anything I thought would help them and whether there was anything there they thought would help me and I really appreciated that. But that was the first time, the very first time.

Your current set-up of wool testing . . . tell me how that started.

That started really because my daughter was at university and, like her mother, pretty stubborn and wouldn't accept any assistance. She said, 'If I can't support myself at university I shouldn't really be there. Let me give it a go'. Well, the trouble was, in the first year she did Agriculture and anyone who's started Agriculture at the university knows the hours involved, and one of the courses was on a Saturday which meant she couldn't even take a Saturday job.

So her father said, 'Well, look, there's this little farmer's unit for testing wool, a little machine'. It's not brilliant but it does give us a correlation of where our wool testing and our wool style is—so he got this thing and she did his samples. It was a terrible method, difficult to do and very unreliable: it was reasonably good but very unreliable. But within six months not only was she doing her father's but the neighbours had seen what she was doing and all the people he'd sold rams to said, 'Oh, will she do ours, as well?' and there was this huge amount of wool. She said, 'Mum, I can't bear it any more. This is like a mountain and I'm leaving.' In fact, she was so upset she ended going to Canberra to university for six months to get away from it. It was huge.

Of course, it left us with all this wool to test and I thought, what am I going to do? I didn't really want to sit there carding wool or testing it, and I ended up getting help—a lovely lady, Rosemary, who still works with me and who knew nothing about wool. By the time we'd been going for two or three years she could tell, when wool was clean and carded, exactly what the micron count would be by the way she would test it.

So that started us off and it was highly profitable. We had very little outlay, just this little machine John had bought and we developed a few easier ways of carding and our own carding machine. We had wool everywhere and it was exciting again: here was this new thing. We'd been testing wool ourselves for twenty years but we didn't know just how many other things were involved and how much you could utilise your results.

We knew that if we were going to really make any advantage out of these results we'd need to put them into something and we'd need to have something we could calculate on, and the computer was the only thing. Well, it took me about eighteen months to get into using a computer properly; just to use the keyboard nearly struck me out. But within two-and-a-half years I'd actually written up my program where we could calculate using fleece weights, body weights, all the information we wanted, plus if we wanted to we could add the current wool prices and we could get a wool value for each sheep.

Then we got into correlations and things like that and that got beyond me. I'm mathematically inclined naturally, but not taught, so there were limits to what I could do until we had a young fellow out who helped us to put in a damn good program. We called it 'Ram Ranking' and we could rank sheep pretty well using any index we wanted to. So everything was going wonderfully and then there was a breakthrough: a young fellow in Perth developed a machine that could actually measure every single micron of every single fibre and give a coefficient of variation (CV) of that micron. To me, that was the breakthrough in the wool industry we had been looking for for a long time, because you could have a twenty micron wool with a coefficient of variation of fifteen to twenty and that is highly acceptable. There are also twenty micron sheep with twenty-seven coefficient of variation and that means the poor old manufacturer isn't buying twenty micron wool at all, he's buying more like something that's spread from fifteen to almost thirty. That's always been a problem. It's been our biggest downfall.

So here we were with this new machine and I knew straight away this was the way to go. My clients were saying, 'Can you do CV?' and I said, 'No I don't have the skill nor do I have that particular machine, so I approached SGS who had the machines and I said, 'I've got clients who would like their wool measured. Can I be involved?' They said, 'Well, yes, if you want to do the core testing and actually scour it, clean it and send it down to us, we'll put it through the machine and send you back the results'. I would then put the figures into the index that I had for each of my farming clients. That suited us all.

That was really fantastic, but it was huge. I was looking at 100 000 samples and I just couldn't keep up and neither could SGS. So I said to my husband, 'Well, the only thing is to buy a machine ourselves'.

At the time I'd come across a fellow in Queensland and, at that stage, twenty-five per cent of my clients were in the eastern states. You know how you meet someone you know you can trust and communicate with? He's ten years younger than me and he has four children at boarding school; he's been through five years of drought and things have been pretty tough for him. He had the advantage of having studied as a wool buyer and he had done all those courses and had a lot more technical knowledge than I had. I'm the first to admit that when you're thirteen years old when you leave school there's a lot of stuff missing. I have tried to study and found that I just don't have the ability to study off paper: I'm a good person to learn hands-on. I thought, this is the guy I need, somebody who really wants the job enough. So I said to him, 'How would you like to be my partner?'. He ho-hummed and said, 'Well, I'd love to work with you. I'll send the samples and I'll work for you'. But I said, 'No, I'm really looking for a partner'. I'm forty-seven years old now and I haven't got a great many years left. To start something like this you need continuity—I certainly do—and you need someone with enthusiasm and with a need. He really had a need—he needed to have an off-farm income.

So after a lot of kerfuffling around and getting through

that reserve that Queensland people have, David and his wife and John and I joined together as partners. We hocked a bit of land at the other end of our place and we bought a machine for here and we have since bought a machine for over there.

But, of course, instead of David and I thinking we could do the work ourselves, we've now got fifteen staff here and seven over there and we're really looking for lots more—certainly when the season breaks in July which is our busiest time. From July through to the end of January we're working around the clock—I work twenty hours a day, and that's every day, to get through, because we just haven't been able to get staff. But this year we'll be a lot better because we're training people now. I can't keep it up and David's been the same over there. We had no idea how much wool would come in, how much work we would get.

This machine was almost the first one out in the industry that didn't have a technician brought over with it. We got it out of the box and we set it up on our floor—the building at that stage was pre-1956, just an old frame. We had things happening—blockages—we didn't have time to learn because we thought, right, what we'll do is not start the business until October because by October the industry rush period is over, so that means we'll do all the last bits. Very little usually comes in October, November, December—or that's how it used to be. Well, you know what they did, of course: they knew I was getting laser so they held their wool over, and instead of having 500 or so samples a week we were looking at 5000 and here we were learning how to use this machine that had its own little idiosyncracies. Oh, God, it was just terrible!

Part of our service is our advisory service to farmers, so when a result comes up through the computer, if it looks really interesting I ring the owner up. If he's, say, a new client, he's never tested before, he's got a thousand ewes and in that thousand ewes, particularly with the price we're getting now, there'll be a bale of wool that's really bad, I can tell him over the phone what, by leaving that one bale of wool in, the value of his bales will be, and if he takes that one bale out what the values of the other bales will be. So by helping in that way, that's our contribution, that's the extra contribution that we make to our clients, even to the top end, where sometimes there's a couple of bales of absolutely outstanding wool. Now, if they've tested the wool prior to shearing they can do something with it.

So it's these little bits and pieces that make it interesting for me, too, otherwise we'd be just like the other companies, the big companies that have been around for a long time.

If you ask any of my staff over there, 'What do you think of your job?', they'll all tell you how interested they are. Now, one lady has been with me nearly ten years and the other lady that's been with me since I started on this says, 'Every day is exciting; there's something new I learn every day'. That means she's enjoying it.

David and I have yet to see a profit out of the business, but then this is only our second year and we've paid money out on very expensive machinery, but what we've gained for ourselves is much more. And in that gain for David and myself we've been able to employ our families.

You don't have trained lab technicians or scientists?

They're not available. We don't have that up here: we're 100ks from Perth and I don't think any scientist would want to come to York and work (laughs). Also, we all learn. I don't see that a degree is a necessity for us. A degree has been used to make the machine that we have and we have access to people with degrees, and we are on-line twenty-four hours a day to the laser scan hotline at CSIRO. He will answer any questions we need, he's our scientist. We're in the throes, in the last few months, of learning to do yield testing properly, absolutely as near as we possibly can. Now, we've been to CSIRO and the Ag Department here and we're getting all the knowledge from them. They're the scientists, they've done all that pre work and it's very well documented. We don't need a scientist to do any trials and things.

The major problem we run into is the cost of machinery for this type of thing because it's 'lab' equipment. That adds $10 000 to the price. We're actually making a lot of our machines now. Now that I've done enough of the work I employ local engineers and welders and electricians to put my machinery together. I very often go to sales and I buy junk cabinets—I'm talking about left-over cabinets that have been used for laboratory machinery—and we put our own machinery into those cabinets. I can't see any point in paying astronomical money for something that we can put together ourselves locally.

You say you're forty-seven and you talk about retiring, you say you haven't got a lot of time left. What would you do if you weren't working on the farm or working up some new project?

Oh, I don't know. I can't see me retiring for a while; I wouldn't know what the devil to do. I would like to have some more time to myself, and know that when my children come home on a weekend I'd actually have time to be with them.

VAL MURPHY

*V*al Murphy's job on the family potato farm begins when
the produce leaves the farm gate. The Murphy potato
farms are in the heart of potato growing country at Thorpdale
in Victoria. Val has worked to make people more aware of the
versatility of the humble potato. She gives talks and cooking
demonstrations all over Victoria and is part of a group that
compiled a cookbook devoted to potato recipes. She frequently
entertains groups of fifty or more to a potato lunch. When I
arrived she had saved me a potato after-dinner mint from that
day's function!

I was a dairyfarmer's daughter. I grew up at Yinnar on a
dairy farm where it was grey, flat soil, and I married a
'spuddie' who works mainly in red, volcanic soil. It was
quite a contrast to my youth, marrying a potato farmer.

I suppose potatoes aren't quite as demanding as dairy cattle?

Probably a little more seasonal, but I don't really see potato farming as very much different, except that it's not the same thing every day of the year. There's certainly challenge in dairyfarming, as there is in potato farming—and isn't it great to have a challenge?

Did you, when you first got married, play very much of a part on the farm itself? Did you drive the tractors and that sort of thing?

To a lesser degree. We've always employed workers, but I've always been able to help in some kind of a way. My husband runs our property with his brother, and men don't always want to have women being their right-hand when they have each other and when they have labour employed, but I've always played some part. Basically it's more, 'this is broken—can you run to town?' and, 'there's extra men to feed' and 'the shearers are here to be fed', just simple things, not the main workforce; the men have always carried that through quite efficiently themselves.

How does that work ... two brothers of a family working the same piece of land? Is it difficult sometimes?

It's all give and take, and the more you give the more you receive. I think we all have to understand each other's needs and I see that as working very well with this particular family. We also now have sons employed on our family farms and as more land has been purchased we've certainly needed that extra employment of a couple of sons coming on.

We have one son and two daughters, and our son's working in his own business now, boilermaking and welding and structural steel. He's got three other men employed with him and that's going really well. He's about to build us a shearing shed, but it keeps getting put further and further back because he keeps getting more and more employment from other areas. Although one day he may come home on our family farm, his father and I both wanted to see him learn a trade and be able to use that trade wisely, one he could also incorporate on our farm in time if and when he wants a farming background and livelihood.

This farm is a series of farms, is it?

Basically Murphy Farms consists of a bit over 1000 acres. There used to be average lots of 160 acres around here being sold as settlements and the like, and as neighbours have had their properties for sale we've been able to see our way clear to gradually buy more land which is certainly something that we're very thankful for. It's not only growing potatoes—we also have onions. Potatoes in the last several years haven't been terribly profitable—in fact they're below the cost of return to produce—so we've diversified a little. We grow about 400 acres of mainly Sebago variety of potatoes, which are a good all-rounder for chipping, baking, boiling and roasting. But we're also growing about thirty-odd acres of onions this coming season. We have first-cross ewes, because you can only crop your paddocks for a certain amount of time and then you have to spell them, so therefore you've got to have something to put on those paddocks. We grow for prime lamb production and our ewes are joined to Southdown and Poll Dorset rams. Our sheep start lambing in about June and July and the lambs are sold pre-Christmas and after Christmas mainly to local markets as prime lamb. We don't say 'fat' any more because people don't want fat—it's prime lamb.

You've also diversified yourself, becoming a potato marketer.

I'm not sure about marketer, but perhaps promoter, if that's fair comment. The farmers don't always have time to see past the farm gate, because they're so busy producing a product and trying to do the best job growing and irrigating and then harvesting. Once the product's on the truck and gone to market they feel then that's the end result for them. I feel that it's more of a woman's role to be able to promote and show people the versatility of potatoes, talk about nutrition and economy. What else can you buy for ten bucks a bag—that's what potatoes often sell for? I just feel potatoes have so much to give that unless we potato growers can tell people of the versatile and many uses the potato has, who else is going to? And with a name like Murphy, what else could I do?

I use potatoes as an accompaniment to chops and with a roast and, of course, in soup occasionally but are there other things you can use potatoes for?

There certainly are. We make lots of different things at field days and supermarket promotions, we've done the Melbourne Show a couple of times and food festivals and so on. We show people how versatile potatoes really are through cooking demonstrations and free tastings. Most of my work is around Victoria and up into New South Wales and I have several other potato farmers' wives who come and help. We do things like potato stir-fry and potato Boston buns and potato after-dinner mints and coconut roughs and potato strawberry balls and wonderful things made with potatoes. Good old potato Boston bun has no eggs and no butter in it, so it's a lot better for people who have cholesterol problems. We're just showing people the many uses of the good old humble potato.

And you've got a cookery book going?

We have a wonderful cookery book, actually two at the moment. The first one was produced in the 1970s and that's sold extremely well here and overseas, and the next one has just been produced. It has 250 potato recipes and all proceeds go to charity or local community projects.

Each year in Thorpdale we have a wonderful festival that produces many thousands of dollars for local community projects. The potato cookbook belongs to the Thorpdale Potato Festival and has everything from potato bread and potato scones to the Boston bun I mentioned, to potato stir-fries and potato after-dinner mints . . .

That's the one that gets me—the after-dinner mints.

That's made with mashed potato, icing sugar and coconut and a little bit of peppermint essence, and it's dipped in chocolate and tastes very much like chocolate truffles. And instead of crushing biscuits and using condensed milk to make chocolate truffles, it's mashed potato instead. So I ask people to pop an extra potato in the pot when they cook the evening meal and they've got the main basic ingredient.

You also have tourist buses coming up here with people whom you entertain for a potato lunch. What would you serve them?

In the last month I've had three different tourist buses, mainly from Melbourne. Our potato lunch basically consists of potatoes in their jackets with sour cream and coleslaw and cheese toppings and bacon and so forth, and salads. I often do a cooking demonstration for their sweets and I do rum and raisin balls or strawberry balls, or peppermint truffles—even potato coconut ice is rather a talking point. I show people how to make these things, give them the recipes and we have a few handy hints and perhaps a couple of jokes and then we go on to the paddock where they see the potatoes being harvested, to the grading shed where they see them being graded into different sizes and loaded onto pallets and onto semi-trailers. We generally load three or four—sometimes five—semi-trailers a day here, each week day, and those semi-trailers come from all over Australia. Our product is marketed in the Sydney and Brisbane markets, so the potatoes go out from your paddock this morning and can be in Sydney markets tomorrow. Every day you're harvesting fresh potatoes. Every day they're loaded onto trucks and by the next day they can be in the markets and sold to Sydney and Brisbane.

Do you wash them here?

We don't wash on our farm. There are some washed potatoes in the area, but very few. We feel a washed potato is inferior, because if you buy your potatoes with the soil around them the soil is the natural immunity until the consumer is ready to use them. In other words it keeps the potato fresher longer. Any potatoes that get a bit of green on are hand-sorted by some of the seasonal workers and tipped in the paddock. Many, many sheep eat those potatoes but for human consumption I think it's always best not to eat the green.

You also mentioned that you were going to a slimmers' convention. Most people have the idea that potatoes are the first thing you give up when you're going on a diet.

Yes. That's certainly a myth that was thrown out the door some time ago. I'm speaking at a big slimmers' convention coming up in June in Morwell, and I'll be happy to tell people that potatoes are no more fattening than an apple, and they have as much vitamin C content as citrus. Of course, your potatoes can be fattening if you cook them in lots of fats and oils or serve them with huge lashings of sour cream and butter, which we all love. But it's not the actual potato that's fattening. In fact, if you eat your potato with the skin on, you also gain a lot more of the nutritional value that a potato has. Potatoes have been underestimated for far too long. They contain iron and magnesium and several of the vitamin B groups and vitamin C, as I mentioned, and they are also high in carbohydrates and have some fibre.

What's the main use of potatoes now? Is it the french fry market?

There are probably many uses and I guess we all fall to something that we have as a favourite—microwave potatoes, for instance, are really quick and easy.

Do you know where your potatoes go—whether they go into the domestic market or into the sort of retail food outlet?

Yes, basically to domestic markets—some to the crisping industries—but we've also got some export markets this year which is great. But mainly Sydney, Brisbane markets and into fresh foods outlets.

Have you got things on the horizon that you are going to work towards developing?

Yes, a lot. I do charity days where I'm invited to perhaps a soup and sandwich lunch that may be put on for anticancer or palliative care or hospital auxiliaries, or whoever are trying to raise funds. And, instead of them asking a guest speaker to come, they'll ask me to do a potato cooking demonstration. I travel all over our state doing potato cooking demonstrations. As I said, with a name like Murphy, what else can you do? It's great to be invited and I'm certainly meeting a wonderful lot of people, and I'll cook four or five different things for maybe a hundred-odd people. While I'm mixing up enough for everybody to try or sample we have handy hints. I've got lots and lots of potato handy hints and one of my favourites is: if you have an insect bite, just rub it with a raw potato and see the difference. I've tried this many times and I've certainly noticed a big difference.

You were telling me about an old lady who used a potato for arthritis?

Yes, I've heard of this many times. I'm told that to carry a potato in your pocket really helps arthritis sufferers. I haven't tried it myself, because fortunately I haven't had a need, but it's not very much to try, is it?

Potato After Dinner Mints

⅓ cup mashed potato
1oz butter
1⅔ cups icing sugar

1¾ cups coconut
peppermint essence to taste
cooking chocolate

Beat butter into potato, gradually beat in sifted icing sugar. Add coconut and mix well. Add peppermint essence to taste. Mould into small balls and refrigerate till firm. Dip half of each ball into melted chocolate and allow to set.

from *Thorpdale Potato Festival Cookbook*

MARJ BOLLINGER

Marj Bollinger, once a farmer, now spends most of her time entering rural road accident statistics into a computer and flying to Sydney to sit on committees while husband Frank takes care of the farm at Molong in New South Wales. In 1992 their son, Neil, survived a fatal road accident in which two of his friends died. Marj then decided to use her considerable energy to lobby for the reintroduction of rail freight and safer road conditions in rural areas. An organisation called the Highway Safety Action Group was formed and is fast spreading to all regions of the State.

I was born in Blayney and I lived there until I was about nine years old. Then my dad bought a corner store in Dubbo, and that's where I spent all my youth until I was married at age twenty-two. I left school rather early, to work in Dad's shop, where I guess I got my basic training in survival. It was a family corner store and Dad, I thought, was a pretty good manager. He always worked on the basic skills of commonsense and logic. They saw you through most problems if you sat back and analysed the situation, asked why, found out why something was wrong and went about fixing it. I guess that was pretty good training for becoming a farmer's wife.

Corner stores are almost non-existent now. In your childhood, did they measure out the sugar and flour?

Most certainly we did. Many a bag of sugar I've tipped into a bin and weighed up into two, four and six pound brown paper bags (roughly equivalent to one, two and three kilo bags)—and potatoes the same way. We were very much a basic post office/corner store, very basic. We were there in early 'fifties when supermarkets first came in and I guess that's also been training to me in what I've been doing over the last three years. I can remember sitting debating with Dad for many hours over if supermarkets can sell things cheaply, why shouldn't people have the right to go there and buy them, and Dad telling me, well, it was the thin edge of the wedge—that eventually they would get the monopoly and it would be the end of the little corner stores. Forty years down the track I can see that as being very true, but at that age it was hard to accept.

Were those also the days when your customers were people that you knew quite a lot about and took an interest in?

Most definitely. Dad used to go out and collect and deliver the orders and I've done my share. That's how I learnt to drive a vehicle, driving the delivery truck around the backblocks of Dubbo through the orange orchards that are now the suburbs of Dubbo. His clientele were a lot of pensioner people and Dad was their grocer, their chemist, their everything. He was the only contact a lot of them had on a weekly basis, and this is something that my husband and I have discussed quite regularly now—that the older generation today have to be able to get out and go to the supermarket. There's no friendly family grocer or milkman or baker, as there used to be back in those days.

Did you ever find that you were also a bit of a confidante, a bit of a counsellor sometimes?

Yes. We would often wonder why Dad would spend all morning going out to perhaps call on ten or fifteen people to collect their orders. But he used to cut the hair of some of the older gentlemen once a month and he definitely was part of the family. It's a very different age today.

They didn't phone their orders in?

No. Dad used to go round of a morning with his docket book and collect the orders and then bring them back to the shop; we'd put them into the cardboard boxes and load them in the back of the ute and go out and deliver them.

So you were his assistant manager in effect?

Well, yes. That's how I came to leave school when I did. We were forced into changing over from our traditional service role to self-service. We still provided the service—same day orders collection and delivery—but we went into self-service, and Dad diversified: it was the only way that he could see at that stage to survive. And I think we were about three weeks into that operation when my grand-mother died and Mum and Dad had to go back out to Broken Hill to finalise her estate. I guess I became the manager unknowingly.

Was it unusual, when you were fourteen, for girls to leave school at that age?

Well, I guess it was. It was probably coming into the era where girls were becoming more educated—I mean, back a generation before that girls weren't. You left school and either became a nurse or got married.

That would have been after the Intermediate?

Yes, I was half-way through third year to do my Intermediate and I missed about two months' school then and it was by my own choice that I didn't go back. I felt that I had missed so much I couldn't pick up, and my labour was definitely needed in the shop, so I felt that was where my priorities were. I was very happy doing what I was doing and helping in the family business. Right throughout my life, which has been fairly diverse I think, everything I've done I've enjoyed doing and I could well have made a life out of whichever occupation I have had along the way. The only difficulty is I've generally had about five other things going at the same time.

So, you ended up marrying a farmer. Was that how you got on the front end of farming?

Yes. I had a cousin a couple of years younger than myself. His dad bought a property adjoining the one I live on today, and Dennis and Frank became good mates, and through Dennis I met Frank and I have no regrets about that either.

What was the property like when you first moved onto it?

We have 1100 acres out in the Molong area. Not the best 1100 acres in the Molong area, but it's home and it will be home until Frank dies—he has no intention of ever leaving there. He's a farmer through and through. And it was definitely very undeveloped when we went there. Frank had been there, I think, about six years in partnership with his parents and about half of it was cleared and the other half was very virgin scrub, and very little water on it and we've just gone about developing it and going on from there.

What part did you play?

I guess the role I would consider many farmers' wives would. Frank and I took over in our own right probably three or four years after we were married, and we were very fortunate, as I believe the whole of my life has been very fortunate, in that everything happens for a reason. Our eldest son had severe allergies, and we had spent everything we had and gone everywhere we could to try to find a cure for him, then somebody suggested we try goats' milk. We set about to try to buy a dairy goat and discovered that nobody would sell us the dairy goat unless we had owned a goat, or knew something about it. People tended to protect their goats as part of their family and didn't want to part with one that wasn't going to be well cared for. And Frank said, there must be a market for somebody who will breed good quality animals and be prepared to sell them to the market. So that's how I became involved in goats. Before we knew where we were I had about thirty goats running around the house. It annoyed Frank a bit, and one morning there were dogs barking and voices yelling and goats bleating, and he drafted them all off and took the dry goats down to the scrub paddock. From that we discovered how well goats clear up wattles. Where Frank's dad had been down there with a mattock, cutting them, all the time the goats were nibbling away we could see that there was improvement in the country. Money being very short as it was at

282

the time, I think I had eighteen goatlings. I saw an ad in *The Land* for somebody wanting to buy them, and I said to Frank, 'I'm going to answer that ad and if I can get eighty dollars each for them, whacko—that will pay the petrol bill and another bill and another bill'. And he said, 'Well, if you don't soon keep a mob of goats down there that will keep the wattles under control I'll buy you a mattock and you can go and cut them yourself'. So I thought, 'Well, short of giving up my six hours' sleep a night, I don't know when I'd have time to swing the mattock', so I went and bought a mob of angora goats—again just at the right time—and the market took off there.

So we were very involved for many, many years, in both the mohair industry and the dairy goat industry, and fortunately I must say they managed to pay off our farm. Had it not been for that I don't know ... probably like a lot of others, we wouldn't have survived. Frank had a job managing another property, and I managed the farm through the week and he came home and, with the children, we all did the drenching and those sorts of jobs weekends, and we survived very well.

Goats were fairly new as a farm animal then. Where did you get the information from?

There was no information. It was all learning the hard way, and we did a lot of research work with Glenfield Research Station, a lot with the local vets. Again, there was my inquisitive nature. If anything ever went wrong, I wanted to know why it went wrong. If an animal died, well, we went about finding out what was wrong and why it died. And, in fact, one disease was identified as a result of our curiosity in conjunction with Glenfield.

When were you producing goats' milk?

We began about 1968 to 1970 and I was in them until about ten years ago when I had Ross River fever and glandular fever at the same time, and that laid me out just a little. I'd also realised that there was a big potential for a dairy goat industry in Australia, but the whole thing was very fragmented. You had to be your own producer, your manufacturer, your marketer. I felt that I'd learnt a little bit about it in my experience with marketing through the shop. I felt also that if there was somebody who understood the industry, that person could be the liaison between the producers and the markets, and maybe we could tie the whole thing together and make an industry out of it.

Most goats' milk was produced, and probably is still, in the metropolitan area, at very high cost for feed and whatnot. We could run them much more economically out on our country where we could turn the dry goats out and have them cutting Frank's suckers so the goats actually worked for us.

There were no government regulations for goats' milk and I set up my scheme based on quality—it really had to be a good product. But we just could not convince the government authorities to bring in some regulations and standards so there was always a low quality product getting into the market which created that 'yuk, goats' milk' image that was a bit hard to overcome. After about two years I decided it was pretty hard work without any support or back-up from any of the authorities and perhaps I had better things in life to do than to be driving a truck from Molong to Dubbo to Mudgee to Sydney and back twice a week at night when I should have been sleeping.

Attiki at Marrickville were a company who were prepared

to pasteurise it and market it for us as pasteurised goats' milk. They still manufacture quite a lot of yoghurt. There was a big potential to spray-dry it and export it into the eastern countries. But, again, you had to get enough capital together to be able to do that, and sufficient producers and get it from here to there and how come *I* was driving the truck around?

I tried to establish it but you'd get in touch with a carrier and he'd say, 'Well, how much have you got?' and I'd say, 'One hundred litres this week, but we're hoping to build it up to a thousand litres', and he'd say, 'Well, when you've got a thousand litres, let us know'. You have to crawl before you can walk, and that was why I bought the truck and thought, if I can establish the business based around the milk trade, then we have something viable to sell and convince to somebody else that it's a goer.

What about meat?

That was the other point that's been a big part of the demise of the goat industry as such. There were never any markets established for the culls, and if you've got cull sheep or cattle you can bring them into the saleyards and you can get rid of them. But goats were very much a supply and demand situation, and when we met saturation point there was nowhere for the meat to go. We did some work with the abattoir at Forbes. Again, they didn't understand that goats are not sheep so they were bringing them in from out west and just turning them out into holding paddocks and throwing them a few bales of hay. But goats that have never seen hay don't know what to do with it, so the animals they were slaughtering were in very poor condition when they came to slaughter and the markets just didn't hold.

Have things changed now?

Not a lot, I don't think. It certainly hasn't gone the way
the potential was there for it to go. It could have been, in
my opinion, a very big export earner for Australia. Like so
many things in rural areas, it is very much knowing what
you are doing, and quite often in the goat industry we saw
people who were going to do wonderful things, but didn't
understand what they were doing and because of that the
whole thing failed.

You decided to get rid of the goats?

Because of my health at that time I certainly wasn't up to
working the hours that I was working, and our children
were all growing and getting ready to leave home.

This was when you had Ross River fever and glandular fever?

Yes—in 1985 that combination rolled me over fairly well.
I still get what I believe are recurring bouts of it. I had four
and a half weeks in Windsor Hospital, where I think everybody but me thought I was going to die, and I didn't particularly care, I was so ill. It gave me the effects of having
heart attacks—I was having massive heart arhythmias—and
I completely lost my memory.

To sit and have a conversation was nigh-on impossible
because I couldn't remember the last sentence I'd spoken. I
still have some problems with the recall button, remember-
ing things from back there. Most of my children's growing
up I don't remember until they say, 'Mum, do you remember doing so and so?' Then, yes, I do'. The Ross River fever
affects your joints and gives you arthritic pain and the glandular fever obviously affected my brain and my muscles, so
I wasn't much good for quite a while.

I'm not sure you ever really get over it. I certainly had it on a pretty regular basis for two years, and then recurring at intervals right up to this day.

Did you go back to working on the farm?

Yes, I did. Again, we had another fortunate/unfortunate set of circumstances where we had a bushfire that came through. We lost most of our grazing land—our sheepyards, our cattleyards—we were still left with our house, and we were all intact and safe so we believed that we had enough there to start over again. I took a job for about six months, driving another smallgoods truck around the area, hoping to earn some money to put back in to rebuilding what we had lost, and that was just at the time when wool was pretty good. I earned my income from driving my truck and gave it and about $2000 more away in tax, so I thought, well, this is not really the way to go. I went home and, again from watching Dad as a handyman around the place, picked up the welder and started rebuilding the yards. I became the repairs and maintenance person around the place.

These were metal cattleyards?

Yes. Frank put the posts in, collectively we did, and I welded up the gates and the agreement is if I make them you swing them. So we're not a bad partnership really.

I guess you don't think of bushfires affecting country people.

If you've ever lived on a country property you certainly would think about it affecting you. Our property is in the middle of about 3500 acres of State Forest and I guess from the day I first went there fire was my worst fear. Over all the years we worked out the strategies as to how we would cope if it did occur, and the day we saw the smoke I was certainly not afraid. I thought I knew what I had to do, and again it becomes a matter of survival. All of my calculated assessments didn't work out the way we planned, but we were pretty lucky. We still had our house, and we didn't lose any animals that day. There were so many people who came around to help. The bush spirit certainly took over. We had had another fire only a fortnight before that burnt out about 4000 acres to the north of our property. This one started at the south, it was burning east and the wind changed a full ninety degrees and brought it across us. And certainly we lost most of our property, but had the wind not changed, probably Molong, Orange would have never held it with the wind that was going that day.

So your pasture gets burnt and your buildings get burnt. What do you do with your animals?

Goodness, I don't know. You just pick up and you start again, I guess. What do you do? It's your home and it's your livelihood and we were very thankful for what we had left. And with that you start again.

Tell me about how you got involved with road safety.

Well, in the country we depend on our transport for our commodities in, for our raw products back out to the sea-board, and in the good old days we had a rail system that functioned fairly well for freight and for passengers. That has become pretty much non-existent right throughout all of inland New South Wales that I'm aware of. I guess most of us sat back and said, 'well, that's the way it is to happen'. In the interim, I guess, once I got most of the farm back together I was in limbo where I was sitting back creating a nice garden and doing some of the nice things that women on the land are able to do.

Unfortunately our youngest son was involved in a pretty horrific road accident that took the lives of two of his friends, and he was quite adamant that we had to do something about getting some of the heavy freight off the roads, back onto rail. And I offered to help, and I guess that's where Topsy's picked me up and taken me. I certainly am very dedicated to the task that I've been doing for almost the last three years.

Neil was in a car that followed a semi-trailer for about five kilometres to an overtaking lane. They pulled out to overtake and another vehicle, a truck coming the other way, crossed the double lines and hit their vehicle. As I mentioned, Neil said that he wanted to see something done about it, that he didn't want to see his friends written off as statistics. He was fortunate. The space he got out of was about eight inches wide and he had a broken big toe on his left foot. He was conscious throughout the whole thing— watched the lights go out, rescued the girl from the back, and I guess I'm a bit biased but I'm pretty proud of him in his actions then and ever since.

He went on ABC radio and told his story as to what had happened and what he would like to see done about it, and mentioned that his mum had a bit of spare time and was going to help. My phone truly hasn't stopped ringing for the last three years with people who've been in a similar situation and who've tried to do something.

I guess everything we have done in forming the Highway Safety Action Group has been the reverse to the way most action groups go about it. I believe that if we were going to get politicians to listen we had to have faces of people who vote. I didn't think that petitions did any good. I felt that they became fodder for the round filing cabinet.

We called a public meeting in Orange and we had almost

400 people in the middle of winter, which was a very strong commitment at the time, and went about setting achievable goals. We've not asked for anything that was over the top and unattainable. I tried to research fairly well and make sure what I'm asking for is possible, and then go to the most senior person in whichever department it is, look them in the eye and ask them, 'Why can't you do it?'.

Road accidents touch lots of people throughout this nation and so many country road accidents tend to involve a lot of fatalities in one accident. Do you think that it touches country people perhaps more than people in the city?

I wouldn't say more than it does with people in the city, but because we're smaller communities and we tend to all know one another and families are related, it certainly comes much closer to home. I would have been no different to anyone else prior to Neil's involvement. I'd have probably said, 'Oh yes, it's just another statistic'. But you do not realise how many people one accident affects. An example I can give is that probably about eighteen months after Neil's accident I was at the Manildra Show and a woman whom I didn't know came and said to me, 'How's Neil?' And I said, 'Oh, basically, he's pretty good'. And she said, 'My daughter still has nightmares about that accident'. I thought, how could that be? I could understand Neil having it for the rest of his life, but this lass was just a schoolfriend of the girl who was killed in the accident. But you do not realise how many people are affected by one single accident until you get where I've been for the last three years.

So what do you want done to change things, to make things safer?

We believe the three main factors in road safety are the road, the vehicle and the driver. The first section of road we set out to do something about was the Mount Lambie section between Bathurst and Lithgow. I think there's only about two kilometres of the eight kilometres that are not now fixed, and it's all coming to be finished soon. Driver education is a big problem—people becoming impatient. Driver fatigue is a big problem—because of the distances we have to travel. We just get in the car and go because you've got to get there. I've certainly done that. I used to drive my truck at night because you can't work with people who are asleep in the night-time, but you can work through the day. And unfortunately that's what happens, and driver fatigue is a big factor in road safety.

We are not an anti-truck lobby; we have asked for a co-ordinated transport system, making use of rail and road for the commodities that are best suited. We would like to see wheat, wool, coal and the heavy commodities that are suited to rail back onto rail. But you can't expect the ice cream to be delivered to the supermarket in a train; that's meant to come on a truck. So, horses for courses are what we're asking for—in a safe manner, with reasonable driving hours so that drivers aren't forced by bigger companies to drive beyond their human limitations. That's what I've spent the last three years of my life trying to do, get out there and do something about it. I'm very heavily involved now on many RTA consultative committees and with the NRMA—I do a lot of work with them and enjoy it.

At the moment I'm very involved with the alternative compliance scheme as they're calling it, which is self-regulation of the heavy vehicle industry. Personally, I don't believe that can work, and I have told everybody, right to the head of the RTA, why I don't think it can work.

Self-regulation won't work?

No, I don't believe it can work. How can it in any industry with a history like that of the road transport industry? With the opportunity to be able to do whatever you want to do, whenever you want to do it. I mean, my truck was rarely ever in roadworthy condition, and, as I say, I drove when I shouldn't have been driving. Back in the days of Dad's shop, when rail had the monopoly, you had to pay road tax on any commodity that should have been carted by rail, and groceries fitted into that category. Dad's groceries used to come up in a furniture van with two wardrobes behind them that went up and down the highway every night, because furniture wasn't taxable. So what makes it any different today? If they eliminate most of the regulations that are there and say, 'Righto, you fellows, go out and be your own master, write your own rules, and enforce them' and if there's no teeth there to bite, why aren't we going to put another three ton on top, or do what we want to do? I think there's a big danger there for the industry, and for the community, and it's strange how many of the transport industry agree with me.

Are these committees that you're part of regional committees?

No, most are state committees. I spend a lot of my time in Sydney—backwards and forwards on a plane.

Not driving a car at night?

No, not driving a car at night. I have cut back now to about twelve hours a day doing what I do, but I don't have time to be able to drive up and down the highway. Again, I'm thankful to the authorities—the departments who have invited me. They provide me with an airfare to get down there to participate in their committees, which is great.

Twelve hours a day's rather a lot. Can you describe what you do in those twelve hours?

Certainly. When I started with the action group it would have been eighteen hours a day average, I would think, on a very regular basis. You should come out home, really, for a day because it's nice to be here without my telephone ringing quite so much. My phone quite often starts ringing at six-thirty, seven in the morning. I spend many hours on the phone speaking with people and the network that we've put together. That's the only way that I can do what I do—I have to know what's going on out there. As I've become a community representative I need feedback from the community. If we get an issue running and I write a press release and put it out, I have all of you nice people with microphones doing interviews with me, or telephone interviews. And we've got such a wide coverage—from right up the north coast, Wagga, out to Bourke, metropolitan. If our issue is good enough we get very good coverage. That can be very time-consuming.

So what sort of information are you looking for?

We've been very involved with school bus safety and the light warning systems that are on school buses, for example. Children standing long distances on school buses. It's bad enough in the metropolitan area where a child gets on a bus and rides for ten minutes standing up, but in one instance—from Molong to Orange—there were about eighty children, with thirty of them standing for half an hour, driving down the highway at eighty kilometres an hour. We see them as being little missiles—if something goes wrong, they go through the windscreen. We highlighted that and managed to get another bus on the route. The list just goes on.

I have a lot of road transport operators' wives who ring

me up and say, 'My husband's driving a truck—he does a trip, eleven hours, and gets back and the boss says, 'Well, jump in and go. Take this somewhere else'. He says, 'But I've done my eleven hours', and the reply is, 'Mate, if you don't want to do it, there's ten other fellows out there that do'. And if he has a wife and four children and a mortgage he has no option other than to do that. If he stands up and says something about it he hasn't got a job.

Because I'm unemployed, or unemployable, or whatever, we're able to represent those sorts of people.

So you go and see the transport companies and talk to them about unsafe practices, is that your role?

No, I've never gone directly to a road transport company, but certainly I'm the mediator between the industry, and well, the RTA, for example.

Are you documenting all this stuff and using a computer?

My word, yes, I'm beginning to use a computer. Provided my tutor is good enough we'll eventually get there, I think. The NRMA kindly lent us one—a smaller one—about two years ago, that we've outgrown. I've just got used to that and now I'm learning all over again. Being practical as I am, it's all in piles of paper at home too, because I don't have much confidence in my computer skills.

As far as the rail transport is concerned, are you moving the government in any way towards reintroducing that?

Back in October 1992 we identified that fuel transport had been coming into Orange and Bathurst up until May of that year, and then just stopped. And we went out and said, 'Why has it just stopped?' We started counting petrol tankers coming up and down the highway and it took us almost twelve months to convince them that we were right. My example there was a petrol tanker coming over the Blue Mountains. If I were to ask you to stand up against a wall while I fired a missile at you at a hundred kilometres an hour, and hoped it misses by a metre, you'd look at me and say 'no, no'. But in reality that's what happens on some of those narrow corners down through the mountains, and we've said it must be much safer to bring it by rail. We were given some pretty ridiculous reasons why it couldn't be— that the volumes were too small and it was too close to the metropolitan area, the distances weren't long enough. We said, 'But, hang on, you cart it through Orange and Bathurst to Dubbo by rail—why can't you just put the small amount on the back of the train and drop it off as you go by?' And they said that, being a woman, I didn't understand the braking system on trains these days, that if you stop and brake the train it takes forty-five minutes to realign the braking system and time is money and then they'd even-tually lose the Dubbo market. So with some of my contacts we went out and did a bit of a crash course on braking systems, and we discovered that that isn't really the case. We've managed to get I think 500 tankers per annum of Shell back into Orange and Bathurst, so I think we've done fairly well there too.

Are there other organisations like yours in other regions around the state, or around the country?

We established here in Orange, and we are incorporated now as the Highway Safety Action Group of New South Wales. Our membership covers a wide area of New South Wales. We have subcommittees in Lithgow, Bathurst, Blue Mountains, Parkes and Dubbo. Bathurst is our only really active subcommittee. We find it a bit difficult tying all of those in together and the workload comes back basically to me to coordinate it all. So now we're seeing the roles of subcommittees as being not as essential as we first thought. We think it's perhaps better for other groups with a specific issue in an area to set up their own committee as they did with the Parkes/Wellington road. They formed their own action group, but we certainly work in together. That way they can go off doing their own thing, and we just back them up and support them. So it's very much a community network organisation.

Do you see it as the beginning of a growing movement?

Yes. I think it certainly has the potential to be that. My aim initially, I guess, was to convince people that if you believed in something strongly enough you had a right to stand up and be counted. All too often particularly rural people sat back and said, 'Well, look, that's why we pay the politicians—what good will it do me, seeing I am only one person?'. But you get all of those one persons becoming a group of people with a strong voice.

The authorities say they appreciate the input that we have, because they're based in the metropolitan area so how can they know what is going on out here unless we go and tell them. I believe if you go about telling them in the right way, rather than going in and demanding, if you identify your problem, show them what it is and say what you suggest as a solution to that problem, they are all pretty keen to listen.

What about your son, Neil? What does he feel about it all?

Not too many months into the project he came to me one night after a meeting and stood on a stage and put his arms around me and said, 'Mum, if it all fell through tomorrow,

I'm satisfied'. He said, 'Someone has listened. I know no-one could have done more than you have and it hasn't all been for nothing'. So I guess from that point onwards my hours reduced from eighteen back to twelve. I didn't feel the same pressure on me to perform. I guess I'm on a round-about I can't get off, where so many people depend on me, who've tried to do what we've achieved and have been unsuccessful, having lost someone in a road accident. I've still got my son. I'm very fortunate. Many people don't. And I think everything that I've achieved is a bonus to society, and I get a lot of pleasure from that.

I have a massive network behind me. Certainly it was pretty much a one-man band as far as the workload was concerned initially, but I'm getting a wonderful support group around me at the moment, with expertise in many areas. I'm quite happy to continue for as long as I can and while the need is there for it, and I'm finding now that people are saying, 'Well, look, we can do the minutes and we can do the posting for you', and somebody else picks it up from here and I think it's that other people want to become involved too. I guess I'm always going to be the one that does the running around, because I'm unemployed. As long as Frank can continue to maintain me and I'm happy doing it and he's happy for me to do it we'll certainly con-tinue. I don't have a lot of time for anything else, but I've made some very good friends and some wonderfully loyal friends out of what I've been involved in.

We had a Christmas party each year, and we decided at the last Christmas party we should do this more often, so twelve of us are going off to a concert in a few weeks' time. I guess I have a pretty warped sense of humour that keeps me going—if I didn't I'd probably have gone round the twist long ago.

Is there anything you'd really like to do, but haven't had time for?

My roses are still surviving, but everything else in the garden has pretty much gone by the board, and no, I really don't know where I'm going from here. I have three rather delightful little grand-daughters that I probably don't spend as much time with as a lot of grandmas would. I think that probably the whole of my life has been a set of circumstances that I've fitted into.

As I mentioned earlier, every job I've had I could have made a career from had I not had five other careers going concurrently. And I think probably the rest of my life will be much the same. I think I'm on a path somewhere—I'm not just sure where, but when the next fork comes in the road I guess we'll branch off and go down there. I don't think I can continue to do what I'm doing for the rest of my life. I'm not sure I want to continue with it, but for the time being I'm enjoying what I'm doing. I get great pleasure out of helping people, and while ever that's there and there's a need for it I hope I'll be strong enough to do so.

BARBARA MARKS

Barbara Marks was in Brisbane when I met her. She had been fulfilling some of the demands of being named Queensland Rural Woman of the Year. Like many other winners, she found the Award attracted invitations to speak at many rural conferences and functions. Barbara's home is at Charleville where she runs sheep with her youngest son Neil. When her husband died she found the local banks more interested in selling the property than assisting her to manage on her own, but ten years on she has reduced the debt by half and the enterprise is progressing well.

My forebears were all farming people. My own family had a dairy farm outside Dalby when I was growing up, and then we lost our home to fire just at the beginning of the Second World War when rationing was coming in, so my father moved then to Tara to manage a property. When I finished at boarding school I went governessing, and then I had a job in a country store in Charleville doing the book-keeping and so forth until I married.

I met my husband at boarding school. It was a schooldays romance and it just went on from there. His family had been in the Charleville area for generations. His great-grandfather migrated from Ireland. He had bullock teams and followed the railway line up through New South Wales to Bourke, then crossed into Queensland and carted wool for many, many years from all the big properties until he was killed at the age of forty-five when he fell off the wagon, I believe, in a drunken state!

He had five daughters and one son and the one son was my husband's grandfather. He inherited the wagon and the bullock teams and eventually was able to buy a small property west of Charleville. He sold that and bought a bigger one in our area, and afterwards was able to buy two more properties. We're still on one of the properties today.

So you, as a young married woman, moved into a family dynasty of properties and farmers.

It didn't seem to be a dynasty in those days because I lived in a galvanised iron cottage of two rooms (laughs) for five years until my husband and I moved over onto an additional area of 11 000 acres, where we lived in another very, very small cottage that increased to three rooms and a verandah. We were there for probably about ten years or more until the 'sixties drought really crippled everyone.

My oldest daughter was at boarding school, my next daughter in Year 8 ready to go to high school, the other one ready to go into Grade 5, a son ready to go into Grade 3—I was teaching them all by correspondence—and a baby.

What were we going to do? We had no money, we couldn't afford to send a second one to boarding school—the first one had to come home—so I moved into Charleville and we rented a house in there so the children could go to high school. That gave me a respite from teaching for a number of years until we were granted an additional area to the family place, which is 'Ambathala' where I live now. When we moved back out there, I had Neil, my second son, in Grade 6 and Elizabeth just starting in Grade 1. By that time School of the Air was going and they were able to go onto that. Because we were in drought again and my in-laws were getting along in years, my husband had to go and work away from home every week and he'd come home at the weekends and do the station work. Neil, at twelve, was doing a man's work. I took him through to Year 10 in correspondence and Elizabeth was fortunate enough to come to Brisbane and have an education at the Brisbane Girls' Grammar School when things looked up in the 'eighties.

Did you have any time for farm work as well?

I did. The properties were about twenty-five miles apart and where we were we had no shearing shed, so the sheep had to be driven back the twenty-five miles from our place to the main homestead for shearing, and that was a two-day trip. The children and I used to go on that droving trip every time it happened and then when the sheep had to come back, and in drought time, we spent lots of time burning down mulga trees and gidgee trees to feed the sheep. After school in the afternoons we'd go out into the paddock where my husband was cutting scrub and we'd light up the trees that had hollows in them and go round the waters and see that there were no sheep bogged; things like that.

So you fitted the farming and the teaching into your life.

We did, yes. The children used to get the cows in in the evening—we milked cows in those days—and one of them would milk the cows in the morning. They had ponies and did a lot of riding. We did lots of show riding and there were always horses to feed and animals to feed; we all had pigs and ducks and chooks (laughs), all that sort of thing, and everyone had a job. I did have a gas stove, but we had no electricity and there was always kindling to bring in to light the fire in the morning: that was usually the youngest one's job. We'd have a roster above the sink and it was someone's turn to wash up and the other's to dry, I'd be hearing dictation while I was making a cake.

How difficult was it to get them to pay attention to school work when there was so much activity going on?

It wasn't difficult because right from the start I decided that school hours were school hours and they started right on school hours. We carried that right through unless we had to go to town for a day and then we'd work late into the evenings or very early in the mornings to get ahead, which people still do today. It just didn't seem to be difficult. My oldest daughter, Denise, was quite capable of doing most of her work on her own, and as they got older the older ones, too, were able to continue. Once they could read fluently they were able to do most of their work by themselves and just come to me for some help.

Sometimes they were very reluctant students if they were playing on the bank of the dam! My second daughter always tells the story of how she got into serious trouble one day because they weren't back in school on time and, as she was the oldest, she was blamed by Mum for leading the others astray. But they weren't really reluctant. I was a bit of a hard taskmaster, I think, looking back now (laughs) and I expected a lot from them—probably too much.

What do you think about their education looking back now?

They've all taken their places in their various fields and have done well, and I can only think it was good. When Denise went to boarding school—she was my first to go away to school in Year 7—the headmistress said to me, 'You've done a good job with Denise', so I felt, well, okay, it's not too bad after all.

Tell me about the properties themselves.

The home block, where my son is, is only 13 000 acres and the property that we moved to after I first married was an additional area of 11 000 acres. It meant we had 24 000 acres which, in today's terms, is just not a living area at all, so in the 'sixties when the drought was so dreadful and sheep were worth nothing, people were crying out for more land. The Ambathala run was 200 000 acres. Its 100-year lease had run out and the Lands Department was just giving them a year's lease, so they decided that they would resume that 200 000 acres and divide it up between the needy small landholders in the area. Consequently, when we were granted 26 000 acres of Ambathala with a homestead and a shearing shed—which was very, very fortunate, although we had to pay quite a bit more for it—we had to return to the Crown the original 11 000 acres because we would have had three parcels of land with a distance between them.

After the original breaking up of Ambathala they were keeping a portion that they were considering making into a sanctuary. It's a lake, just a seasonal lake, but after a couple of years they decided not to go ahead with that and we were able to add that to our lease, so that gave us 37 000 acres of Ambathala and 13 000 of the original home property. They say today that you have to be able to run 10 000 sheep to be viable but we can't possibly do that, so we just battle on as best we can (laughs).

It's predominantly red mulga country but on the little home property we have a double frontage to the Langlo River which goes through it, and where I am on Ambathala we have a double frontage to Ambathala Creek, and the lake that's known as Lake Dart now is in a really good block of semi black soil country. So we're fortunate that we've got two sorts of watersheds that give us good country.

Ambathala Creek is permanent water. The Langlo River isn't permanent but it runs very quickly when there's rain up the top, and we have good dams and a bore. In '86 we had a dreadful water drought and we had every dam on the place dry, and the waterhole behind my house in Ambathala Creek was dry for the first time in forty years. So we had to borrow money from the Agricultual Bank and enlarge all the dams on the home property and put down a bore, and since then we've had no water problems at all.

When, as a young married woman, you first moved into that property, your husband's family was still there. Tell me about the number of people involved in running it then.

There was my father-in-law, mother-in-law and an invalid daughter, my husband and I, and by the time we moved from there we had five children. They also employed somebody permanently. That was on 24 000 acres.

How do you make up for that kind of loss of labour now when there are just one or two people running things that size?

I'm doing work that I wouldn't have done in those days.

For instance, I've had to get a woolclassing licence and I do all the woolclassing, and my son does about six or seven jobs on the place where before he possibly wouldn't have. It's usually a daylight to dark thing: you just get up at daylight in the morning and go, and when you come home at night it's probably seven o'clock in summertime. You just work to the sun and if there's work to be done at weekends it's done; you don't have Saturday and Sunday off, sitting on the verandah. Lots of people think the squattocracy does sit and watch their wool grow (laughs).

We've had wonderful neighbourly support: that's got a lot of us through. If I'm mustering for shearing my neighbours, Bob and Geoff, will ring up and say, 'If you need a hand we're available', so Neil often asks them and then, when they're doing the same, we go and help them. It's the same in the shearing shed: Bob has come and helped me on the wool table and I've done the same for him on three or four occasions when shearing's on. At one time I was able to go and do the cooking for them for shearing. I'd go over in the afternoons and get the shearers' tea ready and wash up and then go home again; it's about twenty-five miles from my place to theirs. That was one time when things were really bad and we were all trying to save as much as we could.

I'd say it's lots of neighbourly help, really. Also, the difference is that today we're not using horses to muster; everybody uses motorbikes and we used an ultra-lite aircraft a lot for mustering. That's cut our mustering time from probably four weeks to two days if we use an ultra-lite but it's pretty difficult these days to get somebody with the wool prices low. When wool prices were good we were able to get the ultra-lite chap to fly down from Longreach and we didn't take much notice of the ferrying costs. But today we can't possibly afford to have him fly down: I think it costs about $600 just to get him there before he starts mustering. So we've had to do all this last shearing on motorbike and it takes a lot longer when you haven't got somebody up in the air telling you where the sheep are.

You have radio connection between the bike and the aircraft?

Yes, that's an innovation we've got; we never go anywhere today without hand-held radios. In the first instance it was rather amusing when my son decided that we had to do that. He strapped a car battery on the back of his motorbike and hooked up a two-way—a big thing—and that worked for a while until he had a buster and the battery fell off. But today we've just got the little hand-helds and they are wonderful because he can call me up at the base at home and say, 'Mum, can you come out to the corner of home paddock? I've got a sheep that won't travel', and I go out and pick it up in the ute. It's just so much better for us all.

Are you involved in the mustering on motorbikes?

Not so much. I'm not on the bike myself. Sometimes I'm trailing behind the sheep on a bike when they're going down to the shed, but I've got a little Suzuki ute that'll go anywhere and I'm usually just round the mob with that or down the fences somewhere, just tailing along behind the mob in the ute. If there's a sheep that won't travel it just gets put into the ambulance, as we call it, (laughs) and gets taken into the shed that way.

Then there's always the drafting of the different mobs when we get them into the shearing shed. Prior to that we always water the yard so there's no dust and that's usually my job: I go down and start the pump and fill the tanks and spend a whole morning watering the sheepyard so there's no dust when the sheep come in. When we do the drafting, it's my job to push them up into the drafting race.

*You now own your own property, but has it always been like that?
What happened when you got married—were you given a slice of
the action?*

When I first married, my husband worked for his father
for a wage and that's how it was nearly right up to my
father-in-law's death. He was a very conservative man who
didn't want to take any risks and he was also a bit selfish,
and I think there was a bit of rivalry between them. My
husband always had innovative ideas and it was always a
terrible battle for him to get anything done. It was only
when we got the additional area of Ambathala that he was
made a partner but my father-in-law died soon after that.

You weren't made a partner with him?

Oh, no. It was only from his will that I inherited a quarter
of his half and my two sons an eighth each of his share. My
mother-in-law was still the predominant partner until she
died and she left her share to be divided between my six
children, so now it's a complete family partnership (laughs).

My husband died of a heart attack in 1984 when he was
fifty-four years of age. His mother was still alive at that time.
It was unexpected although he had had to work hard all his
life and was a pretty hard player—he burnt the candles at
both ends. Looking back now we probably should have seen
signs. I happened to be in Gladstone with my daughter. He
always spoke to Neil on the phone each night and Neil
couldn't get him one night so he went over and found him
dead beside his bed, which was a shock to Neil because he
was just twenty at the time. It was traumatic for us all.

How did you gather it all together and make it work, because the temptation must have been maybe to leave it?

At the time the temptation was great because we were in drought and we had a little bit of a family conflict, because my oldest son had the expectation that he would come home; that I would go to town and live and he would come home and manage the place. But he'd been working in Charleville for a friend of his who owned a motorbike shop and unfortunately this friend had leukaemia, and I said, 'Well, no, I'm not going to town to live. I just want to stay here for a while and think things out and see what we can do'. So Neil and Malcolm and I had to approach banks.

Malcolm was interested in buying the friend's business because he'd worked in it and it meant we had to mortgage the place for him to do that, but the manager of the bank we'd banked with for years and years and years wouldn't entertain the idea, and that was rather an upsetting thing for Malcolm and for us. The fellow who owned the shop went into remission and that was good, Malcolm was still working for him, but within eighteen months he had a relapse. We all tried again but, no, this manager wouldn't entertain the idea, so Malcolm went to a different bank and was able to borrow the money to buy the business. The property just backed him during that time and fortunately it was coming into the years of good wool prices and he did really well. He's still got a good business now and has opened another one in Blackall.

But that was the conflict that I had with the bank manager, because he was quite determined we should sell.

So you had to front up with your two sons to have any currency with him at all?

Yes. It was simply because it was Malcolm who wanted to borrow the money. At that time I'd never had to go and see a bank manager in my life and I was in fear and trembling; I had not ever had to do business with a male in a place of prominence before.

We needed to get the waters done we approached him for the money and he said, 'No, you can't have it'. We'd already got tractors on and the dams were half cleaned out: how were we going to pay this fellow? Fortunately, the Agricultural Bank at that time were giving drought loans and so we got the manager from the AG Bank to come out and they gave us the money to do all the water business.

But then this fellow at the other bank kept ringing me up and saying, 'Have you put the property on the market?'—this was on the old party line—and I said, 'No, I haven't', and he said, 'Well, the bank won't give you a loan; you'll have to sell'. I was really upset and I went to town to see him. We had a family conference: I think $40 000 was the property debt at the time and Malcolm's mortage was $90 000 so I suppose it looked a pretty dicey situation, but we decided that if you were buying a house in the city you'd borrow all that money and that wouldn't be very difficult. We thought, well, there seems to be no reason why we can't get this loan, so I went and confronted the bank manager. He said, 'Barbara, have you put the property on the market?', and I said, 'No, and what's more I don't intend to, and if you won't help us we'll find someone who will'. I just jumped out and slammed the door of his office and burst into tears (laughs). All my kids were waiting for me and they said, 'Oh, don't let it beat you, Mum'.

I'd had a friend whose husband had died and she'd told me years before that she had found that a neighbour badly wanted her property and the bank manager started to put the screws on her, and I thought, I wonder is that happening to me? So I decided that with the kids' help I'd come down here to the bank in Brisbane to the people at the top. When I got into the office this very nice man with all these papers in front of him said, 'Mrs Marks, we can't possibly lend you $90 000', and I said, 'I don't want $90 000; all we want is $30 000'. He said, 'Oh, well, I've got here that you want to borrow $90 000', and I said, 'All we need is $30 000', so he said, 'I'll ring Charleville immediately'. That made us feel better, but the manager in question in Charleville put all the obstacles he possibly could in front of us and that consequently made us change banks.

In those first years what did you do to turn those big debts around.

We went out of breeding sheep because we'd had so many years where we weren't marking many lambs and the ewes were the first ones to go down in a drought. So we gave up breeding and just bought in wethers. We had a good base of wethers that had been bred on the place but then we bought good mobs of sheep and we'd sell off after shearing as they got a bit older. At the time wool was really good and we were able to do quite a lot of fencing—we just bulldozed out old fences that had been there for years and put up all new boundary and internal fencing—and did a little bit of improving to the old homestead where my son was and put on the rural power that came through.

I'm in one shire—the Quilpie Shire—and Neil is in the Murweh Shire. The Quilpie Shire's scheme came on and it was going to cost me $41 000 to have my electricity put on, but within a couple of months of half making the decision that, yes, we would go ahead with it because we were able to pay that off at $4000 something odd a year for so many years, the Murweh Shire decided that they would come on track with their power and that was going to cost $27 000.

Neil had two little children at the time and I was just there on my own, so I thought, well, it's better if he has his electricity than me having mine and at half the cost, thank goodness, so I'm still cranking up an engine at night (laughs). But the electricity's made a great difference to the running of the place where Neil is and he's able to have welders and all sorts of things. He does lots and lots of work; we never have to pay anybody to do mechanical work, he does all that. That's another thing: before, everything went into town or somebody came out to do the repairs but he does everything himself.

At home I've still only got my diesel motor that I crank up and I've got a little Honda motor that I put on at night and that'll give me four hours of watching television (laughs).

What about fridges and freezers and things like that?

I've got a gas fridge, a gas freezer and a gas stove and they're very efficient. It's just the inconvenience of having to go and start a motor and put diesel in a motor and petrol in a motor (laughs). But I'm used to it.

Did you have to work out a whole plan of action to cover the debt and get the farm up to scratch?

Yes, we've got a long range plan of how things are going to go, but it's just up to the vagaries of the weather whether that's going to come off or whether it's not. But you always keep that vision ahead of you. I've been trying to ease Neil into the decision-making position because I'm not going to be there all the time, but he still likes to defer to me. When we go to buy sheep sometimes he'll go on his own but sometimes he takes me with him because I'm the one who sees the wool on the wool table and I can look at the sheep and say whether that line's going to suit us or not. But I'm very pleased to say that he's more or less just taking over the whole thing because, let's face it, I'm not going to be there for ever and ever.

In those first few years after your husband died what sort of things did you have to do that you weren't doing before?

I had to make sure that I was able to keep track of all the money. Like most bush people the bookkeeping was done with a shoebox, and the cheque butts were thrown into the shoebox and went to the accountant every year. I set up a cashbook and religiously keep that so we can see how much money we've got left and how we're going to spend it, whether we can afford it or whether we can't, whereas before things were very haphazard. If you wanted something, well, you got it done and perhaps went into overdraft or mainly had an overdraft, and that's how people got into trouble, I think, because of not keeping a really good check on finances and so forth. That's where my background of bookkeeping helped me, I suppose, because I was able to set up the cashbook and know what I was doing about it. I've been able to get my younger daughter to do the same; she can take over from me if I'm not there and do those sorts of things, too.

I'm the one who goes to the accountant and gets advice from him, and also I'm the one who goes to all the agricultural meetings, the graziers' meetings and so forth. Neil's usually too busy doing something. I'm on the executive of the Warrego Graziers and the secretary of our local branch of the Langlo Graziers and I go there to get all the latest information and know what we can do and what we can't do, especially with the drought loans and so forth. There's so much tied up with filling in forms and things like that, and that's my job.

You just have to keep up to date with all the new changes in government.

Were you accepted easily on these committees?

For a start I was very, very hesitant, especially on the executive of the Warrego Graziers. I found it very difficult to get up and say things, especially when once I was jumped on by one of the men and I thought, goodness, what happened to me (laughs)!

What did you say?

It was about the toxic dump at Chinchilla. I got up and said that I thought it was a very bad thing for Chinchilla and the district and it could seep into the underground water supply, and this man got up and said, 'Oh, the country's worth nothing; it's all some sort of soil, people have been living there for years and they're worth nothing, why shouldn't there be a toxic dump there?' I didn't have any comeback and fortunately my president got up for me and said, 'People want to live there and it's not fair that they have to put up with that sort of thing'. It was my first experience of having something said to me, but I've found now that over the years I've become very used to being at the meetings and having my say and the men, in particular, treat me as an equal, really, now.

Were there many women in the groups you were with?

No, probably only myself and one other on the executive, but in the last twelve months we have two women chairmen of branches and they're very well respected, so things are looking up.

Tell me about the Queensland Rural Women's Network.

That's all eventuated from this Rural Woman's Award mainly through Jan Darlington and Lisa Palu, who were the instigators of thinking that something should be done to recognise rural women. The Network has grown and they now send out a monthly bulletin and we have tele-conferences. It's given women all over Queensland a voice. We've been given an office in the Queensland Farmers' Federation, which is good, and a person from the Department of Primary Industry to collate all our thinking and so forth and, perhaps, get money for women to be able to have better access to things. Telecom's been really wonderful. They've set up these tele-conferences for us and that wouldn't be a very easy job because we're stretched from right up in the north to way out west. It's very, very good to be able to talk to one another on a tele-conference.

What sort of things are generally discussed?

Before I went overseas last year they were getting geared up for their conference in North Queensland and that was the main topic of conversation—who was going to do what up in Cairns.

Are they mostly farming issues?

Lots to do with women's health and communications. Education is a major one, and just now the Correspondence School—well, it's not that any more, it's the School of Distance Education—has this year released new papers. They hadn't had any school papers re-written for about fourteen years, and so this year's been a big year. Some home tutors have been finding it a bit difficult because there's such a huge content of new work in the papers. The Isolated

Parents Association does cover that, but there are a lot of rural women who probably need to voice things to others and it's a way of doing that through the Rural Women's Network.

And also lots of Health Expos and things they've organised through that Network. One I went to at Meandarra was from the Tara Health Expo, and they had workshops on osteoporosis, farm management—every spectrum—and it was a wonderful day and people got such a lot out of it. Meandarra's a tiny little town out on the line from Dalby.

Do you think that there are more children being educated at home now because of the inability of parents to send their kids to city boarding schools?

I know for a fact that there are a lot more secondary children doing schooling by distance education for the simple fact that there's no money to send them to boarding school. Fees don't go down, they always go up and people's income has gone down so far that they cannot afford it. There aren't many hostels. There used to be a hostel in Charleville but it closed down many, many years ago. There was a convent and the boarding part of the convent's gone, and it just leaves people right out on a limb.

That presumably must put an awful lot of pressure on their mothers who do most of the teaching and who often haven't had an advanced education. They've got to Year 10 or something but they're not actually cut out to be teachers, are they?

It's a difficult situation, Ros, because in one instance you've got to be Mum and then you have to be teacher, and your kids probably hate you at the end of the day—mine used to, I know that! (laughs) They're always telling people how many rulers were broken and goodness knows what!

315

It is terribly, terribly difficult, but probably today most mothers have had the advantage of a secondary education. I'd say the generations that are coming on have probably had secondary education and don't find it so difficult.

There's a great student teacher thing in Queensland where student teachers can come out onto a property and give mothers, say, two or three weeks' break from teaching their kids. It's just part of their education and hopefully those students then will come into the country areas to teach. That's the idea of it because we have a great turnover of teachers in Charleville, in particular, at the high school. The young people from the city come out and some of them love it but some of them hate it and they want to get away as quickly as they can. Mainly they're first year out teachers who are sent out there and consequently the experience isn't behind them. It makes things difficult for the kids when they might get half-way through a year and their teacher is transferred or goes somewhere and somebody else comes, some new young person.

I hadn't thought of the role difficulties of being mother and teacher.

Especially after school when you revert to being Mum and you try to leave everything behind in the schoolroom—or you should do, anyway. My kids were really good but they used to be cranky with me at times because I was a pretty hard taskmaster. But we had lots of fun, as well. They're all quite literate and they think it wasn't too bad now.

Those few years after your husband died must have been extremely tough. What keeps you going?

I don't know what keeps me going. A lot of faith, I think. I wouldn't say I'm a very religious person but I used to do a lot of praying to someone there. Thinking back over my life I did a lot of unnecessary worrying. When we were first married and my husband went out in the paddock and he wasn't home by dark, or by half-past five, my stomach would be churning and I'd be imagining all the dreadful things that might have happened. Then, later on in life I thought, well, all that worrying that I did was for nothing, and worrying doesn't make things any better or any worse (laughs). Perhaps it does make it worse for yourself. I've tried to even myself out and just take each day as it comes. If I'm able to solve a problem, good; if I'm not, well, I'll sleep on it and tomorrow something will pop up and alter things. I think that's probably what has helped me, and I've tried to tell the kids when they get into a great state about something, especially Neil, who is a very livewirey person and likes to get things done at a hundred miles an hour. I'm always telling him that he says he can do things in three days that usually should take four and then he gets all cranky because he hasn't got something done (laughs). I try to instil in them that if they just steady down a bit and think things out things usually turn out for the best.

A very strong commitment to staying on the land comes with all that, too. It's not been a question of selling out and living in the town or somewhere else.

I just felt that I'd seen my father's family, from having substantial holdings of land, because of double death duties having to sell all that land in the 1920s, and I always felt my father was deeply hurt that the family land had to be sold for those reasons. Then, when I thought of my husband's grandfather migrating from Ireland with nothing, obtaining and building up those properties and setting up his family, I thought, well, it's not my job to just walk out. There's a family history here that we need to keep going and just for the sake of those pioneer people who went through so much—really, we've got it easy today compared to what they had—it never entered my head that we would sell. It was just a determination to keep the properties. I've got sons and now they've got sons and, hopefully, one of them will be there for generations to come.

Maybe daughters, even.

Yes, maybe daughters. My youngest daughter is a very very capable person on the land and we could walk out today and she could run the place quite easily. But when you've got one property and six kids someone has to go and do something else, and it usually seems to be the girls who get into businesses or something that has a bit of a feminist role about it. But each one of them would be quite capable of coming and running the place.

I know it's difficult to record your whole life on a short length of tape (laughs) but were there any experiences on that property which are particularly memorable to you?

I think one of the most memorable was the cutting up of Ambathala and of us, out of probably twenty people who were given blocks of land, to be given the homestead block which had a big old home on it and adequate water. That's one of the memorable things.

Also, I suppose, when my children did well at boarding school, got their Senior Certificates and probably got As and so forth, that was a memorable occasion for me, thinking that they had had all their basic education at home. Most people think that children in the bush are perhaps a bit dumb and can't do things, and that's also another plus for me when things like that happen.

What sort of difference has winning the Rural Woman Award made to your life?

It's made me more outgoing; it's made me have to get myself in gear and say, 'Right, you have to go here, not say to myself at home, 'Oh, I might go to a meeting at some-where or other' and then when the day comes I think, oh, no I can't be bothered! I've had to do that. I've met so many wonderful people. So many people whom I went to school with, and friends of my mothers who'd been to school with her, have all got in contact with me and it's opened up such a wide lot of friendship. It's just been a wonderful year.

And then I was fortunate to be given the trip to America. When we were in Melbourne at the Australian judging I was the only one who'd been given a prize, as such, for being a state winner, so I felt very, very privileged to have been able to do that. That was a real eye-opener, too, because we went to lots of little out-of-the-way places in America where they were using sustainable agriculture and I really enjoyed that, it was great.

Any messages for women who are working on the land?

Oh, I don't think I can give anyone any messages because all women work in their own field and all of them are very, very capable women, probably a lot more capable than I am. But I'd like to say to them that if they know that this award is being given now, do not hesitate to either enter themselves or have some members of their family enter them, because there was no way in the world I would have entered myself. It was my daughter who entered me, and it's just been a wonderful experience for me. The ABC has been wonderful in taking this and running with it, and I don't think that they realise just how much we people in the bush depend on the ABC. In my area it gives us all the wool prices and that's vital to me. We don't get any newspapers—the Saturday, Sunday, Monday and Tuesday papers come on Wednesday and I wouldn't ever have time to sit down and read them all—but with the ABC we get the reports right on the day that it's happening, the sale prices for cattle and sheep and so forth, and lots of business is done because of that. They just play a vital part in our listening area, anyway, and also ABC television—we look for the weather (laughs) every night.

And pray for rain!

And pray for rain, yes (laughs).

BESS VICKERS

B ess Vickers manages one of Australia's leading Cashmere
goat studs and has become adept at using a computer to keep
breeding and fleece records. She runs sheep alongside the goats
and firmly believes that the two animals complement each other.
Her extensive knowledge of goat breeding brings visitors from
around Australia and overseas to the New South Wales property.
Bess's husband and partner, Ron, died two years ago but she is
carrying on alone. When I met her she had been saving for a
holiday in outback Australia but had just spent all the money clearing out the almost empty dams.

I was born in Blayney. I've lived on this property nearly
all my life, except for a short period when I was getting
a bit of education and doing a bit of teaching. I always
loved working with animals, and I've always been

interested particularly in livestock breeding. This place is home, and I won't leave until I have to.

So, what does it mean to you—looking out the window there to a place you've lived on ever since you can remember?

It means home. It changes of course. We've got a lovely view of the place from here and it's always changing. At the moment it doesn't look very encouraging, because it's all dried off—a lot of the dams are empty—but we've been there before and we'll get out of it again. This is home.

Like a lot of other places in Australia, you have had a bad time as far as rain is concerned. Are there things that you've had to do this time, or are there precautions that you take, to prevent the worst effects?

You can't control the weather, so what you try to control is your fodder reserves, your water supply. We're very fortunate here in that we have a permanent creek going through the property and we pump out of that. In just the last few weeks there've been fifteen farm dams cleaned out on this place—all my holiday money went into that. And now I'm trying to get a bit of water into them from the creek. There is a water supply pipeline that goes through the property that we have a tapping on. It's a very expensive way to get your water, but still it is an insurance. So we're doing that; we're feeding the young stock on self-feeders to give them a good start—hopefully—then they'll be able to withstand a lack of good feed later on. So far we're not bare—we've had a better season than some people. We've still got groundcover which means when we get rain it won't just all wash away, and as yet it's not blowing away. But we've had worse in the 'eighties, and we might get worse yet. I've still got a couple of silos of grain left, and some sheds of hay so I just hope it'll be enough. If it's not enough, well there won't be any holidays for a while.

If we get rain in the next fortnight or three weeks we could be right. But if we don't get rain until the end of April it'll be too cold to get growth, and we'll have to feed through the winter, which is when the stock need the feed. They're OK at the moment while it's warm weather, but when it turns cold they'll need plenty of energy feed. So at the moment we're not feeding anything but the weaners, but you never know when that'll change—you've got to take it day by day.

You mentioned that the 1980s drought was worse than this one—could you give me a comparison with conditions then?

In the 1980s it was virtually, in this area, three years of drought with very little break at any time, and it finished up with all the ground being bare and you watched your paddocks blow east-west one day and west-east the next. We were hand-feeding all the stock that we did save. We sent some away on agistment and they came back with a deficiency that meant we lost a lot of them. But it wasn't very nice. That's when I did a lot of these tapestries. That was my calming drug—anything's better than watching your property blow away. All we could do was feed the stock, and my husband used to drive the tractor with the bin and I'd take the dog and go ahead of him and hold the stock away from the tractor, so they didn't get run over, until he started the trail and then they'd run round behind it. But we used to feed half the stock one day and the other half the next; they were all fed on alternate days. But we never had to shoot animals because of the type of wool we grow. We were exempted from that flock reduction. We did sell some wethers early in the drought, and ours sold—we were lucky. Some of them brought a dollar a head, and others brought twenty dollars for a pen and five dollars for a pen, but that same day there were a lot of sheep that didn't sell, and the people had to bring them back onto their property. We paid sixty-seven dollars in the freight that was excess to the return, so it cost us to sell those wethers. But that's the sort of thing that happens in a drought.

Was this the family property?

This property came into my family in 1864, when my father was a little boy. And then it became his property eventually, and after his death it was split up between the beneficiaries of his will—this and another property that he had and the money that he had. My husband and I took a quarter share of this 2000 acre property but we've gradually put most of it back together. So it really is home, and it has quite a strong psychological effect on me, I guess. This is where I belong and this is the house my husband made the bricks for and things like that, so I hope I don't have to leave. I've been reported publicly as saying I hope I'm found dead in the paddock—the boys seemed to be a bit horrified about that. I just hope they find me before the crows do.

Did you have brothers and sisters?

Yes, but we were all bequeathed equally under my father's will. I have never come across any discrimination on sex or colour or anything else. My father used to tell me when I was a little girl about the Chinese market gardener in Blayney, and he often said that Billy was the whitest man in Blayney—meaning that he was a very honest, decent sort of person, and that that mattered, not the colour of his skin. So I've grown up virtually discrimination-free and, as a child, because I was female I wasn't supposed to watch them cut a sheep's throat, and I wasn't supposed to go into the shed while the shearers were in there, unless somebody told them in advance that I was going in. Now I hear them call out 'ducks on the pond' when I walk in—but I haven't had any problem with discrimination, and my husband and I always were equal partners in everything.

Was your father's attitude unusual, do you think, discouraging not only racial discrimination, but having no discrimination between you and your brothers?

There were things that they were expected to do that I wasn't expected to do, but that was purely a matter of strength, and I never thought of it as unusual. In fact, when I first went teaching, I got a much lower salary than males of the same standing, but then we weren't expected to do certain things in the school that the men did. The men did them for us. And I've always regarded the ladies as being superior rather than inferior. But you see I never came across any wife-bashing or anything like that, and I didn't know it went on until I went out into the big bad world, and I realised that some people are discriminated against, probably originally because of their lack of strength: survival of the fittest.

You trained as a teacher. Did you always intend to come back to the land, or did you intend to have a career as a teacher?

I thought I'd have to have a career as a teacher. I thought it was the only way to make a living. I didn't mind teaching, but I was very happy when my husband was agreeable to coming back here and taking my share of the land. Not every woman's been as lucky as I have. He was a fairly special sort of feller.

He had been born on the land—originally at an orchard

in Batlow. But then the family had moved to the city where he was living when I met him. But he was a person who thought ahead and he made a good farmer, just as he'd been a very good teacher—and he had a tremendous sense of humour, so we all got a lot of fun out of him. Everybody said that I had five boys, and the eldest was the naughtiest (laughs)—meaning Ron of course.

So he had to learn the skill of farming partly from you?

Well, I taught him how to tie wire. He used to call me 'wirebrain' at one stage, because anything that broke I'd fix with a bit of wire. But, oh no, we just worked together, and we usually planned things ahead. Even before the children were born we worked out what we would do as far as discipline was concerned, and that they would never be in a situation where they could play us against one another— things like that, just a little bit of forethought. And because Ron was not bound by old ideas I guess we were more prepared to accept new ideas in our farming and perhaps that's why we did rather well. We've always been successful at whatever we've undertaken.

Where does the education come from—the sort of continuing education of farmers. You didn't do an ag science degree, or anything, so where did you learn?

There are lots of places where you can ask. The Ag. Department's very good. There are ag. bureaux. You learn from other farmers. You learn a lot of it by thinking about it and then asking: none of our boys have been educated on the land either, but I'm sure any of them could make a success of it, because they know how to think. I think most farmers learn. You learn a bit by experience, you learn by your mistakes, and hopefully you can learn by other people's mistakes too—which saves you making a few. But no, it's more just thinking about it.

So thinking and planning are two things you seem to think are very important?

You've got to plan, but you've still got to be flexible, because things don't always go the way you think they're going to go—particularly with the weather. Either you're flexible or you get high blood pressure. You've got to have detours—ways around the problem.

My mother used to have lots of little wise sayings: she always said that people make their own luck, or that luck is more good management. But I had a few that I used to quote at the boys, and one of them was that difficulties were made to be overcome. I thought that was pretty good, till they start throwing it back at me. 'Come on, Mum, difficulties are made to be overcome, you know.' And so they are, and if you stop and think about it there's usually a way around it. And that's why you've got to be a bit ahead.

Can you remember any sort of particular situation where you planned for a certain thing to happen, and, as you said, you had to use some of these detours?

Well, I'd planned to go for a holiday in the wintertime, but, because the dams were getting empty, it was a good time to clean the dams out—the old dams—some of which have not been cleaned for forty years. So I worked out my holiday. I planned how much I was going to spend on it, and spent it on cleaning out dams. When I reached the end of that I stopped. I guess that's a bit of a detour. There are lots of things that you think you'll do, on a smaller basis—you might intend to do a certain job next week, but if the weather changes you've just got to change what you do.

We were going to do some fencing and plant some more trees this autumn. We've done the ripping ready for it, but the way the season's going it will be useless to plant them this autumn. The ripping'll be there but it's no good planting them until the moisture gets down deep. So we'll shelve that—do some more pumping of water into dams, probably carting feed to the sheep in the winter and that sort of thing, watering the trees we planted in the spring. That's what I mean by being flexible. I mean it'd be silly to say 'I've planned to plant trees in March-April' and go ahead and plant them when the season's like it's turned now.

Do you have a routine that you set yourself each day?

My main routine is to get up in the morning. Often I go out for an hour or two before breakfast. I might grab an orange as I go—depends. In hot weather it's much better to do stockwork in the cool part of the day and then come home and have breakfast. People find it very difficult to ring me up because they never know when I'll be in. In those two hours I'd probably move mobs of sheep or goats or cattle from one paddock to another, check them for flies, perhaps bring them in to the shed—those sort of things, where you're driving the stock, where they have to move, because in hot weather you can kill sheep by forcing them to move. It's also more pleasant, not as dusty and you're out there early. If there's a sheep down or something caught in a dam—something having a problem—it's better to get it early before the crows get too active.

Breakfast can vary and can be anything up to ten o'clock. Sometimes it becomes brunch, but I look after myself. I have good meals. But I don't have a routine. Usually I'm in soon after dark. People can't understand that on moonlight nights it's often nice to do something in the moonlight. I watch television if there's something that I want to watch and I'm not too busy, but I don't watch a lot of television.

I never have liked routine. I like to make quick decisions and my idea of an ideal holiday would be to go out—go to the gate and toss a coin and decide which way to go and just be free and easy. I'm not a person that has to have meals on time and because I don't drink tea or coffee I can take a water container in the truck with me and I usually take some sweets in the truck in case I am out very late and I start to feel a bit low in sugar.

Was this originally a sheep property when you took it over?

It had been sheep and cattle—my father used to run mainly Merino sheep. He was very interested in his sheep and his father was before him. Actually they bought rams from Winton in Tasmania in the very early days and I have found a catalogue of a sale in the early 1900s in Sydney of imported sheep from America complete with my father's comments, which are very similar to some of the comments I've put on those sort of catalogues. Things like 'I don't like her' (laughs).

But when my husband and I came here, we ran crossbred sheep for prime lambs originally. We also had an Angus stud. We used to win prime lamb prizes and that sort of thing. But the trouble was you sold what you had bred. You bought somebody else's breeding for your ewes and you didn't have much continuity. There wasn't enough challenge in it. So we switched to fine wool Merinos and we improved the cut, we improved the quality and we improved the yield per head and the percentage yield. But we always had the problem that, as the property built up— with fertilising it and so on—we got a lot of rubbish growing. And after we introduced goats we improved our vegetable matter in the wool from about 1.5, 1.6 per cent down to 0.5, 0.4. But recently we've taken on the lease of another part of the original property, which is infested with thistles, so we're getting vegetable fault back.

Why did you take on goats?

It was sudden, and it was my fault. I had felt cashmere garments and I thought they were lovely. So when we went to England I thought I'd buy a cashmere sweater, and we looked at them and we looked at the price, and I thought: I can do without a cashmere sweater. We did have a lot of fun seeing places, and that was more important. Then a couple of years after we came home from our first trip away to England where we visited our son, I saw an ad in *The Land* newspaper from a lady who had cashmere goats. And I thought: is that where cashmere comes from? That was in mid-1980. Anyway, we had to go up north and just accidentally—only it wasn't accidental—I suggested to Ron that we come back a different way. And of course we happened to go past where this lady who had the ad in the paper lived. And I 'suddenly remembered' and Ron just sort of raised his eyebrows and said, 'Oh, is that why we came down this way'. Anyway, we called in, and she had the goats in the yard and we put our hands on some which had cashmere that was showing through the guard hair and we both thought it felt beautiful. And on the way home I said to Ron 'If we got two or three of those we could tie them up in the orchard'. Now, Ron was always practical. He said, 'If you're going to do something, do it properly. We'll go to the Ag. Department and find out about it.' Which we did and they put us in touch with some other people who were growing cashmere in this area, and we went to one family we happened to know because we'd sold them a child's pony at one stage. They spent half a day showing us what they did and we got in touch with our wool company and their Stud Stock Officer took us out near Cobar and we bought a truck-load of goats. We bought some bucks from the fellow who had shown us around, and we were in business. And then it got to us, because we could see we could make improvements by selecting the right buck to put with the particular group of does, or, if you like the right group of does to put with a particular buck. For a few years we bought in bucks but now if we buy in a buck it's purely as an experiment, to see what happens with that bloodline. Now we're buck sellers, not buck buyers.

Are they much more difficult to handle than sheep?

They're different from sheep. Don't put them in the paddock and then start mending the holes where they're getting through. Mend the holes before you get the goats, and if they never learn that they can get through fences, they don't try. They're much more likely to go under a fence, or through a hole than they are to go over the top, unless you put a big mob of goats into a yard and then 'hoy' and go on, then they'll climb over one another and go over the top. And then you've taught them that they can get over fences. But they don't normally go over fences.

We have very little trouble with them getting out. Some of the wethers do. Wethers are more likely to than bucks or does, I think because they grow very tall and they are not carrying as much weight. A pregnant doe finds it not very comfortable to jump fences. I've never seen a pregnant wether, but I've seen wether rogues. There was an idea once in the Association to lease your wether goats out to people as weed-eaters. My idea is that that would be a very good way to put people against running goats, because wethers are definitely the most difficult to contain, and they're not very nice to handle either. They leap about more than the others, so that makes them a little bit dangerous. I mean, they're not coming at you, but as they go past you they might hit you with their horns.

In a lot of ways goats are easier than sheep. They mob up more easily and stay in a mob more easily than sheep, and they don't get fly-blown, which is a wonderful asset. Anybody that's been through a wet summer with fly-strike and jetting and crutching will be delighted none of those jobs have to be done with goats.

We do handle them in slightly modified yards. We probably have them about six inches higher than you would have to have for sheep. But they never think of going over the top. We have no problem with them in yards. Originally we handled them in old cattle yards that we'd modified because we didn't want to spend any money on them in case we didn't like them, but now we handle them through normal sheepyards. That's OK if we're doing it ourselves, and we know not to rush them. But if we're having people inspecting them I like to put them where the yards are a little higher.

So a lot of the handling is by observation of goat behaviour, if you like. Did you have to learn that yourselves by watching them, or did you get it from books?

People are always telling me I should write a book and I have half-written one but I never get time to go on with it, and I don't know who'd buy it anyway. But it's mainly by observation of what goats do. It's all been a challenge and more or less an experiment, if you like. But, because of the

improvement in our wool vegetable matter and, consequently, our range, it would pay us to run goats even if we
didn't sell any cashmere.

*I was wondering, when we were talking about behaviour, whether
something you learnt as a teacher (laughs), controlling mobs of
naughty children, helped with the goats.*

Well, I guess you do try to think ahead. You're the one
that has to be a jump ahead—not the goats or the children.
Young goats, you know, will be the ones that will test
fences. You put them in a paddock when you wean them—
a paddock where they are going to touch a hot-wire very
soon. By hot-wire, I mean an electrified outrigger. They
learn that fences are something you don't go too close to,
and then you have no problem. But if you put them in a
paddock that had weak fences, and they got out the first
few days when they're trying to get back to their mothers,
then you have fence-trained them to get through fences.
You see goats advertised as 'fence-trained', but you don't
know which way they're trained. A little bit of prevention
is a lot better than cure.

*You were talking about cutting down the vegetable matter in the
wool through having goats. You see them as complementary
livestock?*

Yes. I wouldn't advise anybody to go in for cashmere
goats purely as a money-raiser on their own. But they eat
weeds, and they do eat a little bit of the pasture, but the
weeds that they clear are stopping the pasture more than
the goats would. We haven't had to reduce our stocking of
sheep to make room for the goats, because the goats make
room for themselves. But, there again, you've got to think
about it. There's been a lot of work done in the last fifteen

years, and there are pamphlets available from the Ag. Department which tell you which weeds the goats will find most palatable, and at what stages. So you make use of all that information. At the moment I've got goats eating thistle heads in this newly-leased property, and they're hardly eating anything from the sheep. They're eating the thistle heads, which won't prevent the thistles getting into the wool this year, but it will reduce the number of thistles next year, and in about three years they'll clean the thistles out altogether—and then those paddocks will be clean for wool.

Amazing. Do you run them together, in the same paddock?

You can, and we do, but we don't yard them together. When you want to muster either the sheep or the goats, allow that quarter of an hour extra. Go in and keep your dog on the truck, so that they know he's there, but he's not really worrying them. If you put the dog out they'll all run together. But if you just wait quietly or drive about quietly, it may take five minutes—it may take quarter of an hour— the mobs separate into the species, and then you take in the mob you want. If you yard them together you're risking fibre contamination, either way.

They're temperamentally so different, do they excite each other, or make each other behave peculiarly?

Not really. If you do yard them together and, say, there's only one or two sheep in a mob of goats, the goats will attack—butt them away. But they will do that too if you've been running, say, a mob of white goats and you put a black one in. They'll do the same thing. But we try to avoid doing that and we have two shearing sheds on the property, one for goats and one for sheep. We have no problem with fibre contamination which is very important with quality fibre.

We have never had any comment from our woolbrokers or the buyers, and I'm continuing to go to the wool sales so that I'm there if there is anything that they want to tell us about, but we've had no complaints whatsoever.

They often camp separately, though they will sometimes camp in close areas, but I can't see that you're risking contamination any more with sheep and goats than you are with sheep and cattle. But nobody ever thinks of trying to yard cattle and sheep together. On the camp-sites where the cattle have been lying, it doesn't seem to affect them.

What about shearing? Is it the same process as for sheep?

It can be, but that's the difficult way to do it. Goats resent being 'tipped', as we call it, to shear, but a lot of people do that. When they've been shorn once that way they know what you're about and they don't put up such a fight about it. But the easy way to shear them is with their head in a bale. You can get a specially made bale, or you can use a little miniature cow bale. You hold on to the goat's tail, which is a very useful handle, and shear one side and, in our case, because our goats are fairly dense-fleeced, we find we get a cleaner shearing if the shearer changes hands and shears the other side. A lot of them when they've first seen it done have said, 'Oh, it couldn't be done', but usually fellers don't like to be outdone and they'll have a go. By the end of half a day they're finding it no problem whatsoever and it does give a nice clean finish. There is a method called 'the go-down method', where they shear one side and then come down the other side. That doesn't work with what I consider is a well-fleeced goat, because the handpiece tends to ride out. So we call ours 'the come-up method' (laughs)— the Vickers' come-up method. You're working against the lie of the guard hair all the time, coming up the legs, which means you don't cut the sinews—hamstring them. And you're coming up from the tail to the head on both sides, and it does give a nice clean finish. It makes the handpiece stay in on the skin, not ride out. Second cuts in cashmere or wool are disastrous.

Is the hair classed in the same way as wool? What's the process after that to the wonderful cashmere jumper that you wanted to buy in London?

As it's shorn it is classed, but it's classed differently from wool. You don't attempt to class it into 2A and 3A, 4A and Super 3A and so on. You class it according to the colour. Now we class our goats according to colour before they come into the shed, so that we have our dark-coloured goats running separately from the whites and light-coloured. And that makes it very easy. But then there are things—just as there are cast lines in wool—cast lines like dingy and tender and so on— so there are cast lines in cashmere. But they're different. We have what we call LCV—low commercial value—which is where there's very short cashmere, or very little cashmere, and a lot of guard hair, and that is classed out separately. When I'm doing it, I have a raised table where we shear the goats and I have bags pinned on the edge of the table. I brush into the bags the LCV I know is likely to come from the legs, maybe on the belly of the ones that aren't quite as well-developed yet, and around the tail where there may be some stains. There's also what we call 'cashgora' which is from an angora infusion in the goats and you get some mohairlike fibres mixed in through the fleece. Anything with those we call hybrid fibres or intermediate fibres has to be kept separately and sold separately and it's much lower value.

So, you class those things out as you go and then you class the colour as white—there is a white/white, which must not have any coloured guard hair in it whatsoever but it's very little different in price from what we call WC, which has nothing to do with toilets. We class all our white as WC because often you'll miss one or two coloured guard hairs anyway. And then there is what they call grey, which is white cashmere and coloured guard hair, but any quantity of coloured guard hair; and there's what we call BR, which is pigmented cashmere fibres—usually found on black or dark-brown goats. Sometimes on a tan sort of goat you'll find what they call blond fibres too. Those go separately, but, if you want, you can combine the grey and the brown. It makes an awful higgledy-piggledy looking line, so we don't do that if we can avoid it. There are some what we call broken coloured—bi-coloured—type of goats where it's impossible to separate it properly. We usually cull those. They go to the abattoirs.

And after it's baled or bundled together and leaves this property, what happens then?

Unfortunately there's not enough grown in Australia for it to be worth putting in the machinery required for some of the processing. It has to be separated from the guard hair, which is just like cow hair, and to do that it's sent overseas. It can be done in China, Italy, the UK and America. The UK used to be the best de-hairer in the world, but they have now set up factories in China, where most of the world's cashmere comes from, so that they can de-hair the Chinese cashmere without shipping all the guard hair, and they are doing an excellent job.

I've seen some of the de-haired cashmere from all four places and China and the UK are fairly well equivalent. But, of course, the Chinese do it more cheaply.

Once it's de-haired—of course, it's scoured first—it has to

be spun. It's made into tops and then spun, and there's no machinery in Australia that can spin the fine cashmere so that is done overseas too. There are some processors who are buying Australian cashmere and having it processed to yarn stage overseas, then they bring it back and have it knitted in Australia to Australian designs. It has only just been on the market for the last twelve months and it's very exciting that we are at last getting some cashmere garments from cashmere grown in Australia, knitted in Australia, designed in Australia and sold in Australia and overseas. Some of it is being put in some boutiques in Japan and they will go further than that.

So is it a fast-growing industry?

It grew quite quickly early. Then, like wool, there was a slump, and a lot of people stopped shearing their goats because the income from it was not good enough. If a cashmere goat is not shorn it simply drops its cashmere in the spring anyway, so that it doesn't hurt the goat. You don't have to shear them, not like sheep.

But in the last two years the market has picked up again. At the end of 1993, there was a rise of from 50 to 70 per cent, and in 1994 the sales made were another 73 per cent higher than the 1993 figure on average. So there has been a big boost to the industry finance-wise and I'm getting quite a bit of enquiry now from people who would like to go into it. I think they will be more careful this time.

I had a person call me the other night about a friend of hers who was offered some does that had never had their fleeces measured. They knew nothing about their type of fleece and they knew nothing about their background and this person was asking a hundred dollars each for them. I'm afraid I just laughed and said 'that's ridiculous'. I mean, they should be able to buy those for twenty or thirty dollars at the most. It's a different thing with a stud animal, which has four generations of fleece measurements behind it and they're all good. That's the problem with fleece measurements—they cost a lot and if they're not good you have to send them to the abattoirs. But now we have a new testing authority coming on in Western Australia, and they are testing at a very reasonable price, and from the tests I've had back just recently, I think they're very accurate.

Do you find yourself doing quite a lot of informal teaching of other goat growers?

A lot of people come here, a lot of people ring up. I'm continuing, as Ron and I did, to spend hours showing people over the property, showing them what we do with the goats. If anybody wants to buy a goat from us, and if they have the time, we like to show them every goat on the place so that they feel they know what we're doing. We spend a lot of time on that. I do a bit of judging and all the time you're judging you make comments, because that helps the people who are showing the goats to know what to look for, and it's an opportunity to teach anybody who happens to be standing around. We've run seminars in the past—we're running a workshop here soon, only a few weeks away now—and we've had bookings coming in already for that. It will be held in a shed or, perhaps, if there's only a small number or if the weather's horrible, it will be held in the house and we'll just go up to the shed for the practical part of it. So I guess that's teaching. I've spoken at lots of seminars and workshops and any chance I get, I'll talk.

So you launched into goats. Were they always your responsibility or interest when your husband was alive?

More so, probably. We worked on everything together, but with some things we had a difference of opinion, or it only required one—then I'd do more with the goats and Ron more with the sheep. For instance, Ron never attempted to class the goat fleece. That was my job. He classed the sheep, the wool. But we each watched the other and if something happened either of us could take over.

He had to go to hospital in the middle of shearing one year, and I had to class the wool. I was scared stiff, because I thought I'd be making an awful mess of it, but nobody complained. I was the one that went to classing schools for the cashmere and with the handling machines that we've got I can drench and that sort of thing with the goats. I can do most of the work with the goats, but I don't try to do anything with the older bucks, except tell Simon what to do. They're far too strong for me and it would be silly for me to do things where I might get injured and become useless. I'm very careful that I don't take unnecessary risks.

The other day I did take my mobile phone with me when I was bringing in a cow that was having trouble calving. I didn't know whether she'd belt me up, so I took the mobile phone in case I got into trouble. But she didn't know whether I'd belt her up, so she didn't do anything.

Now you're living alone and you're not twenty-one any more, do you find yourself taking precautions to make sure that, if you are injured, you can get help, or working things out so that you don't take unnecessary risks?

When I first came back from the hospital—because for eleven months I lived at the hospital while Ron was in there, they'd made up a bed for me in his room and I spent all that time there—when I first came home and was on my own I used to remember to take the phone with me. I bought it as an insurance policy and I used to remember to take it with me. But most of the time now I've got more confidence and I forget it. I did take it a couple of weeks ago: we were pumping water from the creek in a neighbour's paddock, and it was rather steep on the bank, and I took the phone with me in case I broke my leg down the creek. The phone wouldn't work in the creek, but I figured I'd be able to drag myself up the bank far enough to get to where it would work. And then I thought: well, nobody in the world's going to know where I am anyway. But I don't often take it. I'm not a nervous person.

With two of you running the property but now only one, you must have had to make an awful lot of adjustments in one year, especially in a thing like a property where labour is such an important part of the thing?

I just have to get up a bit earlier. I do cook good meals for myself, but I don't spend a lot of time in the house. I know it sounds ridiculous, but I do have a cleaning lady come in once a month to make the house a little bit respectable. She's due next week, of course. It's always not the week that people are coming. I certainly am spending a lot more time out in the paddock. But, you see, for several years Ron's health was failing and there was a lot that he couldn't do. We used to travel a bit, which I don't do as much of, so I make up a bit of time there. I can do most of the stock moving. Fortunately we always worked the dogs together, so the sheepdogs all work for me. I often wish that we had more labour, because Simon has his own property to run, so he can only come on average between two and three days a week.

So you have had to rearrange things a bit.

We don't farm as much as we used to when Ron was well. That's cut back a lot of work. But then, at one time we had a full-time fellow helping us, which we can't do now, and I'm very lucky that Simon is happy to go on working with me. There are a lot of men who wouldn't like working with a woman because they've got to do all the hard work, and she does the light work and that means they don't get a spell.

There's a lot I can do—partly thinking ahead again. We developed gadgets for handling the goats; we have a machine we'd had for the sheep which we modified and I use that for drenching and classing and all that sort of thing for the goats. And we did develop a good drafting system. In 1987 we sold two bucks for a total of $22 000 and we put the money into building a shed and equipping it and that's where those machines are. Then, not so very many years before he died, Ron built for me a little kid-marking bale. We worked on the design together and he did the woodworking out of scraps. He had to buy a pair of hinges, which he was a bit upset about afterwards, because he found a pair that would have done (laughs) but that was all it cost. And I can mark the kids in that. In the two seasons since Ron died I've done all the kid marking without any help—marking and identification tagging and recording and all that sort of thing.

How many animals are involved?

Between 500 and 600 a year. There were probably about seven hundred this year. But it's a matter of time. I don't attend the meetings in town as regularly as I used to, but they still put me on their committee; they still talk to me (laughs). I think cutting down on the farming has helped.

When you say farming, what do you mean?

I mean farming in the sense of growing crops, which are fairly time-consuming. We do try to grow enough to keep our own supply of fodder going. What we do, as a rule, is plant oats on nice rain—which we didn't get, so they're not planted—and graze it through the winter, shut it up at the end of August, early September, and then a friend who lives not far away and who's a very good farmer does the stripping for me. Then we put it in the silos so that we've got the grain to feed back. We don't grow our own hay any more. We used to once, but it's not a good area for lucerne and lucerne hay is much more valuable than pasture hay, nutritionwise, so I buy lucerne hay, usually in March, because that's the best hay at that time, so I'm told. The better the hay the less of it you've got to feed out to get the same result. So we buy in hay, where once we used to make it years ago when we had our own four boys home for school holidays, and free labour. People used to ask were we making hay because they could hear the boys laughing. Sometimes I wish Simon could come a little more, but he's got to get his own work done.

Are any of your four boys likely to come back and live on the property, do you know?

The problem is we educated them pretty well—they've all got university degrees. They all say they would *like* to come back on the land, but they'd never make the money that they're making, and they are also involved with educating their children. Financially I don't think it's all that much advantage to them but you always hope that the property will stay in the family somehow.

When the rain comes and fills up all those dams that you've spent your holiday money on, and you get a chance to put a bit more aside for a holiday, where will you go?

I've always wanted to go into the Centre and I'd like to go on safari, so that you're out where the birds and animals are at night and early morning. Ron's health wasn't good enough for him to have been able to stand that sort of thing, so that's what I thought I'd do—being a fit old woman; that I'd go on safari. But I'd go in a group. I don't know enough about that area to drive on my own. And I'd like to learn about it first.

So that's the end of this interview, unless we happen to think of something else ...

I'm glad you didn't say that's the end of Bess Vickers.

MARY SALCE

Mary Salce was the convenor of the first International Women in Agriculture Conference which was held in Melbourne in 1994. It was an idea she had some years ago but it took time to enthuse others, to get funding and organise such a big event. Over 850 women attended from thirty-three countries. Her life is very busy and in recent times she is frequently away, leaving the running of the farm near Sale in Victoria to other family members. I was lucky enough to catch her at home.

I was born in Holland on a dairy farm and my parents migrated to Australia when I was very young, straight onto a dairy farm. They were brought out here by a Collins Street farmer to make cheese on a property in Yarragon, near Warragul, and I spent a lot of my childhood there with the cattle and on horses. Then we shifted, because the owner of that property had died, to another share-farm, and then my parents bought their own dairy farm near Warragul. I worked on the farm there while I was going to school and also while I was working in Warragul.

I was studying accountancy and went on to work in Melbourne for chartered accountants. At that time I was going with Reno who was also a dairy farmer and when we got married he'd already purchased his farm from his parents so I was dairy farming again. Then because the farms were getting so expensive around Warragul, we shifted here to Sale.

Did your parents encourage you to take an active part in the farm as a child?

Being a migrant child you had no choice. You had to help. I always said I was never going to marry a dairy farmer because you had to milk morning and night. It wasn't easy and I remember being involved in all parts of the farming because it was just one of those things that you were expected to do.

Were you the same as other girls, Australian born girls, at school doing that sort of work?

No, not at that time. Going to school with all my friends was just a different world to when you got home. The migrant children always worked harder at home than the Australian children did at school.

Did your parents encourage you to think about farming as part of your adult life?

Because they were migrants and had it very tough during the war I think all they thought about was survival, to have a good job and a good income. They encouraged my two brothers to take over the farm but there was never any suggestion that I stay home and do the farming. And now, out of all the family, I'm probably more involved in farming than any of them.

Why did you choose accountancy as a career?

Because my family were migrants, all they wanted you to do was to leave school and get a job. So even though I wanted to go back to school, you just weren't allowed to. You had to leave school and get a job to earn some money to give to your parents. That was their priority—that you earned money to bring home to the family.

I went to a Catholic school and we had to do Melbourne University exams for Intermediate and Leaving. And if you wanted to go on to do your Form 6—I forget what they call it—you had to do it by correspondence. And that I couldn't cope with as well as working home on the farm. And my parents wanted me to leave school as much as I wanted to keep going. But they did have night school at the Warragul High School in those days, and I think I used to push my bike at night and go and study accountancy. Then I went on to work for chartered accountants in Melbourne, just to better myself and to get the knowledge of accountancy. I never sat for the final exams. I didn't even want to. I just wanted that experience of accountancy and I was happy with that.

I still don't regret not being qualified because I've used the experience in farming and helping the boys. We have three boys, and it's come in very handy.

My father was very strong in cattle breeding. Friesian cattle breeding. And I used to go round the show circuits, so I always had a good knowledge and a love for cattle.

I guess there's no need to ask you who does the books around here, but what else is your role on this farm?

We're not so busy now and because of the international conference and everything else I've slackened off a bit, but normally it would be milking, morning and night. Although not so much at night now because we have a relief milker. My husband and I work together calving down all the cows, just maintaining the cows, the young cattle, drenching them and looking after sick cattle and milking and looking after all the milk records, just doing the farm business.

I don't do any fencing. I used to help with the harvesting—mowing and baling and raking. I used to do a little bit of irrigating but I don't do that now because the boys have grown up. And I used to drive the semis and the forage harvesters but, as I say, I don't do that now because the boys have grown up and also a lot of the machinery has been modernised. Even spraying the channels for irrigation ... where I used to drive the tractor and Reno used to spray the channels, now Reno does it by himself. But I remember they were the days you'd have to take the kids with you on your tractor and they'd just fall asleep in your arms and you're trying to steer a tractor at the same time so, yeah, it was pretty tough.

When the kids were young did you have to take them with you everywhere?

I used to take them milking and they'd sit in the pits. We had a rotary dairy and we worked it from the inside. I'd sit them in the pit there, one would have a fly-screen over him because he was young, and the other one would be doing his homework or his spelling and having spelling and maths tests during milking.

Yet there's a perception that women don't work on farms or that they're not farmers. The reality seems to go against the perception.

Sometimes I say women are to blame for this themselves, but then again it's tough for them to get out publicly and say it's not how it's perceived. I think, too, that often to keep the peace women accept that the guy takes the credit and the benefit, just to keep everybody happy. But at the same time they're doing themselves harm and harm to their daughters and agriculture in general because people think that input is not there and it is. Their priorities of farming are also different to the male and the government of the day has to know that, because if they're trying to attract the female vote on the farm they may have to look at different issues from those that attract the male voter.

When you say their priorities are different, I suppose they'd also have different sorts of strengths. What are the strengths they bring to the family farm?

A survey that was just done a few years ago in Western Australia showed that when a husband and wife are under stress on a farm and financial decisions have to be made it's usually the women that can make these better than the men. It's interesting, because the women keep a lot of their emotions out of it, yet here we are supposed to be so emotional. But at a time of crisis it's often the women that can make the better decisions than the men.

Are they as qualified? Are they as knowledgeable about what goes on on a farm?

I think they're more knowledgeable because it's not just farming itself, it's what's going to happen with the children, the stress, violence in the homes, physical abuse. When women make a decision all this is going through their minds.

A guy might want to buy a tractor and he thinks it's going to be great for the farm work that he's got to do and it's going to pull some implements a lot better than the other tractor. But the woman—this is my own view—would first think, Well, have we got the money? What happens if there's a drought and we can't afford it? And if we have to keep making these payments, who goes without? And the first thing that goes, unfortunately, is the food on the table.

All this would be going through her mind: the food on the table, the children's future, their education, money being there to get out of the place when things are depressed. And also, does she have to lower her standard of living for herself and the family? And the stress when the money isn't there, the emotional stress that is then brought upon that family. She'd be looking at the big picture rather than whether this tractor could do the work that the previous tractor couldn't.

Yet we're always told that women don't look at the big picture, they only look at the domestic details.

I wouldn't agree. Some women don't feel they have the confidence to look at the big picture but I think some self-esteem is needed sometimes to bring that through.

You were convenor of a very big Women in Agriculture Conference weren't you?

Yes in July 1994. I'd been involved in farming organisations since the late 1960s, not just attending meetings but doing a lot of lobbying and what have you. Many times I was the only woman there and I found that the guys weren't as smart as we were all led to believe and I couldn't get over some of the meetings—how long it took them to get to a certain type of question. It was usually about six questions before you really got the true question, and I could always think of that one question straight away. But because you were the only woman you sat back.

It was interesting to see how sometimes it took them an hour to get to an issue. If I had raised it earlier in the meeting it probably wouldn't have even become an issue but you had to sit back and let them create the issue. It's just different ways. There was a lot of time being wasted trying to get the message across. I remember in the 'seventies no one would mention the burden that was put on family life when incomes declined. All these guys could say was, 'Oh, interest is going up and I can't pay my farm payments, can't pay the feed payments'. Not one would ever mention that the kids' clothing was going up or the food prices were going up and their income was going down. They never mentioned these social issues at all and yet I thought, it's these social issues that the government is going to listen to.

I could also see that women's view of farming was a lot different, and I had a gut feeling that women could change agriculture for the better. I thought these guys were repeating the 'twenties and the 'thirties and the 'forties and the 'fifties, and I thought to myself, When are they going to look at something different and better? Women are the only ones that are going to be able to do this.

So then I put my energies towards getting women to support other women because I knew you couldn't do this by yourself. I didn't even want to do it by myself, because I'd sooner work with the team and support others. I got involved lobbying for a Rural Women's Network to be established here in Victoria—it was the mid 1980s—and I've just been putting my energies into that ever since.

The Rural Women's Network had Women in Agriculture workshops which were very successful, but they'd come into a country town and have a workshop and you'd get fifty or sixty women turn up and I think over 2000 women attended these workshops throughout Victoria. But everything went dead after that. The government just didn't put any resources into the next step. There were a few workshops and a few Women on Farms gatherings but the government was quite happy just to let all that happen, just give these women a little bit so they'd all be happy. But I could see that nothing was going to happen. I felt women were being used so the government could say that they were doing something for women. But there was nothing positive happening to agriculture.

I'd heard about the Rural Women's Network in Canada, and at that time I was trying to make the decision whether I'd put all my energy into my own business (because there was plenty of potential in what we were doing) or just give a little bit of my time to the Women in Agriculture.

I went over to Canada and I saw there that we had something in Australia that the Canadian women didn't have. Women in Agriculture here had knowledge and understanding of the land that was far better than that of the women I had met in Canada. They knew far more about business, they were so damn good, and yet we weren't organised. These Canadian women were organised, but I don't think any of them could change a tyre.

Maybe I met the wrong women, maybe the real workers were at home, I don't know. But just talking around, I thought, we're great at passing on information as Australians. It's part of our culture and we don't know that we've got it. We just give it so freely and we're always trying to help somebody.

So, I thought, to make the government and everybody stop and listen we've got one go at this and we're going to have to do it properly and quickly and put everything in the fast forward.

I came back and I spoke to Liz Hogan at Rural Women's Networks and I said, 'Look, two things we have to do are start up a farm women's organisation and have an international conference, because if we don't, somebody else is going to beat us to it'. And she said, 'Oh, I don't know about the international conference'. But I said, 'Well I don't care, we're going to have one and there's going to be no ifs and buts. We've just got to be positive about this.'

I went to see Ian Baker who was the Minister for Agriculture at the time. We'd actually put a submission to him as to why there should be an international conference, and I remember going into his office and he said, 'Look, you've got what you want. It sounds so good I'm not going to argue with you. It's what Victoria needs; it's what you women need.'

He was quite happy to try to get a committee together with representatives from the farmers organisations and from women's organisations and try to get some funding.

But when the government changed we were in a bit of a dilemma because we couldn't get the same commitment from the new government as from the previous government. We got a promise of some money but it was nowhere near enough to get the show on the road. In the meantime we'd done some lobbying in Canberra, to try to get some money. Simon Crean was very, very keen but then again there was a problem because they were going into election mode. We were trying to get some money through the National Landcare Program because the conference was all about the environment and had a strong Landcare feel to it.

Eventually we were able to get $50 000 through the National Landcare Program and with this we employed a program person through the Department of Ag. Towards the end they got more involved because I think they saw that it was going to be a success but in the beginning they shied away from it thinking that it wasn't going to be a success. They even apologised that they hadn't put more into it a lot earlier because they didn't realise that it was all going to happen: we got 860 to attend a conference and we still had to turn hundreds back. They should've been in touch with the community and able to recognise that this would be the response, because all the women on that committee knew that we were going to get it.

What was the time-frame from when you first thought about it to the reality of the conference?

I think it was 1991 when I went over to the conference, so two-and-a-half years, but we didn't get any funding till about twelve months before. For eighteen months it was my own time and, going back again, because we couldn't get this full-time person from the Department of Ag. the whole thing turned around; then it was wholly and solely the women who had to go and get corporate funding, which we did, and we got some other funding for some wages and we employed people, but I'd done it all voluntarily myself nearly full-time for two-and-a-half years. I made one of the bedrooms here into an office and even before the conference, many nights I didn't even go to bed. It was interesting, though, to find out how much energy you had and you didn't know you had.

It sounds incredible. You had 850 women from all sort of countries ... what countries?

I think it was thirty-three or thirty-four different countries. We wrote to all of them ourselves, wrote to the
embassies, got in touch with anyone we knew and the
women were great. If someone was going overseas they'd
take a bundle of pamphlets with them and they'd network,
whether they were touring or whether they were going to
a conference. We had inquiries from seventy countries.

*And this was the first International Conference of Women in
Agriculture.*

It was the first one. There have been agriculture and food
conferences through the United Nations, but mostly Third
World countries. This was the first one that was organised
by women themselves, and that had women from Western
and Developing countries.

I guess you're still feeling the effects of that conference.

Every day there's a phone call or a letter or someone from
the other side of the world wanting information. We took
the outcomes of the conference to Beijing in January 1995
and I was the only international farm woman there. There
were about 120 women there and a lot of guys from China.

There were three of us there from Australia: the Shadow
Minister of Agriculture, here in Victoria, Janet Barker from
Rural Women's Network and myself. It was interesting that
they wanted to know what Australia was about and even
the Chinese women said, 'Australia seems to know more
about China than any country in the world', and because
you're asking them the questions they expect you to ask,
which Australians can do naturally, the Europeans seem to
be—and because I've got a European background myself I
can understand this a little bit—a little bit stand-offish. So,
we got on very well with the Chinese women and the

farmers, we were all asked back to their farms and their villages and asked if we'd come back again and stay with them. At the moment we're trying to get a woman from the Beijing Agriculture University to come out here to look at the Australian networking with agriculture and how we get the message across Australia.

What were the main outcomes, do you think, from the Melbourne conference?

There were so many of them. Recognition, being involved in decision-making, education, a lot of the Social Justice issues—a lot of them felt that we were the new poor in Australia—what we call representation, networking, and that we need government resources to get the message across. I think the main issue that came out of it was self-esteem, the lack of confidence, and that women's priorities were often very different to men's.

Some of those outcomes sound to me the sort of battles that city women have been fighting for most of this century, I guess. Do you think that's right? Is the conservative country just beginning to start dealing with some of those things of work and ownership of work?

Yes, and I think what's probably accelerated it—because I think it would've taken a lot longer—is the drought, the continuous drought that we've been having, and the low wool prices.

In the 'seventies other farming people weren't interested because everything else was going so well, especially in the wool industry, and the grains were doing okay. I'm a dairy farmer and we've had many slumps in dairying but nobody was interested in the dairy: there was a very small population involved in dairying, so you were always fighting your own battles.

But with the drought in the early 'eighties and the fall in the grain and wool prices, everybody has had to accept the jolt and now it's a lot easier to work together as a team. Years ago, if you were meeting with women you could only meet with dairying women, the others didn't want to be seen dead being with these dairying women that were going bust. But now you go to the gatherings and to workshops and they're women from all sorts of farming backgrounds. So, I think they're all coming together and they have the same problem in their own industries that we have in the dairying industry.

What about the men? How are they reacting to change in status of women and the demands by women to speak up at meetings?

I think the men that haven't got any problems with power encourage women because they're so busy themselves. A lot of the time they know that many of the women are better educated and can mix more in the school committees and things like that. I think they prefer that the women go and do this. But every now and again you come across some of these guys that really want to put women down—publicly—so much so that you never see those women again. And sometimes I think that when men are doing this to women the other men should get up and support the women. They won't put a guy down publicly because he's putting down women. I think men have to start to grow up there, because it's their daughters and their wives that these other guys are putting down. Men have to start supporting women publicly. It's probably a culture change they have to make. It won't be easy for them but a lot of men support you privately if not publicly.

Have you had the experience of being put down at a meeting by a man?

Yes but I've had a lot of support from my local community. I think that's what's kept me going because I've got fantastic neighbours and the whole community here is good. And everything is done in a good humour ... they'll have a shot at me and I'll have a shot at them back and it's all good fun.

But I've had some nasty experiences. I remember once we had a member of parliament who was Labor in this area and I used to work very closely with him because he was interested in women's issues, and he was able to get me to meet the minister and lobby on behalf of Rural Women's Network. Because I went to see him about the water situation here with the drought I was called a communist, a 'red ragger', I was called everything, and yet that guy had probably done more for farmers in this area than the National Party members had done, and he wasn't even a farmer. I kept getting that backlash and I was branded 'Labor' and when you're branded 'Labor' in the countryside that's a real put-down, it's not like in the city.

Also, I remember once about 1976 or 1977 I was the inaugural Secretary of the Sale United Dairy Farmers of Victoria and we had Doug Anthony coming to town and we were all supposed to meet him. They asked if every branch in the district council here would put a submission together, and I didn't know what a submission was, but I thought since I was the secretary of the branch, I'd better do something really quickly.

I came in from the shed one morning and I'd milked, got the kids off to school, done the housework and then I sat down quickly to write the submission ... and I didn't even know what a submission was! I just wrote a letter—Dear Mr Anthony—and told him how I felt. I'd had a bad morning that morning in the shed and I mentioned about the kids and the clothing and the food prices and how depressing the whole thing and family life had become.

I remember I went in to the office and the local member and all these guys were in their suits and ties. I don't think any of them had milked that morning but they all had their folders and their typed submissions. Of course, I had to bring this letter out of my handbag and give it to the local member. He read it and he said to me, 'Look, do you mind if we use this in the run-up to the elections?' And I said no I didn't, it didn't worry me, and one of these guys who had his typed submission got so shitty he said he wanted to read it. He threw it back at me and he said, 'You've left the dots off the "i"s!'

A lot of those things are to do with self-esteem, aren't they? If you're a confident person people don't put you down because they know they'll get back as good as they gave. So how do you build the self-esteem of rural women?

The foundation for Australian Agricultural Women is looking at an educational program to build that self-esteem up. We're looking at a program that starts back at the kitchen table, meeting local women in the area. It's like a Tupperware type of thing. Then we want to take them out into a workshop area and then just build up. We're going to try to get a pilot scheme going and look for some assistance, because a lot of women feel more confident when they're with other women.

We've also got to get these women mixing with the men. You work with your husband or your partner most of the day and all the business decisions are made with him, so why aren't male and female making those decisions together outside the farm gate?

My bottom line is always that you do it for your family

and for agriculture. I wouldn't do it for myself, it's that I know we've got to get the women's input with those decision-making areas for agriculture.

Can you see things developing now since the conference?

Only the other day someone from New South Wales said to me that the conference had given women the chance to get involved in the drought meetings, it gave them the official okay that their input was of some use. It's done something back in their own household as well as their own community. It's made them feel as if they're of some importance, where they felt they weren't before.

I think a lot of people forget too that unfortunately, you need a lot of publicity, you need to be involved in the media to get your message across. The ABC has helped here tremendously with the Rural Women's Award. You have to keep it in the media to get that public perception. Women will come up and say, 'Look, I'm not a farming woman, but thanks for what you've done because it's also helped me'. It's just made them feel important that they are recognised no matter what they're doing. And a lot of the city people that have seen what's happening and heard what's happening on the ABC tell you it's more interesting listening to Rural Women than some other boring issues.

Is there any connection between city and country women as a result of some of this?

One that's been dear to my heart personally is that we now have that network with Melbourne city women, with the Women's Electoral Lobby, with the Y.W.C.A. If there's something on in the city that one woman thinks we may need to go to, she'll ring me and then you put the word out. And if there's something on in the country that the city women would like to be at, they feel honoured to be asked. I mean, I didn't even realise this, they feel honoured to be asked to a Rural Women's Day.

So it's just great to have this intermingling, and they're also asking, if there's something on in the city, 'Have we catered for Rural Women?'.

I think we're leading the world.

*Four-and-a-half thousand square kilometres of outback
Australia is now home to former South Australian Val Dyer.
She and husband John run 16 000 head of cattle on their station
south of Katherine in the Northern Territory. Their corner store is
Dunmarra—population, thirty. Regretfully, I was unable to visit
Val at home, so I talked to her on the telephone from the ABC
studios at Ultimo in inner Sydney.*

My father had one of those blocks that were leased in the
lower Eyre Peninsula back in 1954. It was a scrub block and
we were never able to afford to put a house on that farm,
so we lived in the town of Tumby Bay where I went to
school.

We spent a fair bit of time on weekends and school holidays helping clear and do the various things that were

required to start developing the land. It was quite successful and we had a happy childhood in most ways, with the inherent problems that go with trying to be successful as first generation farmers. There is plenty of history to indicate how difficult that would have been then. I matriculated successfully and did all the academic subjects and was awarded a Commonwealth Scholarship.

Was your father earning his living as a farmer.

Yes, there were only a couple of times that my mother had to work in local stores to keep us going, which was certainly something my father didn't like, given he felt that he was the bread-winner.

As a kid did you think about farming when you grew up?

I had quite strong views about what I wanted to do. Firstly I was not going to be around Tumby Bay for long after I left school and secondly I wanted to become a scientist, particularly in agriculture or chemistry of some sort because science and maths were my strong point and led me to think that was my interest. But when I finished my schooling, even though I received a Commonwealth Scholarship, I wasn't able to attend university because in those days it was quite costly. And while the Commonwealth Scholarship would have paid for fees, it wouldn't have paid anywhere near the amount of money for me to board in Adelaide and buy text books. I applied for a job as a laboratory technician with the Waite Institute of Agriculture and Fauldings, which is a chemical company. However it was pretty obvious with the replies that even though my results were extremely good this wasn't to be a female profession and I wasn't successful. Consequently, I did what many other girls did who have an academic background: I became a school teacher, which paid.

I spent two years at teachers training college and was offered a third year but declined. Even though I was only eighteen when I had finished those two years I was fairly keen to get out and about and back into the country where I felt more comfortable. I did a little bit of what was reasonably common in those days, I fast tracked from Primary teaching to Secondary School teaching by offering myself in a small special rules school which existed in South Australia in those days—and still does, I believe. They had a very small High School component and they put on teachers who could teach a broad range of subjects in junior secondary level.

At eighteen you were just about as old as they were.

Yes I was eighteen and teaching fifteen year olds. It was a lot of fun and I didn't have a lot of discipline problems, but that could have been my nature anyway. I have always talked to people on an equal footing so it didn't really matter as long as they were as serious as I was.

My first teaching position was at Penneshaw, a lovely little place on Kangaroo Island, and in central Kangaroo Island there was an Elders GM office—Elders Australia it is called now—and I met my future husband there. We were married in 1970 and I had to move throughout areas of South Australia trying to find a post wherever he was posted. In mid 1971 there was a vacancy for him to commence operations for Elders in Katherine. Being fairly adventurous types (and I was still very young and still a career person) John and I felt that it was OK for us to do that. There was no house or anything available for their managers in those days but they were looking for someone to start developing their presence in the Northern Territory. I went to the Education Department once more and asked for a transfer and we ended up in Katherine in September 1971.

Katherine was very short of accommodation in those days, in fact there weren't any flats at all, there was simply a town Commonwealth-run from Canberra. We lived in the town in a fifteen foot caravan in a caravan park with most of the meat workers from the local Katherine Meat Works and other people. The caravan didn't have any air conditioning so I was happy to be at school every day. I was able to secure a position at the secondary section of the Area School at the time. I would get home from school to find the butter running out the door of the little fridge and I'd spend an hour or so just hosing the caravan down, making sure it was reasonably liveable. At that time John was home on an average of about one night in seven. It was quite different but I managed to survive it all.

The year they decided to put up a house—and we arranged for the plans and the building of it—we decided to change career paths and moved down here to Hayfield. John was the agent in the sale of the property and we were considering having a family. My definite philosophy was that I wouldn't work once I had children. I can recall those couple of times when my mother had to work and wasn't at home when I came home from school. That was pretty awful for me at the time so I considered it a fairly important thing. We were looking to change when this particular position was offered to us. John had always wanted to be on the land and I'm certainly of the land and I had reached the stage of being acting deputy principal at the area school with a school population of about three hundred and sixty but we decided to try something else before we had a family because you can work on a cattle property doing book work and other things and raise a family at the same time.

John came in here as manager and I came in as the book-keeper but I spent a heck of a lot of time cooking because cooks were pretty hard to get in those days—well, good ones anyway. If they weren't schizophrenic they were alcoholic or escapees from gaol back in the early 'seventies. So between cooks I cooked and did the bookwork. John managed the property.

We came down here in January 1974 with a caravan and a Toyota. There was a kitchen here at the time but because I wasn't going to be the cook—well, I thought I wasn't going to be the cook—we brought a caravan for quarters for ourselves.

The beef crash came with a vengeance in 1974, within six months of us arriving and within six months of the new buyers owning the property. Then from 1977 onwards the owners tried to sell for three years. They decided they weren't able to sell at a price that would be good for them and eventually offered it to John and me to buy on a long term, pay back arrangement. Our view was that these things always turn around, having been involved in primary industries all our lives in one form or another. Things do turn around and, lucky for us, with some hard work and cutting back drastic costs we have been able to be the owners successfully since 1981.

I have talked to a lot of country people over the last couple of months and I have come to the conclusion that optimism is an essential ingredient for anybody on the land.

It's optimism and understanding of the cyclical nature of primary industry commodities. You know that there is always something better round the corner, but you don't know when.

Tell me about the property.

We're situated 320 kilometres south of Katherine. Our property surrounds the Stuart Highway and our nearest roadside inn is a place called Dunmarra. It's four and a half thousand square kilometres. We are at the moment running 12 000 head of Brahman and Brahman cross cattle, plus another 4000 agistment cattle for a live exporter. They bring cattle through from Queensland and they depot them here and take them on to Darwin when they are required for the boat. We have a permanent staff of John and myself and two others—sometimes one other—for the twelve months of the year, but then we have seasonal workers from the end of April through until early November that's another twelve or thirteen people including a governess and a cook and stockmen and the people who help with fencing to do all the things that need to be done from April through to November.

So from November until April basically we run the place with our children and look after all the bores. We have twenty bores on the property. The watering for the cattle is all by underground—ground water it's called, which is actually pumped up from 100 metres. So all of those things need to be looked after. We supplement all of our cattle to overcome the phosphorus deficiencies in the country and nitrogen deficiency in the wet season.

The majority of people we employ are Aborigines from the local town of Elliott which is one hundred kilometres away. There is quite a large Aboriginal community there.

What is your role on the property? I know you started off being the bookkeeper but I guess you have expanded it since then?

I'm still basically the bookkeeper but it's certainly a

greater role than that. John is quite happy to leave me with a lot of the financing, the arrangements with accountants, banks and solicitors, what we should spend money on and what we shouldn't spend money on and what returns money rather than a dead cost; he's happy not to have to do those things.

I also oversee what's happening in the school room by taking smoko over every morning to make sure that I keep in touch. I look over all the work that our children have done before it goes into Katherine and the School of the Air. I understand where they are at and what they are doing.

The Aborigines here during the year create a lot of work—medical assistance and general looking after. I get their stores and their food. I order the stores and bring other things in, answer the phone—I'm the receptionist—and I also look after my own home. And I cook for myself. We don't eat with the rest of the staff because we prefer to have a family life so I do a full mother's role in the house as well—washing and ironing and cleaning.

I am also with the Northern Territory Cattlemen's Association and the CSIRO advisory committee which takes me away a little bit, but John is very capable in the kitchen as well so that's not a problem and we still keep our family life together.

How did you get involved in the Cattlemen's Association and are there many women in the Association?

There are certainly interested women who attend meetings. There are no other women in the Katherine branch and there are no other women on the Executive at the moment—there has been one other in the past. Because we have two leases here we actually have two votes and I have attended Cattlemen's meetings from the time we came down here in 1974. We were still living in a past-type situation with animal husbandry and politics, very much a last frontier, and we needed a little catching up ... being part of the world. I always think if you feel you have a vision of things you tend to be involved as a natural course.

Were you accepted easily?

Oh I daresay it's not as easy as if you were a man, because they just simply cannot understand that women have these thoughts and can have vision and are capable of becoming involved in policy. It took a long time but I persevered and stuck with it and I think gained respect. John and I are very much a team, we don't always agree with each other—he has great expertise in one area and I have expertise in another—but a lot of the things we pushed as a team. When I was elected Chairman of the Katherine Branch at the dinner following, it was his job to introduce me—he was the MC or something. He introduced me as the only person who had been Vice President for 32 years. That's his joke but I *had* been Vice President for five years and couldn't quite manage the next step. I wouldn't be aggressive, that's just not my style, I just had to be patient.

Do you think that now you are Chairman—it's a very male title isn't it, Chairman of the Cattlemen's Association in Katherine— that's encouraging other women to attend some of the meetings and perhaps contribute?

Absolutely. When I first started attending meetings in 1975, I was twenty-six and there was one other woman who would attend. Mind you, that's a long time ago, nearly twenty years, and the whole situation has changed. It would be nice to think I had something to do with that by just being there.

I've never been afraid of men. I had a very good relationship with my father in discussing matters of business and there was nothing held back in those days. I lived with farmers on Kangaroo Island because there was no accommodation for teachers in those days and I was just as interested in business. I have always been able to talk to men about business because that's been my interest.

And now you're doing a degree in Agricultural Economics.

I am, yes. I've just recently returned from the latest compulsory residential school. I am still completing first year subjects and I'll be on second year subjects next year. This is my third year and I've been quite successful so far with credits and distinctions so I am keyed up to continue. It will take me another five years but then there might be openings for consultancy work, given the experience of being successful, probably against all odds, on this property.

We can't be isolated in a situation like this for ever. We'd be pretty happy to move out at some stage and have someone else take over. Whether that is one of our sons or daughters or a manager we don't know, but we have to start looking to the future and that's why I am doing a degree.

One way and another there is a lot of education going on your place. You taught your own children as far as Primary School didn't you?

No, we've always had governesses, but I've taught them on and off. One of the things I decided when we came here was that I was the mother and not the teacher. I've seen too many situations where you teach the child all day and when the child wants to let down from school that child has nowhere to go. When you are forced to teach, and many are through financial reasons, when school finishes the mother doesn't want to see the child for a few hours and the child wants to go and probably let down somewhere else. That's always something I said I wouldn't do—apart from the times between governesses when I've taught them and they've enjoyed that and I have, too, for short periods of time. But it creates far too much stress on the family situation, in my view.

You've had a lot to do with the Isolated Children's Parents Association too.

Yes. Back in the early to mid 'eighties I was very involved in the ICPA and I'm still a member. I'm not as active with that as I was, given that one of my children is now out of education entirely, one is in secondary school and Lisa is in Year Seven.

We achieved a lot over the early years. You find that the women in the bush, specially up here in the Territory, are particularly strong, have good views and are well educated. It's probably quite common throughout the rural areas of Australia that the women have a good education, possibly to a higher standard than the men, and if you get strong characters who can see things that need to be done and achieved, they tend to do them. I was involved in the early time with the School of the Air and ensuring things like the children going into town once a year for a whole week for an in-school, when all the children sit together for a week and have classes. We also have another in-swim school later where we all go into town and do the swim programs—our eldest two boys missed out on these developments. There has been extra funding available so children get into town and don't miss out. It's great and we've achieved quite a lot in those areas over the years.

For years some people couldn't get to town because of

the cost, but also some people spend money on other things. There are choices to be made on where your dollar is spent. I always made sure my children could go to town for these things but some others had different priorities.

One of the great successes I felt being Chairman of the School Council was that we actually got the principle accepted that there must be funding made available for travel and accommodation to help people go into town for their swim schools and in-schools. Now it's the common occurrence and is accepted as one of those things that need to be provided, whereas before it was seen to be a grab for money.

Is the Northern Territory your home now?

It is now, oh yes, most definitely. We spend most holidays at Tumby Bay and my husband has a greater connection to it than I do. He loves the fishing and we have a boat down there and he has a great relationship with my father who is still alive. But it's really not my scene any more and South Australia isn't either. Certainly the Territory is our home; this is where most of our friends are.